Hu[illegible]
[illegible]
from
Cecil & Mayey.
—:—

Aug 22ⁿᵈ 1935.
—:—

THE ANCIENT WORLD

LONDON
Cambridge University Press
FETTER LANE

NEW YORK · TORONTO
BOMBAY · CALCUTTA · MADRAS
Macmillan

TOKYO
Maruzen Company Ltd

Plate I

The Winged Victory of Samothrace

THE ANCIENT WORLD

A BEGINNING

by

T. R. GLOVER

The Labarum

CAMBRIDGE

AT THE UNIVERSITY PRESS

1935

PREFACE

THIS BOOK is written to enlist recruits for a study which the writer feels to be of supreme interest— the study of the opening chapters of a story still being unfolded. For many years he has been teaching Ancient History, and reading it for many more; and he hopes that he has so written that at least some readers will feel with him the appeal of the subject. The book is not a text-book for any known examination. Battles, dates and constitutions have been omitted, where they seemed of minor significance in the march of events. The writer has so far followed the example of ancient historians, that he has ignored politicians, permitted himself to digress, and repeated that the cause is as important to learn as the event. He has tried to keep a firm hold upon the thread of the story; but he has remembered that it is a story of men, and he has lingered at times to hear what they say and to give it (in English) to the reader. Legend, drama, art, adventure— the swallow-songs of the Rhodian children, the life of Alexandria as shown in the papyri, the beginnings of the Christian Church, the characters of men—all these belong to the story; and much more. But this is an outline merely. Readers who would wish a somewhat fuller treatment may find it in the *Cambridge Ancient History*.

Cambridge
October 1934

CONTENTS

PLATES

TEXT-FIGURES

MAPS

Chapter I

GEOGRAPHY AND HISTORY

ROBINSON CRUSOE has been a classic for two centuries, read and loved all over the world. It was written in the first instance for men to read, but boys soon discovered it. There is something fascinating about desert islands and new lands, where the world is all before you, and you have to make your home and find your way in solitudes untrodden of man. Robinson Crusoe is repeating, so far as an individual can, the experience of the human race, moving about in worlds not realized. He has to work out every problem of the earliest man for himself. He has, in the story, the advantage of coming of a civilized race and of knowing something of the use of the tools he has saved from the ship, but he has also disadvantages from which the savage and primitive man do not suffer. But the universal need of food, clothing and shelter, and the nearly universal passion for discovery, set him to work on the oldest lines which human energy has followed. He gives us in a romance something like an epitome of what we now call pre-history. Wrecked on such an island, what will be the first thing a man looks for, when it is once clear that he will not get the ship off the reef? Probably shelter, and then fresh water. When he has fetched all he can from the wreck, he will set about finding out what the island can offer. After that the "solitaire" will wish to learn what food the island produces or can be made to produce; what natural

fruits it bears; whether it has wild animals, useful or
dangerous; whether he has savage neighbours; and so
forth. He will wish, sooner or later, to travel over the
island, to climb its hills, to search its forests, to know all
about it. So new races in new lands have ever done,
French in Canada, ancient Britons in England.

Can we treat Geography in the practical spirit of
Robinson Crusoe? Can we take England, or Greece,
or Italy, and ask ourselves how the land looked to the
people who first settled in it, how they pictured it in their
minds, and how they managed to fit themselves into it?
For a new land is not always ready or comfortable; and
as you cannot at once fit the land to yourself, you have
to fit yourself to the land.

A. RANGES, RIVERS AND ROADS

To-day we know all about isobars and isotherms—if we
are under thirty. Older people, like the Greeks, never
heard of them. But there are three things, much simpler
and more essential, to keep in mind when we start
thinking about the geography and the history of a land
—Ranges, Rivers and Roads. This is a simple formula
to remember, but it will be a sort of key that opens the
door to a great many interesting things. The traveller
about Britain, or indeed any land with a history, is
brought face to face with questions. In Britain and
other European lands he constantly comes upon old
castles, on towns whose names end in -caster or -chester;
why do so many of them stand on rivers? and how far
are they from the river-mouths, or from mountains?
What is it that really decides where a fortress or a town
shall be? Why do some towns grow to great cities, while

others never seem to grow at all, and others again dwindle away? Another question that we can hardly avoid asking is, why battles are so often fought in the same places, or very near them?

The most fixed things in a changing world seem to be the mountains. How they were made, how they came to stand where they are, men have wondered from the beginning. The Greeks wondered. A great Greek thinker, Xenophanes, travelled widely about the Mediterranean, and on hill-tops of Sicily he found the remains of sea-shells. How had they got there, he asked? Oysters have never been climbing creatures, nor had men taken them to the heights. Then, thought the Greek, the only explanation is that the Earth herself heaves up her floor sometimes till it is sky-high, and lowers the mountains into the sea. There he anticipated modern geologists. The Greeks also remarked that sometimes rivers take part in big changes; but the rivers must wait for a moment.

Look at the map of England. Three main kinds of scenery are shown there; great flat lands, sometimes rolling (as we call it), sometimes as dead flat and dull as Cambridgeshire or Lincolnshire; and again regions full of masses of rock in every sort of confusion; and thirdly, the long stretch between the Midlands and the Scottish border, where a Range (the Pennine Range) is a kind of spine to the country. The same thing is to be seen in Italy and South America; the Appennines and the Andes are the spines of those lands. North America has two great ranges, the Appalachian near the Atlantic, separated by a vast flat land of prairies and buffaloes from the Rocky Mountains.

Beginning, then, with the Ranges, we quickly get a

clue to the Rivers. Water, as all the sages tell us, and as we all know, will run downhill if it is let alone; and it will take the shortest, quickest and straightest way down. If Nature were as tidy and monotonous as a modern Town Council, we might find the great Range down the exact middle of the country, and all the Rivers on one side or the other of it, running at right angles to it straight for the sea. But Nature is not so dull. The Ranges are never quite straight themselves; odd hills and mountains are thrown up in odd places and turn the rivers aside; even stray rocks may do it with a stream, and it has to wriggle and twist its way as it can, always looking for the easiest path down. Sometimes, in Greece, the river cannot get out, and, as the rocks are limestone, it will dive underground, and find or make its way there, till in some suitable place it gushes out again in full volume, and runs in the open. Sometimes it is blocked altogether, and a swamp is the result. Virgil describes the river Ufens "looking for his way"; in modern times people have helped him to find it, by digging a channel for him; he takes it at once, and the land that was swamp can be used by man to good purpose, instead of merely breeding mosquitoes and agues and such things. Thessaly is a famous plain in Northern Greece; once, the Greeks believed, it had been a huge lake; but somehow—some people said a god did it, and some said an earthquake—the wall of mountain between it and the sea was burst open, and the river Peneios ran out, leaving a rich land to men. The gorge was a famous one, and an English traveller of a hundred years ago says it is very like the Avon Gorge below Bristol.

We must now think of Roads, but of something else first. As we travel by train across England or Ontario to-day, we go through a pleasant land of farms and fields; there are hedgerows in England, wire fences (because of the snow) in Ontario; in both there are trees here and there, or little clumps of wood. In old days in both countries the land was covered with thick forest. So was Europe. It is said that a squirrel might have travelled from Moscow to the Atlantic without having to set foot on the ground. Probably no squirrel ever thought of doing it; and it was ages before man dreamed of such a journey. Why should he want to travel?

There we touch a main-spring of History. How does a people get its food? Most of us know that the earliest men did not sow fields and grow grain. When they passed from the hunting stage, they took to feeding cattle. Hunger was the spur that set them looking for new kinds of food; and animals, once tamed and kept by them, were more quickly to be found than wild ones, and easier to kill. But flocks and herds need grass, and like man they need water. Again, as families grew larger, and tribes bigger, they needed more room for themselves and their beasts; sometimes, too, they felt strongly that they needed more beasts, and that by a war-party they might get them. These and other reasons set tribes afoot, to find their way to new lands and fresh water. Here, if you recall what you have read of Indians in North America, on this side of the great prairies, you will understand what Roads mean at first, and how much more they mean later on. The Indian hunter travelled immense distances. Sometimes he paddled in a birch-bark canoe, which was easier and more interesting than going afoot, but it meant difficulties when he got out of the regions where the birch grows. Sometimes he went on foot through forest; and his road was a mere trail. In very ancient

England the earliest men's trails lay along the moor tops in Yorkshire, in order to be out of the swamps. Threading their way, then, through forest, between rock and swamp, men mapped out routes, as we call them to-day, which became Roads. Not the sort of roads we see; for these are quite modern. In 1786 the poet Cowper had to ride out of Olney to look at the roads along which his cousin Lady Hesketh would have to drive when she came to stay with him; it was a question whether the mud might stop her getting through. The student of History must get rid of all notions of a Macadamized or tarred road (such roads are scarcely 150 years old yet), and remember the rhyme made up in the Highlands after the Forty-Five—

If you'd seen these roads before they were made,
You would lift up your hands and bless General Wade.

The Romans built roads, as they built walls; the Greeks found trails, travelled over them, and left it to the feet of men and of mules to make the roads—or the roads could make themselves. Sometimes a river bed served them well enough. There we touch Rivers again.

Any one who will look out of the train windows as he travels, will be apt to notice how often the train seems to be running along a river—the Thames on the Great Western, the Hudson river and then the Mohawk on the New York Central, the Fraser river on the Canadian Pacific. Why? Because the first men to build railways thought things out, and reached the same conclusions as the earliest men. The river was sure to look for the easiest way, and by sticking to the river (if it does not take too much room, as it may in gorges or after winter rains) they would find the easiest way. An early map of the Eastern

United States will show how settlers went up the river valleys—not for scenery, but because there lay the water, and hardby were the river meadows. For rivers are careless travellers, spreading themselves out and dropping their baggage; in their case, it is mud brought down from the hills—swirled along as long as the river has to rush in a gorge, dropped when it spreads itself over level ground. Note then the easy way, the water for drinking, the meadows to graze the cattle on (and by-and-by to plough and sow), and you begin to understand the first importance of Rivers and their connexion with Roads.

But men are not always going up into the country or coming down out of it. They may want to go along the coast; and that is often far more difficult. In the time of the early American settlements it was easier to go by sea than by land from one to the other, and so it was in Greece; and in some cases it still is. Few of us ever forget the young Lochinvar, and how "he swam the Esk river, where ford there was none", or more strictly his horse did. We remember, too, the "hundred pipers, an' a', an' a'", who marched or swam across the Solway and "danced themselves dry to the pibroch's sound". Lochinvar was in a hurry, and the Scots pipers had reasons for crossing where they did. But the dislike of getting unnecessarily wet explains a great deal of History. Men preferred to find a ford; a ford is handier for cattle, for mules, for men carrying packs, for women and children. Roads then will go up river valleys, and cross rivers by their fords. Mountains may have to be crossed, and man will look for the pass which means least climbing; and, as a rule, it takes him from the head of one river valley over to the head of another.

This is a point to remember in reading History, however far down the story of man we go. Whether it is a primitive tribe raiding its neighbours, or a modern army, the pass and the ford (that is to say, the Road) will decide where the battle is to be. At Barrington in Cambridge-shire some years ago people turned the stream for some purpose, and, digging in its channel, they found skeletons more or less in armour, some with cracked skulls; and some of the armour was Danish, some was Saxon; it was a fight for a ford. Often, in England, and no doubt elsewhere, men in the Middle Ages would build a fort at the ford, a wooden fort, at first; and by-and-by a huge stone castle succeeded it. Any raiders, like the Danes or the hundred pipers, would then be forced to find another place, less convenient, at which to cross the river; and an armed force from the castle might quickly be upon them while they were at it and in no good trim for fighting. Look at York, Newcastle and Berwick on one side of England, and at Manchester, Lancaster and Carlisle on the West. If the Scots are invading England, they must come on one side or the other of the Range; nobody can bring a *large* body of armed men over mountain crags or through swamps. Look again at the map of Greece. Why are there always battles at Mantineia in Arcadia, in the heart of the Peloponnese? Four big battles are recorded there. Why, but that the place is at the mouth of the pass? The Spartans cannot get out northward, nor their enemies into their land of Laconia, but by that way. The Rivers then play a large part in fixing the direction of the Roads from the beginning.

B. CLAN, CANTON AND CITY

As time goes on, and as the number of families increases, and men are more and more in number, and as farming begins to take the place of hunting and warring and grazing, the tribe settles down about some river; and houses begin to be built. At this stage another formula may help us, or at least remind us what to look for; the Clan, the Canton, and the City. The clan needs for the moment no explanation. The canton is the early community settled perhaps on the flat or sloping lands among the mountains, near the river, or in some place in the forest as far as they could fell the timber and hold the clearing against enemies or neighbours (they are the same thing, at first). In England the Saxons were the first pioneers in making these clearings in the forest; primitive man had not the tools to fell the trees. Afterwards, when houses in some sort of order give you streets, you have the village or hamlet, as you may prefer to call it, which will sometimes remain a village, but sometimes it grows to a town, or, larger still, to a city. "City", however, is a vague word, with different meanings in different ages and countries. Look at a map of modern London, and note the places whose names end in -gate, or in any town of Eastern England look for the church of St Botolph (the patron saint of travellers), and you will get some idea of the size of the town in old days. The first houses will be built somewhere near the river, so that the girls going to fetch water may not have too far to go, nor be cut off by robbers from neighbouring towns or by pirates from overseas. "Maiden Lane" in old New York tells the same tale. Besides the human beings the cattle will want water, too. The village will be built near the ford, or on both sides of it, for the convenience of the tribe in crossing it, and to keep others off it. There is another advantage in having first the village, and then the town, on the ford; it will be some little way (or even more than a little way) up the river, and less liable to surprise by pirates. Three things, then, or four, fix the town on the River—the water-supply, the Road into the heart of the country, the shore Road (which needs the ford), and protection from trouble threatening from the sea.

Other things come into the story. Gold, for instance, is washed out of the rocks of the range, as they crumble, and is swept down into the river mud or gravel. But, widely spread as gold is over the world, there is not enough of it everywhere to make this very important. What matters more in a small land like Greece is that none of the rivers is navigable. In ancient France, as in Canada in the seventeenth century, much of the trade and travel was in boats up such rivers as the Rhone, the St Lawrence and the Ottawa, much further up than modern ships will go; for to-day the ships are bigger, and in some lands the rivers are silted up with mud. When you reached the head of the river, you "portaged"—that is, you carried your goods and your boat as best you could over to the head waters of another river and then paddled down that. A great deal of the trade between early Britain and the Mediterranean was carried on in this way, though, later on, the ingots of tin from Cornwall were packed on the backs of mules and went alongside the rivers instead of on them. But the Greek word for river tells its own story—*potamos*; the Greeks thought of a river as something above all to *drink*. If there was enough of it, the women would wash clothes in it, as we see in Homer's story of Nausicaa; but in Greece proper there was no river big enough for sailing or rowing a boat.

When once one has mastered the outline of the map with its Ranges, Rivers and Roads, the rest of it is simple. Other things come in, of course. We have seen the risk of pirates from the sea, and that reminds us of sea-faring. You cannot very well sail a sea-going ship further up the river than the ford; so at the City on the River, on the Cross-Roads (the words come again), you will have to unload and sell your goods from overseas; and in time a great port may grow up there—a centre of distribution, as it is called, a place to which the tribes or townspeople up the country have to resort for manufactured goods. Thus if the people of Italy wanted, as they did, such things as wheel-made and glazed cups and pots from Samos, or fancy slippers from Miletus, they had to go down the Tiber to Rome. The woollen clothes, which the Greeks in South Russia needed for the Russian winter, also came from Miletus, the city with the great Downs up behind it, where the sheep throve. And when one thinks of Miletus on the Aegaean shore of Asia Minor, one thinks of the long Roads all the way from Babylon and beyond, which came down to the sea at Miletus—the Roads along which came all the goods and the wonders and the luxuries and curiosities of the East, on muleback or on camels, to be sent from Miletus to a hundred Greek towns by sea. Later on great armies marched down those Roads.

Watch the shore-line when you are studying a map, and count the places where there are good harbours. Greece with its bays and islands abounds in harbours, but where will you find one on the East Coast of Italy?

Brindisi (Brundusium) had to be *made* by man; there *had* to be a harbour there when once Rome began to trade and to fight in Greece and beyond. But there was no Venice up at the top of the Adriatic in ancient days. Why not? The answer is quite simple: there was no civilized Germany to the North of the Alps wanting goods from the Mediterranean and the East. A port, as we saw, depends on a River—we might have added, or a bay; but it also depends on the Road. If there are no people worth talking about beyond, or no corn-fields, or nothing but waste lands and sea, there will be no road and no port—or not very much of a port, unless for pirates who do not want company. The harbours in the Greek islands have served pirates well. *Hinterland* is the German word which we have borrowed to sum up the country inland from a port, which sends it goods and gets goods from it. Venice then is not on the maps of the ancient world; in the Middle Ages it is a great power; but from 1500 it declines. New sea-routes had been found to the East (by the Cape of Good Hope) and to the West; and thus the Atlantic became more important than the Mediterranean, and new ports—Glasgow, Bristol, Liverpool, Antwerp, Hamburg, Brest, Bordeaux, Lisbon—sprang up which did the business of the Northern peoples with the spice merchants of the East and with oversea colonies of the West, which grew more and more populous. But Marseilles holds on, the most ancient of them all, a port near a great river mouth, linking North and West with East and South, to-day as it did in 600 B.C.

C. CLIMATES

Yet other things have to be remembered and thought about. Look at the map of the Mediterranean and the lands round it. It is neither a small sea nor an Ocean. To the North-East lies the huge flat land of Russia, over which blows the wind from the North Pole. Here is the description that Tertullian gave long ago (about 200 A.D.) of Northern Asia Minor: "The day never open. The sun never glad. Every breath of wind from the Pole. All the year winter. Nothing warm but savagery". And it was fairly true. Just as the North Wind blows across the prairies of Canada and the river plain of the Mississippi, and makes sea-faring dangerous in the Gulf of Mexico, so it comes down into the Aegaean. No Greek wished to go to sea in winter or when the North Wind blew. To the South of the Mediterranean is the huge African desert, and when the South Wind blows hard, you have the Scirocco in Sicily and Italy—a burning, dry, hot, hard wind full of dust and sand; and the air becomes as thick as London fog and everybody grows irritable. Both these winds blew upon Greece; some places were sheltered from one, some from the other; some caught both. As a result, there was a large variety of climates in Greece and Asia Minor, and a large variety of products of the soil. The olive and the vine throve in Greece and on the Aegaean, but not in South Russia; but wheat grew abundantly then as now on the Russian plains. The great rivers of Russia washed down endless mud into the big bay we call the Sea of Azov (Maeotis in ancient days), just as the St Lawrence brings down the soil of Canada to the banks of Newfoundland; in both cases you find a shallow sea; and the great fisheries are found where the shallow seas are. Fish do not like great depths. So the Greeks lived then on dried fish from the Black Sea, as they do nowadays on dried cod from Newfoundland; on bread, and on the olive. The olive is one of the best and most nourishing fruits that man has discovered—a splendid food for children, the Greek poet said.

So much for the scene in which Greeks, Romans and their neighbours lived. In another chapter we shall have to look further afield; here let us end with what Herodotus, who wrote the most splendid travel book of ancient days, said about his own country, the Western shore-lands of Asia Minor and the Ionians who lived there: "they set their cities in places more favoured by skies and seasons than any country known to us. For neither to the North of them, nor to the South, neither to the East nor to the West, does the land do for its people what Ionia does; for in one region it is afflicted by cold and wet, in another by heat and drought". The Ethiopians far up the Nile, he says, may be long lived; India may abound in gold, and the Arabians may have frankincense; the ends of the earth may have the strangest and the strongest creatures; "but it would seem that Hellas (that is Greece) has the seasons tempered by far to the kindliest". Another Greek looked at the peoples of the lands: the colder countries of Europe, said Aristotle, had inhabitants full of spirit, but lacking intelligence and skill; the Orient reared men, gifted with intelligence and invention, but born to be slaves; but the Greek was high-spirited, intelligent, and a lover of freedom. History justifies both of them; but leaves us with a question. For centuries the Turks have lived in these same lands, and have shown none of the great qualities of the Greeks; and we may ask why; and all that we can say so far is that climate does not explain everything, but that race counts far more. But how to explain what race is, is another story. We know very well from History who the Greeks were, and the English, and perhaps the Americans; and every one of them prompts the same questions, What is Race? and how is a Race made, or how does it grow? can it absorb alien strains, or is it the absorption of alien strains that makes a race?

These questions are not easily answered, if we can answer them at all. Some simpler questions have to be asked in the next section; but even to them the answers are not easily to be found.

D. THE RECORDED AND THE UNRECORDED

So much for our prelude, then, and the scene. But before we start upon our story, we have to note something else. Not all the story is told us. Men have written, over and over again, about wars and battles, as if they were the whole of History; and others have discussed constitutions and political struggles, with details which interested them immensely (and posterity very little), about wards and parishes, "demarchs" and "select-men"; and some have given us dates, always useful in their way, if one does not surrender to them and make a mere almanac of History. Men have written political biographies, some full of life and interest, some studying great characters, and others giving us mere chat and gossip. But some things, very important things too, are hardly mentioned in ancient history, and often not even in modern. A rapid string of questions must here serve as a challenge to the reader, questions which the writer cannot answer for him; but to brood over them and try to puzzle out the answers—or at least to ask the questions—is essential, if the study of History is to be of any use at all.

How fast does the population grow? If it doubles in every fifty years, as it has done in Japan, for instance, since 1880, how much bigger should it be in four hundred years? What effects does its increase produce? When a city is ten or twenty times the size of the original village, what difference is made in water supply and water carrying, sewage, street-paving and cleaning, police, or in getting about from one place to another, in summoning town-meetings? Is the difference to be measured by ten or by twenty, or is it not arithmetical at all? All these matters, it is clear, will be affected by the character of the country, hill and dale, and by the distribution of springs or streams.

Another question concerns food and crops. If there are ten times as many people, they will want ten times as much food; where will they get it? If the land will support five times as many people as at first, how will the rest be fed? How often can the farmer get the same crop out of the same ground? Can he keep the earth up to the mark, by digging, ploughing, manuring, or will it become exhausted? If nothing is done to help the land, what will become of the crops? If men, for fuel or for house-timbers or ship-timbers, cut down all the forests, what difference will that make in climate, in the fertility of the land, in flood and drought? If food has to be imported from overseas, how can it be preserved all winter? How are the cattle to be kept alive in winter? If they have to be killed in November, as in England till 1700, what effect will the meat have on the general health by May? Navigation, in the ancient Greek world, stopped in October; how could people in a great city like Athens be sure there would be enough food in the town to last till ships could go to sea again in spring?

Crops do not grow equally well in all regions, nor are they the only things that man must get out of the earth; nor do fish haunt all seas alike. One of our inquiries should be as to the sources from which men derived not only their food, but their metals, their timber, their colours, clay, wool, and other things used in building up the framework of life. These things are distributed about among lands and seas, and the knowledge of where they are sought will help us to map routes of travel and sea-faring, and give us hints as to trades and alliances based on trades, and perhaps as to the movements and growth of population. In the same connexion we have to ask what sort of tools the people used? Were they apt at improving them? or at finding out fresh arts? Did these affect their ways of living, or their ways of thinking? We have seen how electric light, the telephone, the motor car, have changed our habits; have they changed our thoughts? Did anything change life for the ancients in any big or sudden way, as these things have changed it for us? Or were there similar changes, less sudden and less noticeable, if just as real?

When Anglo-Saxons came to Britain and mixed with Britons, and when Danes and Normans and Flemings and French Huguenots followed, how did our race change? Did English ideas develop—did Englishmen somehow come to think in a different way? Did ancient life change, when populations were mingled? We shall have to notice in our story great cities, centres of dis-tribution, where traders brought goods to be distributed in new directions. Can we find any laws running through all commerce? Can we find any general effects produced by the sea upon sea-faring people as opposed to inland people? Why do art and philosophy, and ideas generally, thrive best in such a city as Athens? Or is that disputable?

When small states are linked up into big states, like the seven Saxon Kingdoms into England, is it a good or bad thing? Does it mean more peace, or worse wars? Are the people's characters changed by the growth of these united nations? Is their thinking the better for it, or is it worse? And, generally, how do ideas alter life? We shall see in these pages something about slavery, coinage and Christianity—very different things, no doubt, but behind each of them lies an idea. Can we tell what that idea is, or see at all clearly how far it made life different for those who held it?

From matters economic we have moved to the thoughts of men; and we have never to forget that, if History is conditioned by the need of food, of water and air and land, imagination shapes it and emotion again and again is the driving force in great movements. Such things the ancient historians rarely chronicle; who could chronicle them? But if we are to make anything of History, we cannot overlook them; we have to try to learn what things most stirred imagination and emotion, and then, by imagination, to enter into them, till, as emotion is stirred within us, we begin to understand how men felt of old, and how their life was shaped by their feeling.

This is a long string of questions; they will not be answered in these pages; perhaps the reader may forget, as he reads, that they were ever asked. But, once more, it depends on our asking these and similar questions, whether we learn much or little from History. For, as someone says in one of Xenophon's books, "a question, then, is education".

Chapter II

CITY AND STORY

A. "THE CITY TEACHES THE MAN"

To all of us nowadays it seems natural for boys and girls to go to school, and to learn reading and writing; and in all educated homes they grow up surrounded by hundreds of books. It was not always so in England; compulsory education and girls' schools are very modern indeed. Printed books are not yet five hundred years old. In Chaucer's day there was no printing-press and all books had to be copied by hand; and even a scholar was proud and glad to have at his bed's head twenty books clad in black and red. In early Greece, if there were any schools at all, they were only here and there; and few indeed were those who went to them. It is a question how many people could write, if any could. But it must not be supposed that people who cannot read or write are always uneducated, or stupid; very far from it. Indeed Heraclitus, one of the cleverest and wittiest of the Greeks, to whom we shall come in a later chapter, used to say that learning a lot of things did not teach the mind. A man may load his memory with all kinds of things, and still be, as the English poet wrote,

> A book-full blockhead, ignorantly bred,
> With loads of learned lumber in his head.

There was nobody of that sort in early Greece before they had the alphabet (see page 70); but later Greeks knew and detested them.

But if one looks at the things one has learnt, if one counts them, and then weighs them, it is surprising how much we learn out of school. Simonides, one of the older Greek poets, said: "The city teaches the man". Without schools or books or playrooms, without examinations or newspapers (for if Chaucer had no printing-press, the ancients had not even paper), boys and sometimes girls (when the girls were not yet locked up indoors) learnt many things that modern boys and girls, yes, and modern men and women, never learn. Some things, no doubt, they learnt in the streets that did them no good. But all round them was real life. Men made things in all the shop fronts, and a boy could watch them. Here, in one street, were the people who made sailcloth for the ships; and at the foot of it were shipyards, where shipwrights and carpenters were building the ships of wood; and there is immense interest and education in watching a boat being built. Greek boys were not told not to ask questions; or, if they were so told, they asked them all the same. A wise Greek, as we have seen, once said: "Then a question is education". Why is the boat built so curved at the bow, so cut away at the sides, with so flat a bottom? And the sails, why that shape? Then a sailor would come along and talk to the boat-builder, and the boy listened and heard wonderful tales of the sea and the lands beyond it; and when the sailor saw him listening, he would tell of the strange beasts in the sea, of rocks that crashed together on the ship, of the strange faces and stranger ways of foreigners. Little as he thought it, the boy was learning Geography, in a far more delightful way than we do; but he was also learning something better. He was being taught to wonder; and wonder, said the Greeks, is the mother of thought. He was being taught to expect strange things, and to look out for them; and, by and by, perhaps he too went to sea, and learnt anew that, as the Greek poet said, "many are the wondrous things, and nought more wondrous than man".

There were no newspapers to tell what had not happened; but there were plenty of people to talk as wildly about politics, to argue about nobility and blood, about the price of food, about the need to change the laws, about the bad ways of rulers and shop-keepers and food-sellers, and the need to fix the prices of everything, to let the poor live. And the boy could listen to all of it, and note that, whatever argument one man might use, another man could always argue for something different. Children grow up more intelligent to this day in houses where things are argued out; and in every Greek street and market people argued, and often talked sense, and the boy grew up with an instinct for argument, and a quickness to see reason and to trounce nonsense. The Greeks lived in the open air far more than Northern peoples can; there was always a market-place, an *agora* they called it; and foreigners noted that Greeks loved the *agora* and its talk—they were born talkers, born arguers, and loved, as St Luke said of Athens, to hear any new thing.

But there were old stories, too, to hear, and to hear again. For, with all their love of what was new, and of the latest thing, Greeks had great memories, and they used them and they trained them. They could carry in their heads immense pedigrees—who was so-and-so's great-grandfather, whom the old man married, and his brothers and cousins and great-nephews; all this as correctly as savages in the Pacific remember such things, and for much the same reason. There were no registers of births, deaths and marriages; and a man's fortune or his citizenship might depend on some detail in that old pedigree; and besides, there are many to this day who will tell you it is interesting. But beside such family chat, there were old tales—tales of great heroic deeds, of wars and voyages and discoveries, telling how Greeks had found their way about the world, and proved their mettle, against beasts and barbarians, fought the sea and its monsters, and turned all to account. Some of these stories were recited in the market by men called *rhapsodes*; long poems they repeated by heart, and people came to know these poems, and to love them, and to know when they were wrongly given. If you love a story, and if it is in a good swinging metre, it is not so difficult to get it by heart. There is a story of a Greek who told Socrates about his education; his father had wished to make him a good man; so he made the boy learn by heart the *Iliad* and the *Odyssey*; "and", he concluded, "I could recite them to you now". He owned that, though he knew them so well, he still loved to listen to the public reciters repeating them in the streets.

It may seem a strange way to educate a boy—to make him learn two long poems, of about 20,000 lines each. But I have met a Finnish girl (she was a cook in New York State) who had learned by heart the epic of Finland, the *Kalevala*, at school in Finland. It had taken her three years. Why should she learn that long poem? It is not as good as the *Odyssey*. No, but it is the poem of her people and her race; and the rulers, who made that long task a part of her education, had a real idea and a purpose. Finland was newly free from Russia; all the education had been more and more Russian; they would make it Finnish—the ideas of the children, their memories, all they learnt and all they admired, all they had in their hearts, should be Finnish. Without any such political purpose, but with the same sort of result, the Greeks learnt the poems of Homer, till they throbbed with pride for Achilles and with pity for Hector in the *Iliad*, and thrilled over the adventures of Ulysses in the *Odyssey*. And they did not forget that there were people still living, who were descended from the heroes (see page 221). There are worse ways of educating a boy than to familiarize his mind from childhood with great tales of splendid deeds and heroic men; and to this day there are no stories to match the *Iliad* and the *Odyssey*. People read them all over the world. Even in America, where Washington, and Ben Franklin, and Edison are the national heroes, in hundreds of schools boys and girls read the *Odyssey* in English; and probably it is the best part of their education. There is nothing like living with noble characters to make a man's character noble; and nearly all that was best in Greek character was linked up somehow with Homer. No one knew who Homer was; but every Greek loved Homer's poems, with "a reverence and an affection that began in boyhood".

But tales of heroes are only one kind. All over the world, it would seem, men have loved fairy tales, tales of magic, of youngest sons who do what the big brothers could not do, who have fairies and magicians to help them, who marry princesses and live happily ever after— tales of monsters and miracles, of jinns and elves and "thim ones"—queer stories that make you creep, but come out all right in the end. There are changes of fashion in story-telling; and the ancient world, like our own, has seen times when people thought it "modern" to say they liked disgusting stories, though the ancients never quite reached the modern fancy for tales of such very dirty little people, living dingy lives and doing mean things. Not all vulgarity is modern. But, if the fashion for such stuff appears and re-appears, it never lasts very long. Dirt and dinginess lack variety and are not really interesting. Esquemeling's stories of the pirates, for instance, are in the end dull, and they would be a great deal duller but for the seamanship that enables the pirate to scour the Caribbean, and the great fighting qualities, courage, strategy, tactics, and so on, that help him to sack the Spanish towns and capture his thousands of pieces of eight. The rest of his story is tiresome enough. It takes a lot of virtue to make vice interesting; and the great Greek poet saw (and, as the Greeks said, he was always right) that the splendid qualities in men and women are the interesting ones. Let a poet remember that, while he works in third sons and princesses and fiery bulls and raging seas—let him make the enemy a good fellow too—and the chances are that he may make a great story that people will love for ever.

One of the great arts that the Greeks perfected was story telling. In these pages only a little of the skeleton of each of three stories can be given; the whole story is quite a different thing, for a skeleton is a dead thing, without colour or life or movement. When one reads Greek stories, it is worth while to watch how the Greeks tell them, where they begin, how much they suppose that you know or may be able to guess, how much they leave out (a great thing in story telling), how they lead up to the point, how quietly they do everything, how they let you forget the story teller in the story and do not tell you (like some people to-day and in ancient Rome) how clever they are, but fix your mind on the man about whom they are telling, and make you see what he sees and feel what he feels. One great Greek said about tragedies (and it is true of all stories) that a tragedy must have a beginning, a middle and an end. If this seems very obvious, we have only to listen to some people telling stories, and to notice how they mix these things and never let you know where you are, they get to the end too soon, and hark back; and the story draggles on, for ever, broken-backed. Not so the Greeks.

B. JASON

The oldest (in one sense) of our three stories is that about Jason. Homer, who lived about 1000 B.C., knew the story, but we have to learn it from later poets. It was a favourite subject with Greeks and Romans, and William Morris has told it over again in English verse and Charles Kingsley in prose. It gathers up, as great stories do, the matter that makes many stories—the lucky young man who becomes king, the strange task, the princess, the fairies, the magic, the monsters; and the sea and the discoverer are in it; and the whole tells us what the Greeks were thinking about.

To Pelias had come an oracle of cold fear, from the central stone of tree-clad mother earth (in the temple of Apollo at Delphi), that he must in any wise "be ware of him of one sandal", whether citizen or outlander, coming down from the mountain homesteads to the sunny land of Iolkos. At last, then, he came, a hero, wondrous to look upon; two spears were in his hand; and he had raiment of two sorts, the garb of the Magnesians close fitting upon his goodly limbs, and about his shoulders the skin of a pard to ward off the chill rain. Nor had his splendid locks been shorn away, but like a flame they rolled down upon his back. And forthwith, to make trial of his dauntless spirit, he went and stood in the market-place of the thronging people. And they knew him not; but one said to another, "Of a surety this is not Apollo, nor Ares lord of the brazen chariot. And this one and that of the great heroes are gone". Anon, with his mules and his polished chariot, came Pelias, in headlong haste; and he looked, and wondered as he saw the sign, the sandal upon the stranger's right foot, one sandal and no more.

So Pelias knew that his doom was near. But he dissembled his fear, hiding it in his heart, and asked who the stranger might be. And the splendid youth told him how he was the nursling of Chiron in the hills, bred in noble thought and true word, a prince by birth saved from death in his cradle at the hands of a usurper; and, now that he was twenty years of age, he had come to his own land to claim his own from Pelias; and the divine creature that bred him called his name Jason.

Thus our hero strides into the market place—and into the story; and claims his own from Pelias, and from all who listen to the legend. But Pelias uses subtlety; would not Jason fetch again the Golden Fleece from the halls of Aietes at the far end of the Black Sea, and thus lay the spirit of Phrixos, who of old flew through the air on the ram of the Golden Fleece? Trap or no trap, Jason was ready for the task, and he sent forth messengers to tell of a voyage preparing; and heroes from far and near, the sons of gods and mortal women, gathered to him; none would be left behind, to abide at his mother's side, nursing the life that knows no danger. So to Iolkos gathered the flower of seamen, and they built them the Argo to sail to Colchis to fetch again the Fleece. And the soothsayer chose for them the lucky day for sailing; they heaved high the anchor and made it fast to the prow; and Jason took a golden goblet and emptied it into the sea, calling on Father Zeus and the rushing waves and the winds to prosper them upon the sea, and to bring them again in peace. As he prayed, Father Zeus thundered in the clouds, and gave the lightning flash as a signal to the heroes. They sped on their way, and came to the swift-moving Rocks that clash upon the ship; but the Lord of all ships and of the sea stayed the Rocks, and fixed them fast for ever; and the Argonauts sailed between them, and came to Colchis.

But there Aietes had fresh tasks for them, before ever he would yield them the Fleece. There were the magic bulls with hoofs of brass, breathing fire; could Jason yoke them, and plough the land, and sow it, and then—What then, but other perils? But Medea, the princess, had seen the beautiful stranger, coming to her father's palace, as he came to the market place of Iolkos; and she loved him. Night came, and she took a casket of many drugs, some for healing and some for slaying; but she would not slay herself, she would succour Jason, and at dawn she went to him and gave him the charm that should conquer the bulls. And for the dragon's teeth that he was to sow, and the armed men that should leap from the furrows, she taught him what he must do. So he tamed the bulls, and ploughed the field, and sowed the teeth; and when the warriors rose from the ground, they fell one upon another. And, next after that, with her aid, he lulled the dragon to sleep that guarded the Fleece. So, with Golden Fleece and princess and all upon the Argo, he got him away in secret and in safety, to sail back to his father and his country.

But now we in our turn have trouble to meet. For some said that Jason sailed up the river at the far end of the Black Sea, and when he reached its head waters, he portaged (as we saw in the first chapter that explorers did) over to the Ocean, and thence into the Nile, and sailed down the Nile into the Mediterranean, and so home. This was at least the longest way round, and it seems confused. Or, again, the Argonauts sailed up some river to the North of the Black Sea, up into Russia (as we call it), and portaged somehow into the Baltic, and sailed out by Copenhagen, and round France and Spain, and so to the Aegaean. And a third story said it was the Danube up which they sailed, and reached the Adriatic, but had no luck, and had to sail up the Po in North Italy, and portage to the Rhone, and so round Italy and Greece, back to Iolkos. After all this it seems commonplace to be told simply that some said they sailed back exactly the way they came, and made no discovery of the Atlantic at all, never saw the Indian Ocean, never portaged all across Africa, nor sailed on the Nile, the Rhone or the Dnieper.

But why all these confused stories? It was evident, men saw it and said so, that one ship could not come home from one and the same voyage by four different routes. And portaging, as we saw, is very well from the head waters of the Rhone to those of the Seine, if it is a canoe or small boat you are carrying. Who could carry the sea-going Argo across Africa, and do it in twelve days? What does it all mean? Was the Argo a whole fleet? Miss Janet Bacon has given us the clue. The great old stories (third son, fairy princess, magic and monsters, and so on) are apt to gather round one and the same hero; it is quite easy to be a third son, and any third son may

marry a fairy princess, why not? And once these stories
began to cluster round Jason, so did the other stories of
travel in strange lands, and they became terribly mixed
as they did. Of course in a fairy tale, the difficulty of
portaging a ship for twelve days across Africa becomes as
simple as that of marrying a fairy princess and yoking
brazen bulls. And what we really get out of all this
confusion is that, away back in those early days, men
were telling tales of adventures up stream into Russia,
up the Danube too, away into further Asia; and of course
there was the Nile (and we shall return to the Nile); and
why leave out the Ocean that flows all round the World?
Why leave out the Eridanus? In later days they said this
was the river Po,

> Where the water of Eridanus is clear,
>   And Phaethon's sad sisters by his grave
> Weep into the river, and each tear
>   Gleams, a drop of amber, in the wave.

Yes, that was the way by which the amber did in fact
come to Greece from the Baltic. The Greek women of
old loved amber beads; the Phoenician trader in the
Odyssey has "a golden necklace, strung with amber
beads". And the Rhone? But it is clear that the great
story has been growing for ages, and the dates like the
Geography are all mixed. We need not mind that, but
be thankful there were Greeks who knew such splendid
tales of daring, of travel and exploration. That was how
Greek knowledge grew and Greeks became Greeks.

C. TROY

Troy town, they tell us, covered roughly as much ground as New Street Railway Station in Birmingham, perhaps a little less; but, as the Greeks said, "charm goes with the little". Troy has meant more in History, and so far has done more for human happiness. The story is told by Homer; and men have debated who Homer was, and how many people he was; was he a guild of hereditary poets? or was he some one, perhaps a prince like Pisis-tratus of Athens, who collected all the "lays" of the "bards", and wove them rather carelessly into one story? Are there not contradictions? One wonders if people who talk so have read *Don Quixote*, the author of which, in his Second Part, gently laughs at his carelessness in the First Part. Nobody approached Homer in story telling till Cervantes wrote of the Don and the man; and we have been asked to believe he was a sort of committee. To-day the scholars incline to let us believe that poems so great as the *Iliad* and the *Odyssey* needed a poet to write them. Homer, the ancients said, "wrote Homer-fashion"; he told you the story in his own way, and that is worth watching. In a mere history everybody wants things explained and put in lists with dates; but Homer began at the great moment, and let people pick up the tale as he went on. Some have realized that this is the real art of a poet; and some find it of interest to watch for clues in a story you do not know very well.

Sing the wrath, O goddess, the baleful wrath of Achilles son of Peleus, that laid on the Achaeans ten thousand sorrows, and sent many goodly souls of heroes to Hades, and themselves it gave to dogs and all the birds; and the counsel of Zeus was fulfilled, from the day when first Atreides, king of men, and the divine Achilles quarrelled and stood apart. Who among the gods set them twain to fight? The son of Leto and Zeus; for he was angered by the king and sent a sore plague upon the host, and the people began to perish, because Atreides had done dishonour to Chryses the priest.

For Chryses had come to the fleet to ransom his daughter, who had been carried away captive and given to Agamemnon. But the king answered him roughly and sent him away; "Her I will not set free; nay, before that old age shall overtake her in Argos, far from her own land". And the old man went, in silence, along the beach of the loud-sounding sea, and he prayed to Apollo; and he was heard. Down from the heights of Olympus came the god, angry at heart, and the arrows rattled in his quiver as he came in his wrath, descending like the night. He let fly an arrow at the ships; and first the dogs and the mules he smote with plague, and then the men; and ever the funeral pyres of the dead were burning, full many. Nine days the shafts of the god fell on the army; and on the tenth Achilles called a council and bade inquire the cause; and their prophet told them it was the wrath of the Far-darter, angry for his priest's sake, nor would the plague cease till the girl was sent to her father. But Agamemnon was angry, and taunted the prophet and Achilles; yet at the last he consented, but to Achilles this he said: "Mine own self I will go to thy hut and fetch away the fair-cheeked Briseis, whom they gave thee for thine honour, that thou mayest know that I am greater than thou; and another hereafter shall abhor to match his words with mine, and beard me to my face".

Grief came to Peleus' son, and he wondered within himself whether he should draw his sword and slay

Atreides, or check his soul in its wrath. And, as he was drawing his sword from the scabbard, Athene came from heaven, and stood behind him, and caught him by the golden hair, seen of none but him, and bade him hold his hand. (It is a wonderful touch, the unseen swift presence of the goddess, her "there-ness" on the instant.) So the sword goes back, and Achilles taunts the "folk-devouring king", "heavy with wine, dog-faced and fawn-hearted"; when did he take pleasure in battle? A longing for Achilles shall yet overtake the Achaeans. Take the girl; ye gave and ye have taken away: but see to it, ye take naught else.

So the heralds of the king come and lead away Briseis, they twain unwilling and she unwilling. And Achilles, aloof from his comrades, stood on the shore and prayed to his mother; does she see the dishonour done to him? And his mother heard him in the depths of the sea, and she rose from the sea as a mist rises, and sat before her son and stroked him with her hand. He tells her the tale; "but go thou to Olympus, beseech Zeus, bid him remember how thou didst help him, and clasp his knees, and pray him to give aid to the Trojans, and let the Achaeans perish at their hands among the ships, that they may make trial of their king, and that he may see what he did in that he honoured not the best of the Achaeans".

The story moves rapidly. Homer does not pause to explain that Achilles' mother was a sea-nymph; there are no footnotes to his tale, you must listen till your heart beats; and beat it does. There is the quarrel, wrong on both sides; and Thetis goes to Zeus, and the prayer of Achilles is granted. It is his undoing, and the undoing of his people; and it costs him his best friend Patroclus, whom Hector the Trojan slays and spoils of Achilles' armour. Prayers are strange things, and the noblest of men may go wrong; but Homer does not moralize; he tells his tale for those who love a tale, and still more for those who will think of it.

But who were they all? This we learn, not from any list; but as we sit on Troy's wall with old Priam the king, and he asks Helen of one and another: who is that man, taller than the others by a head, never a man so beautiful nor so royal? It is Agamemnon. And who is he, shorter than Agamemnon by a head, but broader of shoulder and chest? That is Odysseus (Ulysses) skilled above men in cunning. And Antenor the Trojan joins in, and tells us (but in graceful words) that Odysseus was what we should call long in the body and rather short in the legs— a very curious touch. And over there is Ajax, a huge man, bulwark of the Achaeans. Helen looks to see if her brothers are there, and does not see them; "but them the life-giving earth held fast there in Lacedaemon, in their dear native land".

Now we are in the Greek camp, now on open plain, and again we are in Troy. There we see Hector bid farewell to Andromache, while the handmaid bears in her bosom the tender child, Hector's son, whom the people called "king of the city", for only Hector saved Troy. And Andromache wept and held his hand; why must he go? All she had, have perished; he is father, mother, brother to her, as well as husband; have pity lest the child be an orphan. "Surely", says Hector, "I take thought for all these things, my wife; but I think shame because of the Trojans and the Trojan women of the long robe, if I shrink like a coward from the battle." Yes, he knows: "the day shall come when holy Troy shall fall"; but he must go. He reaches out his arm to take the child; but the child, in fear of the bronze and the horse hair plume nodding upon the helmet, with a cry buried his face in the nurse's bosom. "Then his dear father laughed aloud, and his lady mother; and Hector laid his helmet on the ground, and took his son in his arms and kissed him."

He must go; that is the Homeric note. "Friend of my soul," says one Greek warrior to another, "were it so that once thou and I were escaped from this war, we should live for ever ageless and deathless, neither would I myself fight among the foremost, nor would I send thee into the battle that gives renown. But now—for, none the less, fates of death stand over us, ten thousand of them, which mortal man may not escape nor avoid—*let us go*, whether we yield glory to another, or he to us." The horse of Achilles speaks with a human voice to his master and warns him he must fall. "Why this talk of death?" cries the hero; "I know it; but for all that I will not cease, till I give the Trojans enough and more of war."

Zeus grants the prayer of Thetis; and trouble falls on the Achaeans; an embassy is sent to Achilles to beg him to fight; but he is angry and will not fight. But later he lets Patroclus go to the battle, and loses him. Then he will fight, too late; and wonderful new armour is made for him by the god Hephaestus, at the prayer of Thetis, notably a shield on which are pictured scenes of Greek life, very revealing; and it shows, too, how Homer and the men of his day loved art. Achilles slays Hector, and will give him to the dogs; but in the night, led by a god, comes old Priam, and touches the hands that slew his son, and would ransom the body—"fear thou the gods, Achilles, and have compassion upon me, remembering

thine own father". Thus spake he, and stirred in the
heart of Achilles desire to make lament for his father;
and he treats the sad old man with the courtesy of a hero,
and gives him the body of his son; and Priam bears it
back in his chariot to Troy. With the words, "Thus held
they funeral for Hector, tamer of horses", the poem ends,
that tells of the wrath of Achilles.

> What gifts hath Fate for all his chivalry?
> Even such as hearts heroic oftenest win:
> Honour, a friend, anguish, untimely death.

D. THE ODYSSEY

The other great epic, the *Odyssey*, is quite different from
the *Iliad*. The long war of ten years about Troy is over;
and ten more years have gone, and Odysseus has not
yet come again to his home. Once again Homer tells
his tale "Homer-fashion". All the gods felt pity for him,
all save Poseidon (the god of the sea) who was his enemy.
But it fell that Poseidon went away to the Ethiopians afar,
to feast with them; and Athene seizes the moment to
entreat Zeus for Odysseus, the wise and luckless. Him
a goddess holds captive on an island in the midst of the
sea, wooing him with enticing words that he may forget
Ithaca; but he yearns to see were it but the smoke rising
from his own land, and he would fain die; why dost thou
hate him so? But Zeus does not hate him; why should
she say so? Despite Poseidon, let us plan for his home-
coming. So Hermes is to go and tell Calypso that the
will of the gods is that she let Odysseus go. And Athene
comes to Ithaca, in the guise of a merchant who sails
the sea to fetch iron.

There she finds the house of Odysseus thronged with

suitors from the western islands, all seeking the hand of Penelope; and, till she consent and choose one, they feast in the house of Odysseus, day after day, living riotously and consuming his wealth. But Penelope puts them off; she must weave a shroud for Odysseus' father, the old man Laertes; and weave it she did, day by day, and night by night she unwove it, till the suitors came and caught her at it, and she must perforce finish it. Yet she would not marry. Athene gives counsel to the wise Telemachus her son. He summons an assembly of the men of Ithaca, and raises protest against the insolence of the suitors; and one says one thing and another another, and, as generally happens in Homeric assemblies, no very clear conclusion is reached, but you come away with the feeling that something may follow, whatever it is. The suitors do not wish Telemachus to have a ship and go travelling in search of word of his father. But by the aid of Athene he gets a ship and a crew, and goes; and they lay a plot to kill him when he shall return. But he does not tell his mother he is going.

He sails across to the mainland, and talks with Nestor, three generations old; and the wise old man tells him of his own journey from Troy and of some others, but of Odysseus he cannot speak. Still he sends Telemachus with his son Pisistratus overland to Sparta to ask Menelaus whether, in his longer and wider wanderings, he has learnt anything of the lost hero. In two days the young men drive across to Sparta, by a road which no mortal has since found again—a fact to be noted by those who would tie down Homer and Odysseus to the modern atlas. But pleasant as is the house of Menelaus and Helen, and pleasant the tale of their travels, and pleasant the drug *nêpenthes* that Helen puts in their drink to take away sorrow, all that is heard of Odysseus is that he is held captive by a goddess, on an unknown island. So Telemachus must go back. All this time (for four books) we do not see Odysseus; we keep hearing about him; this one and that one speaks of him, tells over old memories of him, wonders about him, speaks of his prowess and his wisdom; our minds are always upon him, and we build up our picture of him, and watch for him. That is "Homer-fashion".

At last Athene speaks again to Zeus; and Hermes flies to Calypso's isle and finds the Nymph busy at her loom, singing with sweet voice, as she plies her golden shuttle. "Hard are you gods, and envious!" she cries; had she not rescued and cherished Odysseus? and now the gods say he must go; so be it then. She goes to tell him of his release, willed by the gods, and she finds him sitting on the shore, gazing out with tears upon the sea. He will hardly believe he is to escape; he makes her swear it is no fresh trap for him; and then he builds his raft, hewing him tall poplar and pine with axe of bronze, twenty in all. She gives him a sail, and with braces, halyards and sheet-ropes all is made shipshape. With a fair wind he set forth, and day and night he sailed, seventeen days, steering at night by the stars, "with the Bear on his left". (So he was sailing East, we note.) But on the eighteenth day Poseidon saw him, stirred sea and sky against him, swept the rudder from his hand, broke the mast, and hurled him into the sea. But Ino, the sea-goddess, saw him and had pity; and she gave him her wimple to float upon; "but, when thy hands shall touch the shore, untie it, and cast it into the wine-dark sea; but turn away thy face as thou doest it". So he came to land and was thrown upon the rocks, but at last found a river, swam up it and scrambled ashore. He cast Ino's wimple into the stream; and found a bush and went to sleep in it.

He was in the land of the Phaeacians, which of old they said would be Corcyra, but it may well have been a little nearer Fairyland; life was so happy and so good in the realm of King Alcinous. If Calypso's isle was twenty days westward, where was it, then? Two things said by the Greeks may be remembered; "we may hope to map Odysseus' travels, when we have found the tanner who made the bag in which Aeolus sewed up all the winds for him"; and yet "to invent everything is not convincing, and it is not Homer's fashion". For Odysseus is rescued by Nausicaa, most charming of princesses, a queen among girls, and comes to her father's house; and there, after true Homeric hospitality, he at last reveals his name and tells of his travels, a tale as joyous to read to-day as to hear recited three thousand years ago.

"We were the first that ever burst into that silent sea", and he tells of the cave of the Cyclops. (Did he really live in Sicily, where Etna rolls down the rocks, hard by the site of Greek cities we all know?) The Cyclops, with one eye and horrid ways, penning his sheep night by night in his filthy cave, would eat the Greeks, but, for the sake of Odysseus' wine, will eat him last. But Odysseus is too clever for him; he tells him his name is Nobody; and in the night he blinds the Cyclops with a hot stake, and the stake hissed in the eye, as iron hisses in the water when the smith tempers a great axe blade. The friends of the Cyclops gather to his cave, as they hear his shouts. Does any do him wrong? they ask. "Nobody", he cries; and they go; and the Greeks escape.

They come to Circe's isle, where that enchantress gives his men drugged wine to drink, and with her rod trans-

forms them to swine and pens them in a sty. But Hermes
gives Odysseus the root *moly* which protects him against
the enchantress, and she brings his men to human shape
again, and becomes his friend, advising him of his
journey. He goes, far West it would seem, down into the
world of the dead, and sees the ghosts; he gives them
blood of a sheep to drink, and life comes into them, and
they know him and can speak. He sees his mother, she
drinks of the blood, and tells him of his young son and
his poor forlorn old father in the fields. But he cannot
embrace her; three times he tries, and she slips from
his arms like a shadow or a dream. ("What is man?
What is he not? The dream of a shadow is man", said
Pindar long after.) He sees Achilles, and bids him
remember his old glory and be comforted in death. Nay,
says the hero,

> Speak not soft words concerning death to me,
> Glorious Odysseus: rather had I be
>   A thrall upon the acres to a man
> Portionless and sunk low in poverty,
>
> Than over all the perished dead below
> Hold lordship.

So dim and sad and dull is the life beyond.

The Phaeacians in one of their miraculous ships take
Odysseus in a night to Ithaca, and leave him sleeping
on the shore. He finds his way to Eumaeus, the divine
swineherd, in whose hut he meets his son Telemachus.
Of all they do and plan, of the return of Odysseus to his
house, of the deeds and words of the suitors, of their
slaying by Odysseus and his son and his two friends, and
of the recognition of her husband by Penelope, the last
twelve books of the *Odyssey* tell; twelve books, but they
are not too long. Instead of analysing them further, let

one half page suffice; why, asks an old Greek scholar, Dionysius of Halicarnassus, does it appeal to the reader and charm him (it does in the Greek); is it the words?— but they are quite ordinary words; then what is it? The reader shall have the passage, and answer the old critic's question.

So they two in the hut, Odysseus and the divine swineherd, were getting their meal at dawn by the fire they had lit, and they sent forth the swineherds with the swine. But on Telemachus, as he drew near, the wild dogs fawned but did not bark. And the divine Odysseus marked it, that the dogs were fawning, and the sound of two feet came to him. Forthwith he spake to Eumaeus at his side: Eumaeus, surely one is coming here, a comrade of thine, or one known, since the dogs bark not, but fawn upon him; and I hear the sound of feet. Scarce was the word all spoken, when his own dear son stood there in the doorway. In wonder up leapt the swineherd, and from his hands fell the vessel in which he was mixing the sweet wine. And he ran to meet his prince, and kissed him on the head, and both his beautiful eyes, and both his hands; and down the big tear fell.

E. THE WORLD BEHIND THE EPIC

Seven Grecian cities fought for Homer dead,
Through which the living Homer begged for bread.

So runs the famous epigram, and the first line seems to be true. No one knew exactly where Homer was born, nor when. Herodotus put Homer and Hesiod together, very definitely, at a date four hundred years before himself—say about 850 B.C. The Greeks built up legends about Homer, and made him the author of epics which are lost to us, of hymns to the gods, and a burlesque of the heroic epic. There things stayed till at the end of the eighteenth century a German scholar, F. A. Wolf, "made a 1793" for Homer, as a Frenchman put it—a regular French revolution, with a guillotine cutting up the great poems. For a century no scholar could profess belief in a single Homer; it was the rule to detect additions and alterations, and to discover an original *Iliad*. The mood of the times has changed, and there is a feeling that a great poem implies a great poet and not a big syndicate.

But, waiving the author, what were we to say of the world he described? Did he tell of what he saw and knew, or was he an acute antiquary who reproduced the past? Or, to compromise, did he set heroes of the past in an age closely resembling his own present? Or was it all imaginary? Surely there was too much gold for the Dawn of History?

About 1820 a German boy was born, who in his early schooldays fell in love with Homer. He did not learn Greek, but he loved the stories in German. He had to go into business at an early age. But he had a gift for learning languages, and he never forgot Homer. He had adventures too, and took his chance in Russia, New York and South America. But at last he had made money enough to retire, and he went to Greece to begin life again, digging up the scenes of Homer. Excavation had revealed Nineveh; might it not tell us something of Homer's Achaeans? Of course, it would; and, over-coming the obstacles of Turkish officials and neglecting the doubts of German scholars, he took the hint of a local Englishman and excavated the mound or hillock of Hissarlik. Later on he did the same at Mycene and Tiryns. He was not a skilled modern excavator, and his methods shock archaeologists to-day. But he dug, and dug deep, and got there. He found seven Troys, one on top of the other, and one a long way down had been burnt. He found the grave of Agamemnon, where the Greek tourist Pausanias (see page 353) had said he would; and in it were gold masks; Mycene was amazingly rich in gold, as you can see to-day from the most hasty visit to the Athens Museum. So Homer was true!

But, as others followed Schliemann, questions arose. Fortress walls, beehive tombs, the Lion Gate, these were familiar, they had not been lost; but when the ground plan of the houses was unveiled, it did not quite fit what Homer says of the house of Odysseus; and other divergences were noted, in time a great many. The men whose cities were dug up were no mean artists; the gold cups found at Vaphio show wonderfully living scenes of bull hunting, work not primitive in the least. From representations found of men and women, it seems they did not dress like Homer's people. Needles, buttons and scissors are not primitive appliances, and clothes made without them have to be simple. The archaeology of buttons has perhaps yet to be written, and it should be interesting. The Homeric man wore the *chiton*, a loose sort of woven shirt; the Mycenaeans wore loin cloths, which represent surely an earlier stage. Homer's women had brooches, the Mycenaean did not, and it means a fundamental difference in dress. Homer's heroes were "long-haired Achaeans"; these people wore their hair in three curls on the crown. The armour was different; the Homeric shield was round; the pictures discovered showed a long, almost oblong, shield. The Homeric sword cut with a stroke; the bronze swords found were made to wound with the point and had small hilts. (All Homer's heroes were big—"bigger than men now".) Homer's heroes put iron heads on their arrows; in the graves and ruins the arrows were pointed with obsidian. (This is a natural glass, of volcanic origin; in the earliest times the island of Melos seems to have been its chief source.) Iron is constantly mentioned by Homer; hardly any was found in the excavations.

Other discoveries followed, as other sites were excavated. In 1897–8 the Turks lost Crete for ever, and left it; and excavation began at Knossos. Knossos before that was a mere name; now the name stands for a civilization. Elaborate buildings and staircases are found, evidently not the work of beginners; statuettes of goddesses (or women) with full skirts and wasp waists, oddly suggestive of Parisian fashions of the 1880's; and what amazed the discoverers perhaps most of all, a sanitary system flushed with water. Gradually what was found was classified and dated. Egyptian art was no new field, and its history was accurately known; and, from loans and likenesses, it became possible to put a date on this and that; and by degrees it came to light that in the days before Homer there had been in and around the Aegaean a civilization of a very high order, which lasted for centuries, rose, flowered, declined, and perhaps was ended by violence. The people, it is clear, were not Homer's heroes, but men of a different build, stature and mind; and they are assigned to the vague Mediterranean race, from whom masses of people in Italy and France are obviously descended, and not a few in Wales and other parts of the British Isles, dark-haired, rather short people, neat-handed, with heads of a distinctive shape. All over Europe, as we know, there broke in historic times another race, "big blonde beasts" as a German humourist called them, big splendid men and women to match the dying Gaul, familiar in the sculpture. Again and yet again we know of tribes bursting into the Mediterranean area from North or Mid Europe or beyond, Scythians, Trêres, Bithynians, Gauls, Cimbri and Teutons, Goths and Vandals. Is it possible that Homer's heroes came of some such stock? Their build and their light hair suggests a Northern origin. But this is guessing.

One thing is clear. Centuries of civilized history are lost to us, between say 1200 B.C. and some date long before it; and older again there must have been half-civilized people in these areas. A history of their art and of their crafts can be written, with shrewd deductions from works of art imported from other civilized places, as well as such things as bits of amber (proved by chemists to come from the Baltic) and jade from China. There were kings who had wealth to spend on buildings and ornaments, kings rich in gold, who used and perhaps controlled the sea (so archaeologists interpret Knossos), but their names and stories none can tell. "Brave men there lived ere Agamemnon was", said the Latin poet; and there we must leave it for the present.

With one last word, however, or perhaps two. The period of Man's development on the earth grows longer and longer with the discoveries of recent decades; civilization has a history far older than anyone, in days before Schliemann, had guessed. Early man in favoured regions had to the full the instincts we see in his ablest descendants; the history of ancient metallurgy discloses a gift for experiment and a surprising ingenuity in the treatment of ores and the use of tools, and then in the early flowering of the arts. The ancient craftsman wrought in gold, he carved stone, and he built ships. The modern world, it has to be remembered, had to re-discover by experiment the proper lines, the true curves, for a ship's hull, which the ancient world knew and the Middle Ages lost. Very great developments indeed there were in the arts, in these days before Homer, in large measure swept away (we are told, and we can believe it) by barbarian invaders, just as Roman civilization largely was between A.D. 400 and A.D. 800, but in neither case was all lost. Civilizations do indeed decline and fall, but, as Cassius says, in Shakespeare, who took it from Brutus in Plutarch, "the cause...is not in our stars, but in ourselves". Civilization fails from within, and there are many causes, from too much patience with over-government to no patience with any government. "The moral of Knossos", said a Scotsman, as he boarded his ship after a visit to Sir Arthur Evans' excavations and restorations, "is that good plumbing will not save a civilization." What *will* save it? is the question that comes again and again to the reader of ancient history.

A lady of Tiryns

Chapter III

THE EARLY GREEK WORLD

A. THE UNKNOWN MEDITERRANEAN

THE surface of Greece is broken up by mountain ranges and by great bays, and a large part of the Greek lands were cut off by the sea. For hardly any part of "Greece" was so Greek, or remained for ever so Greek, as the islands in the Aegaean. These, they tell us, are simply the mountain peaks of a land sunk beneath the water. There are no great plains in Greece, no great rivers; there is no Thames, no Hudson, nor St Lawrence; no stream on which a boat of any size can be sailed. So when the Greeks came into their country, mainland or island, they settled down, as it were, into compartments. Indeed, the map of Greece might be compared to a long coach on a modern train with its different compartments; it is possible to reach the one from the other by the corridor, but the people in one compartment are a family party and do not want to be interfered with by the people next door. It was something like that in Greece, and the sea was the corridor. Lands of different sizes, some pleasant in climate, some harsh, were separated by mountains, sometimes by swamps. On the ford of a river, or a bay of the sea, a town might grow, or, failing ford or bay, on a hill-top, which could be defended against invaders. Readers who know Edinburgh Castle or Dumbarton Rock will have a picture in their minds of the fortress high in the air, safe against every enemy who has no long-range guns, and round the rock at its foot there grows up something of the town. Such a town was Corinth, on a neck of land between two seas, with a towering mountain that gave the widest view over all Greece. The main things to remember are these: that town is cut off from town by mountain or by sea; that few had very much land about them; and that many and many a Greek town saw its population outgrow its food-supply.

When food for its people failed ashore, the Greeks had to take to the sea; sometimes to get fish; sometimes to cross the sea and find new lands where they could feed cattle and grow food; sometimes to be raiders and traders. Raider and trader are different things with us, but in the early Greek world the same man might be both. In speaking of the Mediterranean in the first chapter, mention was made of the winds that blow upon the Mediterranean—the cold stormy North wind from Russia, the hot stormy South wind from the Sahara. There is something more to be said about the winds. Even to-day, when all the ships are steam-ships, winds matter far more than landsmen think; but we have to deal with an age of sailing ships. The student of Nelson's voyages and battles finds that the winds of the Mediterranean, when they are not stormy, are light and fitful; they change quickly, and they drop. The wind drops, and the ship has lost the power which enabled the captain to control it; it may very easily be at the mercy of currents, or it may lie almost helpless. This made the navigation of the Mediterranean a very difficult art; and the wonderful thing is how clever the Greeks became in sailing their ships. In our times, nearly every day a liner starts to cross the Atlantic, and she reaches the exact port for which she starts, whatever the wind or weather. The captain to-day has charts of every coast and of every sea, which show him all the rocks and many of the currents and the depths of the bottom. He has, like all the sailors of the last six centuries, a compass; but, unlike most of them, he has special instruments for finding out every day at noon where he is, by "taking the sun". He has also "a log", which trails behind his ship and tells him roughly how many miles he has travelled since noon yesterday.

The Greek sailor had none of these helps; he never dreamed of them. He was very reluctant to cross the open sea, even with the help of the sun and the stars to guide him. Sometimes, as in St Paul's voyage, they failed him. His aim, then, was to skirt the land, and this meant that he must know the coast-line as a motorist knows the shape of his own town. He must know the headlands, and the rocks and shoals beneath the surface. ("A new boat and old rocks" is a Highland proverb.) He must know where the sandbanks are, and be able to guess how they may shift, and what the rivers are doing in silting up the bays. He must be weather-wise, too, and that means a good deal of local knowledge; "the wise master-mariner", says a Greek poet, "knows what wind will blow on the day after to-morrow, and is not wrecked through greed of gain". When he gets out of the known regions, he must be able to guess, from shapes seen in the twilight, what the coast-line really is, and to guess from the colour and movement of the water how deep it is, what lies beneath the surface and what the currents are, and, again, what the wind is likely to do. So much for the voyage out. But, to come back, he must know all this from the other end, which may be quite different; and he must know it all both ways, in storm and sunshine, in good light and in bad light. It was centuries after the Greek took to sailing about the Mediterranean before he had an anchor; and to be afloat in a small sailing ship on a more or less unknown coast at night when you don't know exactly where the currents are, nor what the local winds will do from hour to hour, means danger and anxiety. So if the early Greek sailor could see towards sundown a safe-looking bay he was always rather apt to run his ship up on the beach. He at least knew where he would find it in the morning, and it gave him a chance of fresh supplies of drinking water. If a ship is to be constantly beached, she must be built to do it safely; this is one of many problems which the ship-builder has to think out.

Broadly there are three things always to be remembered when one is thinking of the sea. The first is that a landsman never knows what a ship can do; and the second is that he never knows what a ship cannot do; and the third is that he generally forgets that there are no frontiers on the sea. England is England; it leaves off definitely at the Straits of Dover, and after some centuries of fighting it left off in the North at the river Tweed. It is impossible to draw lines on the sea: and, wherever the sea reaches, a ship may go. The Mediterranean is all *one* sea. If we talk about Greek history or Roman history, French or Egyptian, that is only for convenience. The Mediterranean touches all those lands, and links them up; and, in a sense, it invites the people of every land to come and see the people in all the other lands—always provided that you know what a ship can do, and what a ship cannot do. Those two points you will only learn by handling a ship; everything turns on that; and one of the first rules is that the master-mariner has to know his ship and all her ways; and very often they take a lot of knowing. Ships are as individual as people, and as wayward.

Let us take the story of a famous voyage made about the year 600 B.C. by a sailor called Kolaios. He sailed out of Samos, an island in the Aegaean, to go to Egypt, probably in the late spring when sailing began to be safe. The North Wind would take him down among the islands to Crete, and, as it still held, he dropped across to the African shore. This was the regular way to Egypt. Kolaios landed on a small island off the African coast, where he found a marooned man, left by another ship which was to return; and his food had run out. Kolaios gave him food, and then set out to sail Eastward for the mouths of the Nile. All had gone well, so far, and now all changed. The North Wind dropped; the wind chopped and changed; and before very long he was in the open sea, out of sight of land, with no idea where he was. All he knew was that he was being driven headlong by a gale— he could not tell from what quarter, because he could not see sun or star. But his ship was a good one, and she did not strain her timbers like St Paul's ship long after, in the same waters; or, if she did, he knew what to do, and was able to do it. The gale continued for days, and then it stopped; and on a fine clear day, with the sun on his left, which meant he was sailing Westward, he saw two huge rocks and the open sea between them. Kolaios must have known a good deal about the Mediterranean; stories travel far and wide; and, though he had never been there before, he knew where he was. He was facing the Straits of Gibraltar, and the two rocks were the famous Pillars of Hercules. Wherever the American sign for a dollar is printed, you have a reminder of Kolaios

and his voyage. On an old Spanish coin the two mountains were represented by pillars, and a garland was
twined about them ($). That coin was the ancestor of
the American dollar. It is worth while sometimes to
remember the links that bind us to the past, and to
remember that through all commerce runs a pedigree.
Men still sail the same seas as did the ancients, and very
commonly with the same purposes.

Kolaios knew where he was, and he sailed out on to
the Atlantic, the first Greek of whom we know to reach
it. He turned Northwards up the Spanish coast and
sailed into the port that we still call Cadiz, which, like
London, is the remains of a very ancient name. All we
are told next is that he sold everything he had on the
ship at immense profit, and came safely back to Samos
and set up a great urn, as the offering of a tenth, in the
temple of the goddess Hera (Juno).

In modern money he had made about £150,000, a
good profit for one voyage. The question arises "How did
he do it?" What was he carrying on that ship? What
did people produce on Samos? Pottery and wine. Greeks
were always sending wine in great jars to Egypt. Samian
pottery was famous all over the Mediterranean. We
lose a great deal of History because we do not think
of the familiar things. The most ordinary cup or basin
to-day is round, and is glazed; it is handy, and you can
clean it; it has been made on a wheel. An unglazed pot
soon fouls past cleaning. In ancient days, whatever the
uncivilized tribes of Italy, France and Spain, used to
hold water or anything else, they had nothing to match
the graceful, rounded, and glazed pottery of the Samians.
Kolaios, then, had reached a country where the people
would buy every bit of pottery he had at any price he

liked to ask, and where Greek wine was a new experience. Like more modern navigators trading glass beads for lumps of gold, he knew how to make a bargain.

But what had the Spaniards to offer him? There was a Hebrew prophet writing at this very date. "Silver spread into plates is brought from Tarshish", says Jeremiah (x. 9). "Tarshish" was his name for the region to which Kolaios had come. From the very dawn of history down to to-day Spain has been a land producing silver. The clever Greek traded his pottery and wine for silver, and his bargains took his breath away. The next thing was to get home, and that was a new voyage of exploration Eastward. He was, in a sense, starting from the wrong end. He had to discover the way to Samos. That was not all. There were other traders on those seas, the Carthaginians; and, like the Spaniards in the days of Sir Francis Drake, they did not want interlopers in their seas, nor on the Spanish mainland; and their practice was to capture every Greek ship they found in their waters, and sink it, men and all. Kolaios had to get a picture in his mind of the coast-line, as we have described it. He had to dodge the Carthaginians, or, if he met them, to fight them, or to show them a clean pair of heels. He may have gone Northward, round the long coast-line of Spain and France, passing Marseilles and down Italy, and through the Straits of Messina, or else along the North coast of Africa. This African course takes a modern tramp steamer three days and three nights; and he plainly could not sail by night; he had to know the whole coast. But, at any rate, he found his way back, and we may be sure he went to Spain again, and many another Greek after him.

About the same time another great traveller made a

great land journey; his name was Antimenidas. He came from an island near the home of Kolaios; and, whether he went overland all the way, or took ship to Tyre or Sidon, he struck right down the Euphrates to Babylon. There he enlisted in the army of the Babylonian king, who may have been the Nebuchadnezzar we read of in the Bible. He served his time and came home again; and his brother, who was a famous poet, wrote him a song, telling how he had come from the very ends of the earth, and how in that far country he covered himself with renown by laying low a giant near seven cubits high, and how he had been given as a reward a sword with an ivory hilt, studded with gold.

B. COLONIES

These were not the only lands the Greeks visited. We have seen how Kolaios sailed for Egypt, as many another had done, but now we have to turn to another scene. North of Asia Minor lies what we call the Black Sea. The Greeks began by calling it "the Inhospitable"; but, as this was discouraging and suggested ill omens, they changed its name later on to "the Very Hospitable" (the "Euxine"); and it honestly deserved the name. It is a stormy sea, and in winter its northern shores are ice-bound; but on those northern shores lie rich wheat lands, which the early Greeks quickly realized; and, when the population outgrew space and food-supply in the home towns, colonies were planted all along the north shore of the Black Sea. The city of Miletus in Asia Minor sent out eighty or ninety colonies, and it was not the only colonizing city. The words are easily said; but if we think what it means to plant a colony, if we read the history of our own colonies, it grows clear that the thing is hard to do. First, there must be some sound knowledge of the seas and their shores, and the lands inland; and something ought to be known about the climate and its changes, and about the inhabitants. When Europeans colonized North and South America, nearly every first beginning of a colony ended in disaster. One in three of the Pilgrim Fathers was dead within a year. Starvation dogged the French in North America, and the Spaniards in La Plata. Even in the rich land of California the Spanish colony had to be fed by sea from Mexico.

We have hints that Greek colonies began with plenty of failures; but, in the end, they established themselves along that Russian coast. They walled their cities, and they had need to wall them. But the barbarians would trade with them and grew boundless wheat for the Greeks to take to the cities of Greece, where there were more than enough people to eat it. They were able to supply the natives in return with tools, and other necessities and perhaps luxuries, which made the wheat-growing worth while. They bought from home what they needed themselves; on an ice-bound coast we may be sure that woollen garments were needed in winter. Central Asia Minor is a high plateau of downs and pasture, a land throughout the ages of sheep and wool, as every Turkey carpet more than ten years old reminds us;* even its pattern, we are told, is partly Assyrian by origin. The fleeces were taken down the roads to Miletus, spun, and woven into cloth, and the cloth sent to the colonies. The olive, as we have

* Since the Greeks of Asia Minor were transplanted to Europe in 1923, the "Turkey" carpets are made in Greece. They were made in Asia a thousand years and more before the Turks came there.

seen, was one of the chief foods of the Greeks, particularly
in the form of olive oil; but the olive would not grow on
the harsh Russian soil, so, along with the clothing, the
Black Sea Greeks imported olive oil. Consequently,
ships went to and fro, with plenty of freight both ways;
which means, though nowadays people do not always
realize it, cheap goods at both ends, and better profits
for those who sell and carry them.

It was not only in the Black Sea, but Westward also
that the Greeks planted their colonies. They sailed a
certain distance up the Adriatic, but not far. There the
mountains come down to the coast, and the climate is
colder and more rainy than they liked. So they sailed
across to Southern Italy, and began planting colonies in
Italy and Sicily. Southern Italy, it has often been said,
was the America of the Greeks; and just as we speak of
New England in America, "Greater Greece" was an old
name for Southern Italy. Very populous and very
renowned the cities became, and many of them are still
there. Tarentum, Syracuse, Naples, are famous names in
history, and are all Greek. Perhaps half we know of the
tools and furniture of ancient life comes to us from the
Greek city Pompeii; the name of it was Roman, but the
city was Greek. Marseilles, near the mouths of the
Rhone, was a Greek foundation of about 600 B.C., not
so important in early days as Syracuse, for want of a
civilized world to the North of it. Syracuse was a western
town, to begin, but as civilization spread Westward, it
came to be more and more in the centre of the world.
Marseilles, till Roman days, was on the very outskirts of
the world, and, like Montreal in the days before General
Wolfe, and Winnipeg long after, a centre for trade with
barbarians or half-barbarians. But when Gaul became

populous and civilized, the old Greek town rose like these Canadian towns to a new importance.

Southward, the Greeks planted Cyrene and other towns on the stretch of North Africa between Egypt and Carthage—towns between the desert and the sea, but on a good soil; and they reached a high prosperity. Cyrene, for instance, had a famous dynasty for eight generations, who introduced the Greek world to a new variety of horse, bigger and stronger than Homer's heroes ever saw; and this meant new interest and new sensations in chariot racing. The African desert was not in those days quite what it has become, and there was prosperity beyond what we might have expected.

All this navigation, exploration and adventure, land-travel and sea-faring, had its effect on the Greek mind, with ceaseless contrast, challenge and question. It got the Greek out of the parish, as we might say, into the world; but much as he wanted to see the world and make it his own, he loved the parish. Few races have turned homeward like the Greeks. To this day when the Greek in America has made his fortune abroad (it need not be a big one), he will wish to go back to Greece.

C. TYRANTS OR STATESMEN

The word "tyrant", it is guessed, came from Lydia, a foreign loan-word, perhaps used at first as half slang, much as Englishmen at various times have borrowed such words as Nabob, Begum, Mohawk, Bashaw; but "tyrant" had more staying power. It may have meant "king" in Lydian or whatever the language was; in Greek it came to mean a usurper who has made himself master of the city, and remodelled the laws and rules to

please himself. There has been much abuse of tyrants in
the ancient world, and not a little since "tyranny", in
the Greek sense, has reappeared in modern Europe. But,
as was suggested by the historian Polybius, of whom we
shall hear more in later chapters, "the cause is more
interesting than the fact". What were the circumstances
that made a tyrant possible? Again what did the tyrants
do, to give the bad taste to the Lydian word?

First, then, how tyrants arose. We have to remember
the Greek city, one among dozens, with its limited fields
and its unlimited population outgrowing altogether the
food-supply from those fields. If the numbers of a
population double every fifty years, how are they to be
fed? It is clear at once that the land, even if badly farmed
and less and less fertile, comes to be more and more
valuable; where else can food be found? Then the owners
of land will prosper, and the landless starve—is that it?
And where the farmers are tenants, rents will go up. Add
to this the quick adoption by the Greeks of the Lydian
invention of coinage. If a rent is to be one-sixth or even
five-sixths of the farm produce, the farmer has indeed to
reckon with the changeableness of seasons; but the landlord shares his plight or his prosperity. But if he has to
pay his rent in coin, he has to sell his produce first, and
must reckon on the market being as irregular as the
seasons. One year he does well on the new basis of rent
in coin, the landlord not so well; the next it is the other
way round; the farmer never really knows how things
will go; and we learn that he often got deep in debt.
Overseas trade may relieve pressure; younger sons and
livelier spirits take to the sea and shipping life, for love
of adventure clearly stirred the Greeks; life was not all
economics. But whether the farmer or his landlord

makes or loses year by year, the man who buys the produce and sells it again, at home or abroad, seems to do very well; he makes money hand over fist. So we find this combination: a crowded state; pressure on the land; scarcity of food-supply; the growth of debt, with money-lending at dreadfully high interest (the security was so bad); farmers growing poorer; noble landlords, at best, much as they were; and traders and newcomers and odd persons, foreigners perhaps, overflowing with money. The old balance is upset, people do not know where they are, still less where they will be; money is in one lot of hands, land in another lot, and in many hands there is nothing; there is the ugly outlook of sheer starvation; something must be done to prevent famine and the food riots that may mean revolution and fresh muddles.

Relief was found mainly in three ways. A shrewd city government, like that of Miletus, pushes the idea of colonies; and, after some bad failures, it catches the public imagination, and Miletus founds her eighty or ninety colonies. But such an expansion must have meant a new and big development in trade—ship-building, tool-making, cloth-weaving; and the appearance of brokers who gathered up woollen goods, olive oil, etc. and took them in bulk to the Black Sea; for it is evident that the farmer who grew the olives could not always have oil enough to make a full cargo, nor always have a ship in which to carry it, if he were sailor enough to do it. As a result dealers, traders, middlemen, and the smiths, weavers and other craftsmen counted more in the community, making more and more money, and creating fresh problems. A second way out of those difficulties, which were partly economic and partly

political, was to appoint a man to be legislator, with
power to codify and to change the laws, to deal perhaps
with debt and land tenure, in short to save the state, to
give it some good working rules, and then to retire into
private life. *Aisymnetes* was the name they gave him—
a poetic word taken from Homer.

Both of these plans needed some very real intelligence
in the ruling classes; and where they did not possess it,
there was liable to be explosion. Some man would seize
supreme power by force, a popular leader obviously; he
would get rid of the ruling classes, by death, if they had
not the sense to clear out; and then he would rule by
himself. To do this and to make himself tyrant, he needed
several things. First, as the ancients tell us, he wanted
popularity; a man whom nobody liked would have no
chance to become master; too many people would be
against him, they would rally, and he would be killed;
he must be a popular figure. It is pointed out nowadays,
that he must also have money; he will have to pay a good
many people and pay them handsomely in cash. He
needs armed men, who have to be hired, their armour
and rations have to be bought; and a number of people
will have to be bribed. It is a shrewd suggestion that
this combination of popular favour and cash in hand
must mean a man of the new kind, who makes money
earn money, not one of the old landlord class or a penni-
less labour leader. The man might indeed be of the old
aristocratic group by blood, as Cypselus was at Corinth.

At Corinth a noble family, called the Bacchiads, had
ruled for ninety years, and on the whole they had done
fairly well. They claimed to be descended from Herakles,
and married among their cousins. A girl in one of the
families was somewhat deformed; they nicknamed her

Labda, she looked so like the letter L; and nobody wanted her. So she was given to an outsider, which was rather a mistake; the family were warned by an oracle to be watchful. So when her baby was born (who was not like L), a number of the men of the family came to see him. She handed the baby to one of her kinsmen, and the child seemed to smile; he handed it at once to the man next him; it quickly went round the lot and back to Labda. It was rather odd. She came of a clever family, and she had some of their sense. The men went out; and she listened. They were quarrelling; why had the first man not dashed the baby on the ground and killed it, as arranged? They must try again, and they did; but Labda was too many for them. She hid the baby in a chest, and perhaps sat on the lid; and that is why the baby was called *Cypselus* from the *cypsele* in which his mother hid him; or so the Greeks said. But stories of this kind are sometimes invented afterwards to explain names.

Cypselus was a strong man and evidently popular, a demagogue, they tell us, as we should have guessed; and so well liked, so big and genial, that he would not guard himself against his people; he would have no body-guard. He drove his mother's old family out of power, doubtless most of them out of Corinth too. He was tyrant for thirty years, which at once suggests a great deal of practical wisdom. He had a gift for realizing chances in the opening seas; for he developed a lot of colonies up the Adriatic, which succeeded, and lived and flourished for centuries. He also reduced the older colony of Corcyra to some sort of dependence.

His son, Periander, succeeded him and reigned forty-four years, a great soldier, with something of his father's eye for the map. But Greece forgot most of that, and passed on stories which illustrate another side of tyrant life, stories of family quarrels; and a strange one about Periander's dead wife. She had known where some treasure lay, and he did not. So he sent to a shrine where the dead could be brought up by magic; but Melissa would not tell him—she was too cold in the other world. If that was it, Periander would see to it. He announced a great religious ceremony for all the women of Corinth, and they came—the tyrants managed festivals well. But a surprise followed; Periander's guards surrounded them, stripped them of their clothing, and let them go home as best they might. Periander burnt the whole heap of clothes, and Melissa's ghost came again, said she was comfortable now and told where the treasure lay. Stories like this live in what is now called "folk-memory", when men forget about constitutions and colonies. But can this story be true? Some moderns have guessed that Periander had made laws regulating extravagance, and, when he found them broken, determined that the women should learn he was in earnest. This is to make Periander very simple indeed. It has also been suggested he wished to capture the gold, worked into their clothing, which of course would not burn. But, as we learn more and more the beliefs of primitive men (and of modern Chinese), and realize how widely it is thought that to give something to the dead you must burn it, the story about Melissa and the clothes is taken as it stands. It can be believed that an act of this kind caused annoyance, and that everybody remembered it.

Without going into further detail among the tyrant houses—interesting as they are, for, if the tyrants were great sinners, there must be something right indeed, some-

thing interesting, about a man if he is a great sinner—
can we sum up, roughly, the good and the bad in the
tyrants? First, then, the bad; a tyrant's rule, says a Greek
philosopher, is bad, because it is directed to the advantage
of the man himself and not of the community. True—
more or less, as we shall see. Next, the tyrant is arbitrary;
he "gets outside the ordinary thoughts"—he does not
limit himself as we all have to do; and "he disturbs
ancestral customs, does violence to women, and kills men
without trial", it was said; all serious charges, the first
much the worst to the ancient mind, though nobody
liked the murder habit which the tyrant sometimes
showed. Third, they kept Greece weak and divided;
when things looked too risky at home, they might launch
their city on foreign war. The famous Polycrates of
Samos, who seized the power with sixteen armed men
(not a large number), was really a pirate-king, harrying
commerce all over the seas. (The story of his ring, given
back by the sea, hardly needs to be told.) Finally, when
it came to the point, the tyrants were ready to accept
Persian supremacy over all Greece to save their local
power.

On the other hand, some of the tyrants were very
enlightened rulers, who were open to new ideas and put
them through, as neither nobles nor popular leaders
would have done, even if they had thought of them—the
nobles because they were not generally interested in new
ideas, the popular leaders because they have generally
to follow the average man. Polycrates had a tunnel
driven through a mountain to bring a water supply into
Samos; Pisistratus set up fountains in Athens. As there
were no pipes or taps, all water for house purposes was
fetched by the women; and these measures halved their

work; it was a practical service to the women in every household. In the countryside, the tyrant might, as Pisistratus did in Attica, clear out the big landlords (who, perhaps naturally, disliked him very much for it), and turn all the peasants from tenants or serfs into small land-owners, much more prosperous, and anxious to keep the tyrant and not have the landlords back. In much the same spirit the Tudors broke the power of the barons; and we are told that it was peasant farmers who kept Napoleon on the throne of France. As we have seen, the tyrant in some cases guided industry, commerce and colonization. In our own times we have seen how a millionaire, after being furiously denounced in middle life, has exterminated yellow fever. The tyrants by use of their arbitrary power made progress possible, which, if it helped their own interests, gave their critics also the chance of a larger life. Such service of the state must not all be put down to self-interest; the big man sees things in a big way, and some of the tyrants were the best servants their cities ever had. One part of a tyrant's task was to find work for the citizens, and out of this need came (in large measure) Greek architecture. Architects, builders, stone-hewers and quarrymen all profited from temple-building; and the big new temples brought people to see them, and made men proud of their cities. Here once more the tyrants led their age. They developed great popular festivals—not of the modern bank-holiday, cocoanut and charabanc type—but such festivals as centred in acts of worship, and out of which came the Greek drama, sculpture, painting and other arts. It is a curious thing to reflect upon—how much has been done for the human mind, for culture, science, literature, by men of whom no common politician or moralist could approve, men whose hands were perhaps bloodstained, but whose minds ranged into regions where the ordinary good patriot would be left gaping. Only one of the Greek tyrant dynasties lasted as long as a century; two generations were generally the utmost; and the ground was left clear for a forward movement in democracy and (at least in Athens) in culture.

For we always come back to Athens. Athens was made by two men, if ever a state could be said to be made by individuals. A backward community out of the mainstream of Greek life, these two men made it possible for Athens to become what a great Athenian called "the education of Greece"—and that means, literally, the education of the world. What with currency, agriculture, debt, and unintelligent land-owning nobles, Athens was in as bad a way as any Greek city. Then Solon is made legislator, to "do something", as the English say. He seems to have been an elderly man, who wrote poetry of the genial comfortable kind that ordinary people could understand. Men spoke of him later as one of the "sages" of Greece. He had been a trader and gone a good deal about the Mediterranean; Egypt is mentioned, and he must have known the Black Sea. He was a patriot, who had done something (a poem, men said, did it) to rescue the island of Salamis for Athens for ever—the island you can see from the Acropolis. He was a kindly old man, very human, and great enough to be very simple; he understood common people and their ways of thinking.

Solon began by making life endurable for the farmers. He cancelled out of hand all debts on land; and he forbade the selling of a man's wife and children to pay his debts. One has only to think what it meant; he called this first group of measures *Seisachtheia*, the "shaking off of burdens"; and so it was; the horrible fear of a break-up of the family was gone for ever, the burden of debt was rolled off, and the farmer was free to work in hope. Hope was the secret, Solon saw; and anything that would get men to work and keep them working. So he did away with old-fashioned laws that tied men's hands in making contracts and wills, and thus discouraged enterprise. He altered the currency to one more generally accepted and understood; and just as if someone could get rid of English pounds, shillings and pence and give us dollars and decimals, it meant more trade. He headed the farmers toward producing olive oil, for which Attica was suited; they could sell that in the Black Sea for all the wheat they wanted. He made Athens a centre of trade and shipping, a centre of distribution to which merchants would bring their goods from everywhere. He encouraged industrious people, clever people with hands and brains, used to employing them and developing them in arts and crafts, and tired of revolutions in their own cities, to settle in Athens; and they came more and more for a century. To sum up the work of Solon, we may put it that he realized the significance of the individual, and set him free in a new way; he altered the constitution, too, to meet new needs; and he gave the impulse which made the Athens that could produce the poets, thinkers and artists of the great fifth century; for art and thought and poetry are intensely individual, and of all things least amenable to state control; they need a real freedom and Solon gave it.

After him came the tyrant Pisistratus, whom the landowners, as we saw, did not like, though the farmers looked back to his reign as the Golden Age. He did not meddle much with the laws; he was not cruel—far from it;

a genial, big, humourous sort of man. One day, the story went, out in the country he saw an old man working a very stony field. He sent one of his guards to ask him what he raked out of all these stones. "Trouble and pain," said the old man to the guard; "trouble and pain; and Pisistratus takes the tenth of it." "Go back, and tell him", said Pisistratus, "that I don't want the tenth of his trouble and pain"; and it was called the Taxless Farm ever after. A story like that made friends for him. So did his law providing at state cost a living for men crippled in fighting for the state. So did his water works, his country roads, his temples, his festivals, his care for industries, his gift for "putting Athens on the map", as moderns say, for making all the world aware that Athens was forging ahead and counted in Greek affairs. He had more "force of nature", says a Greek historian, than any of the politicians; and moderns have called him "the greatest statesman that Athens ever produced", "extra-ordinarily enlightened and successful". He and his sons did all this, and more; for they made their court a centre of poets and architects; and Athens became the very nest of all the genius of Greece.

D. THINKERS AND POETS

When all is said, the politicians of any age are rarely remembered ten years after they die or lose their seats in Parliament. Only historians, pondering sadly over maps, marvel at the short outlook and the scanty insight of those who managed our Colonies before they governed themselves. Ancient politicians were little wiser; and it is one of the touches of genius in the historian Thucydides that he ignores their very names, unless it may be that the murder of one of them shows the temper of the day. So little significant, so little formative, as a rule, are party leaders. Few indeed of the political figures did so much to make Greece as did the poets and the philosophers. An obscure Cambridge scientist wrote a book in the 1850's; and, though Darwin shaped no national policy in those ten years, the book altered, for ever since, the way in which educated people look at any question. And who, one asks, were the bribe-eating princes, evidently persons of importance, to whom Hesiod alludes in his poem about farming and other matters, which he (or posterity) called *Works and Days*?

People, who liked legends and coincidences (and such people were abundant in antiquity as to-day), brought Homer and Hesiod into contact. The two poets competed, it was said, for a prize in song or poetry; and the humourists must have been right when they said the prize was awarded to Hesiod—it is the one probability in the story. We have to guess at the dates of the two men —or of the poems attributed to them; and to say that perhaps two hundred years lay between them would not be the worst guess. The ancients noted that Homer tells you nothing about himself; you have to discover what interested him by reading his works, as you do with Shakespeare. Hesiod talks all the time himself, and a good deal of it about himself and his troubles. His father was poor; his brother was a trial to him; the town he lived in was bad in winter, evil in summer, never good; and his neighbours were not much better. His brother ought not to loiter chattering at the forge; work is the thing— "work is no shame, not working is the shame"; and early rising helps—"dawn takes away a third part of your work, dawn sets a man forward on his way, and sets him forward with his work, dawn that puts many a man on his road, and the yoke on many oxen". Yes, and if you work, you are more likely to buy your neighbour's lot of land, and not he yours;—so private property in land has come in, and the purchase of land, about which Homer is very hazy. Hesiod takes a look at ships, too, though he does not like the sea ("full is the earth of evils, full is the sea"); and he warns his reader when to venture aboard ship, and when to haul his ship ashore; and he adds the curiously modern hint (proved sound in modern commerce) to praise a little ship but put your freight in a big one—and hope there will be no storms. He ends up with a few words on manners—don't cut your nails in public, nor be rude in other ways, which he mentions; and he gives an odd list of things that are uncanny and days that are not lucky. He is a peasant, and a peasant's poet; but you have to forget Burns when you say so.

Theognis, who lived long after, was anything but a peasant. He is an aristocrat, and a city-dweller, whose world has turned upside down. He thought it would— "Kyrnos, this city is with child, and I fear lest she bear a man that shall straighten out our wantonness. Our citizens are yet sound of heart, but our leaders are turned to evil. Think not that that city, how quiet so ever it be, shall long go unshaken, where evil men love gains that bring evil to the state. From this come revolutions, the murder of men by their kin, yes! and monarchs". He prophesied aright—"Kyrnos, this city is still a city, but the folk are other folk, who in time past knew not laws nor customs, but with pelts of goats about their loins they lived and fed, like the stags, outside the city. Nowadays *they* are the noble, and the noble of the past are the base. Who could endure to see it?" Hesiod and he do not belong to the same generation; they are ages apart in outlook; but it is possible to sympathize with both. "A man's a man for a' that", sang Robert Burns; but the democrats of Greece, like those of France in 1793, forgot that aristocrats were men; they may have had provocation.

With one of the thinkers we may end this part of our story. Heraclitus was a man of Ephesus, whose writings are all lost, but stray sayings of his are still to be quoted, and well deserve quoting. Everything, he said, is flux; you never bathe in the same river twice. But if everything is change, some things stand; thus, "if the sun were to leave his track, the Erinnyes [the avenging goddesses] would fetch him back". All is change, but the laws of Nature do not change. Again (in words that may serve to win goodwill, or at least forgiveness, for this volume), "it is not learning *many* things that teaches the mind"; some people even in those days before examinations and certificates thought it did. Men hunt for an explanation of everything, but it is well to remember that "a hidden cause is better than an obvious one"—how much of the thinking of mankind has gone wrong through forgetting that! But it is so easy to miss the true cause;—"Yes", he said, "eyes and ears are bad witnesses for people who have barbarian souls". A barbarian soul—that would be a soul that knew no Greek, did not think like a Greek; —an arrogant claim? But to the end the Greeks were quite certain that no one could match the Greeks in thinking; anything to be first rate had to be Greek somehow; and they were right. A great modern German thinker said a very suggestive and probably a true thing, when he said that "the thoughts of Jesus were never properly expressed till they found Greek words".

E. THE ALPHABET

To this early period in Greek history belong the adoption and the improvement of the alphabet. It came to Greece from the nearer East. Herodotus tells us how Cadmus and his Phoenicians, when they came seeking the lost sister Europa, brought the letters to Europe; and how the Greeks adapted the letters. He had himself seen an inscription at Thebes in "Cadmeian letters, most of them like the Ionic". That the alphabet was a Semitic invention, its name tells us; *alpha* was *aleph*, which means ox; *beta* was *beth* (a house); *gamma* was *gimel* (a camel). Long ago the letters were pictures; *beth* was a triangle, for the house was a tent; *gimel* was the head and neck of the camel. But the chief change made by the Greeks was the invention, or we might perhaps better say the development, of the vowels. In Hebrew the vowels are hinted at by dots or strokes above or below the line of consonants. In Syriac, another Semitic language, two systems prevailed for giving the vowel sounds: one was a series of dots; the other, strangely enough, consisted of the Greek vowels, written above the line or below it. The Greeks also, in their logical way, when a consonant was doubled in pronunciation, wrote two of it; the Semites only wrote one and left the reader to divine how many he should pronounce. The alphabet has been called one of the most wonderful inventions of mankind; and if the Phoenicians were its inventors, we owe them much; but the thought rises, did not the Greeks do almost as much for us, when they realized that the vowels ought to be written? It was ever thus in antiquity; again and again the barbarian thought of something, the Greek borrowed it with genius, and made of it something else, something better, perfect and alive. (This sentence is itself borrowed from a late

Greek writer who says something very like it about ideas; the barbarian might get hold of an idea, it took a Greek to show its real significance.)

The Hebrew, like the Arab to-day, as everybody knows, wrote from right to left. When the Greek first used the alphabet, he wrote *boustrophedon*, as it was called. "The lowing herd *wind* slowly o'er the lea." The Greek wrote from one side of his page (whatever it was made of in the earliest days), and then in the next line he wrote back again; it was like driving cows, first out and then back. But at last our modern way of writing from left to right prevailed. It is still a question which way, if you use the right hand, was the more natural; but in this case usage is stronger than nature.

No one knows exactly when Homer's poems were first *written* any more than when they were first *made*. But by the time of Theognis and Heraclitus men wrote their thoughts, and gained an ever greater freedom in thinking. Cheap paper and the printing press were still far away in the undreamt future; but if a date is sought for the beginning of the "modern world", perhaps as good as any would be the year in which the first Greek *wrote a book*—if we could discover what year it was.

A Syracusan coin

Chapter IV

THE WORLD EASTWARD

A. PEOPLES OF ASIA MINOR

SOMETIMES the name of some common article hides a story. Such words as cambric, damask, muslin, calico, may tell you very little, perhaps; but to someone else who puzzled over the words, English enough by now, but somehow not akin to any other English words, they might say more; they might raise questions and, after a little search, might open up a great history of commerce and adventure, taking him to Cambrai, and on into Syria to Damascus, and further afield to Mesopotamia and Mosul, and at last in 1500 to India and Calicut. The names of ordinary things we eat and drink to-day tell the same tale. Tea is a Chinese word, however variously the Western nations mis-spell or mis-pronounce it, thé or chai. Coffee speaks of Arabia, sugar of India; these words have never been translated. The child who wants chocolate has still to ask for it in Mexican. A series of such names gives you landmarks of trade and travel; they grow half romantic, as you ask who were the men who first reached these distant shores, and what were the tribes they met, Flemings and Moslems, paynims and Gentoos and the people of Montezuma. The very names take you to Hakluyt and Queen Elizabeth, and step by step to Marco Polo and *The Dawn of Modern Geography*.

The Greek language tells the same sort of tale. Most Greek men and women wore a *chitôn*, some sort of shirt or chemise, sometimes covered by one other garment; it was compared to an onion skin by a Greek poet. *Chitôn* is a foreign word; and, since the Assyrian language became known, it is thought to be connected with *kitu* flax and *kitinnu* linen. Even gold and the axe have borrowed names, it is suggested, *chrysos* from *kharasu*, *pelekys* from *pilakku*. A number of names for weights and measures, *mina*, *siglos* (shekel) and *coros* more obviously and naturally come from the East; even the word for brick, our *plinth*; and flowers and strange things like camels, roses and cherries, myrrh and nard, have kept their foreign names. Even the Romans, long after, could not for ever call the elephant a "Lucanian cow".

Very simple questions sometimes open the door to historical inquiry. What colour did the Greeks paint their ships, and why? Homer constantly speaks of a black ship, but sometimes of a ship with dark blue prow or a ship with rosy cheeks. To have rosy cheeks, a ship needs red paint. This the Greek got from a red stuff he called *miltos*, which was found as a natural product in large quantities up-country in Asia Minor, but he did not go to the obvious ports on the Aegaean shore of Asia Minor; he went to Sinope on the North Shore, a Black Sea port, and the *miltos* was called *Sinopic*. Two things may be noted here. It is generally much cheaper and easier to fetch goods by sea than by land; it may cost less and be safer to take them five times or ten times as far by sea. A ship, too, will carry fifty times as much as a waggon, it needs no roads and no horses, pays very few tolls, meets fewer people, and requires far fewer men to work it than fifty waggons. As lately as 1880, it seems, some Greek towns imported their wheat from overseas, when, perhaps a day's journey inland, there was plenty growing for them, simply because transport by mule or horse would cost too much. But you have also to ask who holds the lands between you and your commodity. Quite apart from roads and horses, the longest way round may be politically much the shortest way home.

Who, then, held Asia Minor? And the answer must be, that at different times all sorts of people held it, the remnants of whose tribes remained there in inextricable confusion, the débris of races and religions. A clear impression, if the reader could gain it, would be wrong. Confusion must be the note of this section.

We do not know when or how the Greeks first went to Asia Minor; they knew, or they said so. They calculated somehow the date of the Trojan war; Herakles, they said, was a generation earlier; so his sons would be living at the time of the war; a hundred years of exile was laid on his family; so two full generations after the fall of Troy would give the date when his descendants returned to the Peloponnese, with the Dorians (the ancestors of the Spartans) to help them. They drove the Achaeans up to the Northern shore of the Peloponnese, who in turn drove out the Ionians. The Ionians went across the Aegaean in a body, and settled in Asia Minor, the land, as we saw, that a good Greek would count most blest of all for climate and seasons. Whatever truth there is in all this, the story is simplified and compacted; it all happened at once—which hardly seems likely. Legend said, and it is obviously true, that they had to fight for their foothold, against the Carians—a race which had a great gift for fighting, so much so that the Persians long afterwards called them "game cocks". But the Greeks beat the Carians, took their towns, and inter-married with them; and their children in turn were men of valour in defence of home and country, and joined with their Carian cousins in raiding other lands, as we shall see (pages 88, 89).

Up-country were other races. Asia Minor was already, as it always has been, a mixing bowl for races; some remained distinct, as it were, in pockets; some became blended with other broken tribes. Invaders came, some across the Bosporus, some across the Black Sea, and others by land from further Asia, up from Mesopotamia, Media and Persia, down from Turkestan. The two races who most impressed the Greeks were the Lydian and the Phrygian. The Greeks had only the dimmest idea of the Hittites, of whom indeed nearly everybody else lost sight, apart from references in the Bible which were not really understood. It is only since 1900 that it has been realized that the Hittites ruled at times from the Euphrates to the Aegaean, and were a very great power indeed with strong cities. In one of these cities, called by the modern Turks Boghaz-keui, was found a whole record office, full of documents all written on clay tablets, which proved to be diplomatic correspondence in eight languages. But the Greeks knew nothing of all this; they had some inkling of the people and called them White Syrians; and perhaps the Keteioi of Homer were Hittites. The famous Hittite monument on the road from Ephesus to Smyrna the Greeks believed to be Egyptian, though the man wears moccasins, the footgear of lands of snow. The Greeks knew of raiders of various tribes from Europe who swept over Asia—the Cimmerians, for instance, who went far and upset dynasties, and made Gyges the Lydian king ask aid of Asshurbanipal, king of Assyria (about 660 B.C.). The Assyrian king put a quite different colour on this; on his monument he records: "Gugu (Gyges)

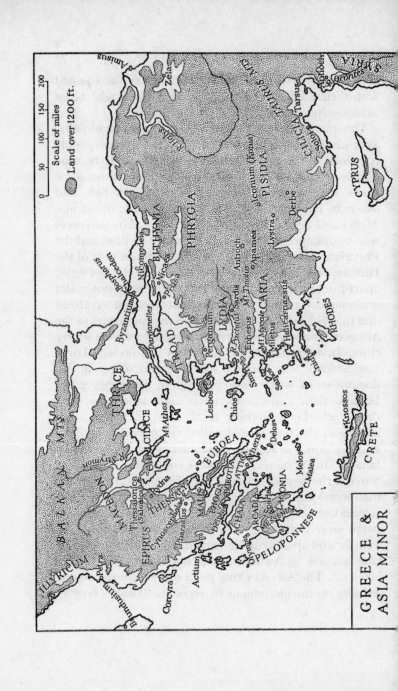

GREECE &
ASIA MINOR

Scale of miles
0 50 100 150 200

○ Land over 1200 ft.

ILLYRICUM

BALKAN MTS.

THRACE

MACEDON

Strymon

Thessalonica (Salonica)

Pydna

Olynthus

CHALCIDICE

Mt Athos

Byzantium

Bosphorus

Chalcedon

Nicomedea

BITHYNIA

Nicaea

PROPONTIS

Dardanelles

TROAD

Lesbos

Pergamum

PHRYGIA

EPIRUS

THESSALY

Cynoscephalae

Pharsalus

MALIS

Thermopylae

BOEOTIA

Delphi

Chaeronea

EUBOEA

Chios

Smyrna

Sardis

R. Hermus

R. Cayster

Ephesus

Mt Mycale

Mt Tmolus

LYDIA

Antioch

Iconium (Konia)

PISIDIA

Apamea

Derbe

Lystra

Actium

ACHAEA

ARCADIA

Olympia

Mantinea

ATTICA

Athens

Delos

Melos

Miletus

CARIA

Halicarnassus

Cnidus

Samos

Cos

RHODES

Corcyra

MESSENIA

LACONIA

Sparta

C. Malea

Petra

PELOPONNESE

Knossos

CRETE

TAURUS MTS.

CILICIA

Tarsus

Soloe

Issus

CYPRUS

SYRIA

Antioch

Orontes

R. Halys

Zela

Amisus

took the yoke of my kingdom". There were Scythian raiders, too, and Thracians, visitors as horrible by land as the Angles and Saxons were by sea on our shores. There was a famous king of Phrygia, up-country, who became a proverb; for everything that Midas touched "turned to gold"; but the raiders were too much for him, and he drank bull's blood and died. There is then confusion of every sort in Asia Minor—races, raids, legends, dynasties, all mixed up with fairy tales, demigods and scraps of legend and of real history. Happily we have not here to sort them out; and it has to be remembered that in the Middle Ages fresh tribes from the East brought in fresh confusion.

There was one race about whom the Greeks knew far more than they desired, the Lydians. They had plenty of legends about them; they worked the universal Greek hero Herakles into one of the Lydian royal houses; and they told splendid stories of Gyges, captain-general to the last king of that house. One was that the king showed him his wife; and the queen told Gyges that either he or the king should die for it; and Gyges chose that the king should die and saw to it that he did die, and then married the queen and was king himself. Another was that Gyges found a ring which would make him invisible, and this enabled him to do much that most of us dare not do, and at last made him king. The real Gyges, as we saw, had to ask Assyria to help him against the raiders; but in vain, for the raiders killed him. But, before that, he had struck out a line which his successors followed. The Ionian cities were what to-day people would call "his natural sea-ports"; and, like Russia pressing for the sea, he meant to have them. It took the Lydians five reigns of fighting to achieve this. Croesus was the king who

subdued the Ionians—the last Lydian king, the hero of
many Greek legends, always interesting, whether we see
him as the magnificent monarch, the friend of Solon, the
victim on the Persian pyre, the counsellor of Cyrus, or
miraculously rescued by Apollo from the flames and
transported by the god to live with wife and daughter in
the happy land beyond the North Wind. It is always
worth while to ask what sort of a figure it is round whom
the legend gathers; it is apt to be a personality, a maker
of history.

Historians and archaeologists have discussed the
Lydians, in some uncertainty, as to whether they were
a creative people, or middlemen who used and passed
on the inventions of others. The Greeks clearly felt their
influence. The Lydians, they said, invented two things,
which profoundly affected Greek life—coinage and the
retail trader. This type of trader could hardly exist where
barter prevailed, and where there was no small change
for small purchasers. There is obviously a widespread
change in all the web and woof of domestic and citizen
life, when the dealer on the market sells things in
penn'orths to married women looking after families;
and the Greeks said the Lydians began it. They also attributed to the Lydians wealth on a scale unfamiliar
to Greece, since Homer's day. Gold comes again and
again into the stories of Croesus; we hear of his gracious
gifts of gold to the Spartans to make an image; of his
splendid offerings to the god at Delphi; of his permission
to the Athenian visitor to take out of his treasury as much
gold as he could carry, and how the ingenious Greek
stuffed his tunic, his pockets, his boots, and his mouth
with gold, and then rubbed gold dust into his hair, and
staggered out, "looking like anything rather than a

human being"; and the genial king fell a-laughing and gave him as much more. Not everybody saw policy in this generosity, a successful plan to divide European Greeks from Greeks of Asia, with whom he had dealings of another sort. With gold, Lydia became a byword for luxury, dye-stuffs, carpets, slippers. But without doubt the Lydian king was the greatest of powers; had he not subdued the Greek cities of Asia, was he not lord of cavalry and chariots, had he not divided Asia with the Medes? So indeed he had; for, when Lydian and Median armies met on the river Halys, an eclipse of the sun surprised them—a sign that heaven would not have Lydian and Mede fight; so they made peace. This eclipse was foretold by Thales, says Herodotus; how he did it, we do not know, but it took place, and it gives us one of our few firm dates, 28 May 585 B.C. Later on, as we shall see, Croesus crossed the Halys to face other barbarians, and "destroyed a great empire", as the oracle said he would.

B. ASSYRIANS AND BABYLONIANS

Our tangled skein of races reaches from the Aegaean to the Euphrates, and at the far end of it we find the Assyrians. Asshurbanipal is a difficult name, and the Greeks and Romans turned it into Sardanapalus, and made the warrior king of the Assyrians into a proverb for the extreme of luxury. Babylon overcame the Assyrians before the Greeks had gained any very certain knowledge from travel in those regions. The influence of these peoples upon the Western world was indirect; but among the Greeks we find echoes of their religion. Year by year the women of those lands wailed for

Tammuz, the lost lover of their goddess Ishtar (Ezekiel viii. 14). *Adonai* is the Aramaic for "lord"; and the lost lover became Adonis for the Greek women, who wailed for him across the Aegaean. Jew and Phoenician had contact enough with the conquerors or raiders, as you may choose to think them, from Nineveh. In one way, however, the great empires perhaps helped Western civilization; for in the days when the Greeks were battling for their foothold in Sicily, Tyre had all it could do to hold its own on the Phoenician shore, and the Carthaginians could not keep out the Greeks.

In 425 an envoy from the Persian king to the Spartans was captured by the Athenians; he carried despatches "written in the characters of the Assyrians", which, on interpretation, revealed that the king "did not understand" what the Spartans wanted; perhaps he did not wish to. There was a whole literature written in those characters, lost to the world till the nineteenth century; for, curiously enough, it would seem that Asshurbanipal, the last king of the Assyrians, and Nabo-na'id, the last king of the Babylonians, had each of them a taste for literature and for history, and amassed great collections of books (if we may so call them), stamped upon clay tablets in cuneiform (the wedge-shaped letters that represented syllables). When the cities were sacked, these tablets were left lying among the ruins; they had no value whatever to people who could not read them; so they survived, to be gathered, deciphered and read in the nineteenth century. Then it was with surprise that the West discovered that, in addition to monuments and sculptures which revealed high artistic gifts, the vanished peoples had a remarkable literature of epics and legends, of history, of law, and of astronomy. The clay tablets preserved the wonderful epic about Gilgamesh, which contains the story of a flood, and of a man who escapes in a vessel of his own, and who, as the waters abate, sends out a dove, a swallow and a raven. People asked at once what connexion there was between him and Noah. When a code of laws, associated with the name Hammurabi, was found and translated, similar questions rose about the laws of Moses; were they borrowed from the older book, or did both codes more or less independently register common Semitic customs? Real achievements in astronomy are credited to the Babylonians, and a great deal of nonsense in astrology. "Babylonian numbers" in the Roman Empire was a poetic figure for a horoscope.

In one or two curious ways Babylonian astronomy still regulates our lives. The seven-day week, with days dedicated to the seven planets (counting sun and moon as planets, which is not usual to-day) was adopted with a strange suddenness all over Western Europe in the first century A.D., in the Roman Empire almost within the lifetime of Christ. To the Jews a seven-day week had been familiar before. The week spread, further, among the tribes of Germany and the North, who translated the names of the days, which we should all be reluctant to change. But it is a strange reminder of Babylon, and not the only one. Every hour with its sixty minutes, everything in fact counted in sixties, speaks to those who know, and reminds us of an empire long gone, and of thinkers, whose work did not die with their imperial glories and their great city.

"An oiled and curled Assyrian bull"; "the Assyrian came down like a wolf on the fold";—the phrases remind us of boastful kings telling in great sculptures of their wars, their destruction of cities, their slaughter of men. The modern historian would have us pause before we believe all that an Assyrian conqueror proudly records of his devastations; but it appears probable that too great an expenditure of treasure on building palaces and magnificent monuments, and incessant waste of human life in extending a rule that constantly broke down, and in crushing revolts that blazed out anew with every fresh reign, may explain in some degree the final collapse of Assyria, and the almost total disappearance of the race. The Romans mixed them up with the Syrians, who called themselves Aramaeans.

We learn more of these two great peoples from the Jews than from the Greeks, little as the Jews saw to admire in either. Babylon interested the Greeks far more. It was a living city of immense size, built in a great plain, in shape a square, they said, each side one hundred and twenty furlongs in length, surrounded by a moat deep and wide and full of water, and a wall fifty royal cubits thick and two hundred cubits high; and the royal cubit is three fingers broader than the common cubit ($20\frac{1}{2}$ inches as against $18\frac{1}{4}$); the wall is of brick cemented with hot bitumen. Through the midst of the city runs the great river Euphrates, wide, deep and swift, from the Armenian mountains to the Red Sea (the Indian Ocean). A second wall is within the outer one. Herodotus, whom I am quoting, probably saw the walls and moat, which are somewhat similarly described by Nebuchadnezzar, who made them; he says of "the great waters" (his moat) that "the crossing of them was like the crossing of the great sea, of the briny flood". Babylon, says the Greek, was famous for two queens, Semiramis and Nitokris. Three hundred years before his time there had been a real princess Semiramis, who married an Assyrian king; and in later days the wildest legends gathered about her name. Nitokris is a puzzle; could she have been Nebuchadnezzar himself, perhaps, spelled in the Persian way Nabukadracara? "Her son, Labynetus", in Greek, was perhaps Nabo-na'id, the last king of Babylon; but three kings separate him from Nebuchadnezzar, and he was not of the same family. So obscure is the memory of the great.

A few lines from an inscription of the Persian king Cyrus, matter-of-fact enough, and dated by scholars in 538 B.C., form a pendant to the other king's boasts. (The months are modernized.)

In the month of June, when Cyrus, in the city of Upe (Opis), on the banks of the river Zalzallat, had delivered battle against the troops of Akkad, he subdued the inhabitants of Akkad. Wherever they gathered themselves together, he smote them. On the 14th day of the month, Sippar was taken without fighting. Nabo-na'id fled. On the 16th Ugbaru, the governor of the country of Guti, and the soldiers of Cyrus without fighting entered Babylon. Because he delayed, Nabo-na'id was taken prisoner in Babylon.... On the 3rd day of October Cyrus entered Babylon.... Peace to all Babylon did Cyrus proclaim.

Babylon had a long history still before it, even if the queen city of the world was destroyed. Every one knows how the Jews had been taken into a Babylonian captivity, and the name became a proverb for the oppressor. In the Christian book that ends the New Testament Rome appears as "Babylon"; the popes went into a "Babylonian captivity" at Avignon in the Middle Ages. But it appears, and it is a curious revelation, that a large number of the Jews, in spite of the freedom given by

Cyrus, refused then to return to Palestine as they refuse to-day; and Jewish scholars tell us that those who remained in Babylonia looked on themselves as the pick of Jewry. The 87th psalm, when it is unravelled, is a protest that the Lord counts a man born at Babylon as much a Jew as the child of Jerusalem. Jewish learning flourished there, and one of the rabbis lays it down that "to live in Babylon is the same as to live in the Holy Land".

When the House of Seleucus succeeded to the Eastern part of Alexander's Empire, one phase of its rule was "the resurrection of Babylonia"; there was a revival of cuneiform literature, a restoration of old temples and cults, but, as far as possible, not of the power of priest-kings. Greeks, too, in great numbers came to the country; they had no competing "Holy Land" to call them away. Greek words passed freely into Aramaic, the wide-reaching language of the East from Tarsus in Cilicia to China eventually. Of late years the Greek town of Doura on the Euphrates has been excavated, a town which had been re-founded, re-named, and "Hellenized", and then reclaimed for the Orient by the native wives of the Greek settlers. If modern Law gives a man the legal nationality of his father, History chose that mothers should as often, or more often, fix their race upon their sons.

C. EGYPT

Of all lands that Greeks visited, or of which they heard tell, none was strange as Egypt; and modern discovery of the world has found nothing like it. "It has more wonders than all the world beside", wrote Herodotus.

Here was a country, which consisted of one river, its banks and its delta, a country some eight hundred miles long and perhaps thirty miles across—nothing but the river and the fields it overflowed. Other lands look to rain to keep them fertile; when it rained in Egypt, it was counted a portent, a warning from the gods that trouble might be expected; yet Egypt, thanks to the river, was immensely fertile. The creatures of the river were as strange as the river itself. Lizards there grew to the size of nightmares, but they were real; for crocodiles were new to the Greeks; and, more than once in Greek travel-stories, when we hear of a river with crocodiles, the question quickly follows, could it be the Nile? The hippopotamus again was new, a thing incredible in Greek waters. Strangest of all, the river reversed the obvious laws of Nature; Greek rivers were torrents in the time of winter rainstorms—even small streams could do furious damage then; but they dried up in summer. Yet summer was the season when the Nile was at its fullest and overflowed. The Greeks made many guesses why it should be so. Strabo, the Geographer, in the time of Christ, at last gives the true reason; the overflowing was due to the summer monsoon rains far away in what we call Abyssinia.

The people of Egypt seemed to do everything the wrong way round, that is, in the opposite way to the Greeks; and yet, it seemed to come out right. In Egypt the women go to market and buy and sell, while the men remain at home and weave, but not as the Greeks weave. Men there carry things on their heads, but women shoulder their burdens. What the Greek does indoors, the Egyptian does out of doors, and *vice versa*. There are no priestesses in Egypt, but plenty of priests—and such remarkable gods! When a Greek would shave his head, as for mourning, an Egyptian would let his hair grow. An Egyptian does not object to living with animals in the house; he will not eat wheat or barley. Their dough they knead with their feet, but clay with their hands. They make their boats, and handle them, in a different way from the Greeks. They write from right to left, yet they are great in calculations. They are much fussier in some ways than the Greeks, less nice in others. They are far more particular about religious usage than other races; their religious usages are peculiar; their religious traditions are longer; and in regulating the year (which was bound up with religion) they show a far better grasp of astronomy and have a far more sensible calendar. Nowhere in the world are men more interested in death and the soul, or take more care of burial. No other land can show anything like the pyramids; and Egypt was the first place where the doctrine of the immortality of the soul was taught and believed; and those who preach it about the Greek world have borrowed it from the Egyptians. "I know the names of those who did this, and I do not mention them", says Herodotus. Strangest of all, the Egyptian regarded the touch of the Greek as pollution, and would not kiss him, nor use his knife. The Hindu in the same way counts English and American as unclean and defiling for himself—"Mleccha" is his polite name for us.

One may compare the effect of Egypt on the Greek mind with that of Japan and Australia on the modern European. The customs of Japan are all different from ours; the animals of Australia are incredible; and yet nothing seems very wrong. We may recall, too, the shock to European thought, when it was discovered that in

EGYPT   87

Peru and Mexico, utterly untouched by Greek, Roman
or Arab, very high civilizations had been developed, even
though it was not yet known how wonderfully precise
and accurate was the astronomy of the Maya in Mexico.
Egypt was in every way a challenge.

There was a Greek called Hecataeus who went to
Egypt, and was injudicious enough to talk about his
pedigree, which began sixteen generations, i.e. about
five hundred years, ago with a god. The Egyptian priests
took him into the inner court of a certain temple where
stood a number of wooden statues; every high priest
there, they said, inherited his office from his father and
set up a statue of himself. They numbered three hundred
and forty-five; at three generations to a century, this was
11,500 years; and the priests were all *men*, and there had
not been a king who was a god in human form. ("What
the priests did for him, they did for me, though I told
them no pedigree of mine", adds Herodotus.) Here was
a range of history far beyond anything chronicled in
record or legend or myth by the Greeks. Egypt had a
people incalculably older than anything in Europe or
Asia; it had known thirty dynasties, according to the
common reckoning of the ancients. Modern archaeo-
logical discoveries reveal that Egypt had a history far
older even than the Egyptians claimed, just as Stone-
henge and the flint arrow-heads and axe-heads found
about our fields tell us of peoples here centuries before
Julius Caesar.

It would be needless to give here a list of those dynasties
or to try to chronicle their campaigns into Palestine and
the Sudan, or their temples and pyramids, the marvels
of art that Tut-ankh-amen's grave has only recently
revealed. Greeks knew nothing of Chinese history and

culture. Even if the Egyptian was not really known to the Greeks, nor to anyone else till the Rosetta stone, with its clue to hieroglyphic, was found in the nineteenth century, yet an age-long civilization, amazing architecture, science and religion, both immeasurably old— it was no wonder that thoughtful Greeks were fascinated. The Greeks watched with amazement the practices of Egyptian religion, and in later days they had a half-proverb about an Egyptian temple, splendid without, and inside was a priest singing a hymn to a cat or a crocodile. But that was not the whole of Egyptian religion. Herodotus was quite clear that many Greek beliefs about the gods, many of the religious practices of the Greeks, were borrowed outright from the Egyptians; and he clearly thought some other things, such as the calendar, might be borrowed too.

It was a wonderful land, and it was very strange how the Greeks got there. There had been one of the recurring bad periods of Egyptian history, and the kingdom was divided among twelve kings, but they dealt justly one with another, till on a day of festival a strange thing befel. The twelve kings had to pour libations from golden saucers, but the high priest counted wrongly and brought only eleven. Psammetichos the last in the row used his helmet instead. Then someone remembered an oracle that that man should be king of all, who should pour a libation from bronze; and now Psammetichos had done it. The other kings did not however kill him, but drove him out into the marshes. But another oracle came to him that vengeance should come from the sea, when men of bronze appeared. This seemed unlikely; but suddenly word was brought him that men of bronze had disembarked from ships and were foraging on the plain.

In an instant he saw what it meant; he ran down and made friends with the raiders; they were Ionians and Carians in bronze armour, and they served him well, and made him master of all Egypt.

From that day on, as we can believe, Greeks came more and more to Egypt, traders and soldiers. Away up the Nile at Abu Simbel, carved on the legs of the colossal statue of an old Egyptian king, are the names of Greek soldiers, led there by Psammetichos (perhaps the grandson of the first); and it is the oldest, or one of the oldest, of all Greek inscriptions. The soldier from Colophon spells his city's name with a Q. There was in time a native reaction against the Greeks, but even the king, who profited by it, could not do without them; they were given a town of their own, Naucratis, which was excavated in 1906.

By this time Greek architecture and sculpture had made such progress, and these arts had become so stereotyped in Egypt, that little Egyptian influence is to be traced in Greek sculptors and architects. But for Greek thinkers and philosophers Egypt had a fascination. Plato tells how Solon the Athenian legislator went to Egypt and was there treated with high honour; but when Solon began to talk of the antiquities of Greece, the Egyptian priests smiled, and one of them, a very aged man, said gently: "Ah! Solon, Solon, you Greeks are always children!" What did he mean? "I mean, you are all young in your souls." They had no traditions of any real age, he meant; but his words have for us another meaning. Egypt was old, and the past crushed the present; but the Greek was young, with a child's love of asking questions, a child's freshness of mind. There is something fascinating about the past; it can bewitch;

but the Greek was not yet bewitched by it; he would use the past, and live in the present, and shape the future. And he did all three.

D. PERSIA

At the beginning of the nineteenth century, a scholar, named Grotefend, set forth the idea that an inscription in an unknown lettering could be read, if you had a clue or two; and to prove it he read two short phrases from a Persian monument—"Darius, king, son of Hystaspes" and "Xerxes, king, son of Darius". It proved that he was right. Thirty years later a young British officer in the Bombay army was sent to Persia, and became interested in the country, its history and its inscriptions. A great solitary rock, 300–500 ft. high, stands at Behistun, with a smoothed face, on which is carved a long story—two, in fact, but one is high above the other and much older. Henry Rawlinson had himself lowered from the top, copied the older inscription, took squeezes of it, and sent back to England in 1837 a fair translation of two paragraphs. He was called away to Afghanistan, but happily in 1843 he returned to copy and translate the whole of the Persian text of this famous inscription of Darius. Till then all we knew about ancient Persia was chiefly derived from Herodotus, complicated by the romances of a Greek physician, called Ctesias, the ancestor (one might say) of Sir John Mandeville and Baron Munchausen. The Greeks recognized Ctesias as a liar, and were misguided enough to bracket Herodotus with him. Henry Rawlinson led the way in establishing the credit of Herodotus; nothing can be done for the other man.

It is interesting to note that, though Persia was the national enemy of Greece, and came so near to ending

Greek freedom (and one wonders what would have befallen Greek literature and art in that case), there were Greeks who had no hatred for the Persians. Three names stand out of Greeks who really knew the Persians and quite clearly admired them—Herodotus, Xenophon, and Alexander the Great; and, as we gather up what the Persians have done in age after age, it ceases to be surprising. To begin with our gardens, the Persians were lovers of flowers, of the rose perhaps above all. But the lilac is Persian, as its name tells us, and so is the tulip. (Tulip and turban are originally the same word; and anyone who has seen the big coloured turbans of the East understands it.) The peach is Persian; its very name is a worn-down attempt to say so; and the orange reached Europe as the "Median apple". The Persian was interested in animals; a Persian noble would have a "paradise" (a Persian word again), where wild animals roamed at large, though his interest was not zoology but hunting. "Paradise" has taken on other meanings, because the ancients pictured Adam and Eve in something very like a Persian hunting-park. Persian character impressed the three Greeks we have named. The Persians were such splendid men; "their names", we are quaintly told, "are like their bodies and their magnificence",— long rolling impressive names, all ending in S, says the Greek, and adds that the Persians had not noticed this. They did end in S in Greek, but not in Persian; Xerxes seems to have been called by his parents Khshayarsha; no wonder foreigners got as far astray as Xerxes and Ahasuerus. They taught their boys three things—to ride the horse, to shoot with the bow, to tell the truth. Two of these were too often left out of Greek education. They thought it dishonourable in a man to be in debt; a man in debt generally tells lies, they said. Moderns have noted a fourth thing in Persian training—an intense loyalty to their King; the Greeks said that Persian nobles jumped overboard to lighten the ship, when Xerxes was in danger on the sea. The Greeks also noted that in the early days the Persians were water-drinkers; but this virtue, and others, they lost when the world was theirs and they fell into strange company.

The Persians created the greatest Empire of antiquity before the Roman; and they held it for two centuries. The Assyrians wore themselves out with wars and extravagant building, but the Persians last to this day. Cyrus was the founder of the Empire; and Herodotus tells us that the Persian stories about him go three ways, and he will choose the way of the Persians who do not wish to glorify Cyrus; even so his story borders on fairy tale. Yet he brings out that Cyrus was a great soldier, swift in movement. When he defeated the Lydian king across the Halys, Croesus had thought he might fight next year again. But Cyrus "was his own messenger" and met Croesus at once outside the walls of his capital. He had the ready wit to disorganize the Lydian cavalry by turning his camels upon it; horses hate camels to this day; the horses of the Lydians bolted in terror; their riders dismounted as soon as they could and fought on foot like men; but Cyrus had won the battle.

Darius was, if less of a conqueror, a greater administrator. He organized the provinces, and had an eye for trade and prosperity; he dug a canal to connect the Nile with the Red Sea, and gave his empire a gold currency of very remarkable purity. On the Behistun monument he tells how he became King; how a usurper, no Persian at all, had usurped the throne "and the lie was great in the land"; and how, with six friends, he overthrew him and reigned. Herodotus had told the story, and five of the friends he had named aright, as far as Greek spelling allowed it; which of itself suggests that the Persian friends of Herodotus (a number of whom can be identified) and the man himself were to be relied on.

Persian religion greatly interested Herodotus, who inquired into religion wherever he went. It was not their custom, he says, to set up statues, temples, and altars; they counted it foolish to think of God as like man; they called the whole circuit of the sky Zeus, and worshipped that. He is trying to describe the followers of Zoroaster, who were not worshippers of idols. To this day the Parsis of Bombay maintain that ancient religion, though the old Persian kings (but not Darius) fell away from it. It is interesting to note that Persia gave one of the last great rivals of Christ to the Roman Empire, the sun-god Mithras; that Mani, founder of the Manichaeans, who so much influenced St Augustine and are still mentioned in the Anglican prayer book, was a Persian; that, when Mohammedanism conquered Persia, it took on another colour from the Persians, who are heretics (Shia) to this day; and that in the nineteenth century Persia gave the Bahai faith to America. This is an extraordinary record for a people, nor is it all. For no Oriental people has as yet so much influenced the West with its literature as Persia has through its poets—Hafiz, Sadi, Firdausi, and not least Omar Khayyam—though the Persians do not rank Omar as high as the English do, since Edward Fitzgerald translated him.

Taken in all, this record, from the tulips to Omar, is a unique one. It shows a people of very high gifts, more closely indeed related by blood to European races than to other Orientals, such as their neighbours the Syrians, the Jews and the Arabs. A great race in conflict with another, both full of high intellectual qualities and high courage—it is a great spectacle. In the last big land battle of the Persian war, Herodotus says the Persians fought with a strength and a spirit to match the Spartans, but the Spartans were in armour and the Persians in linen shirts. They were bowmen rather than swordsmen, and on their gold coins set an archer.

Imperial government, the fact of a whole race being one nation, and perhaps ruling other nations, is no new thing to us. To the Greeks, we must realize, it seemed somehow unnatural; man could only be at his highest and best in a city-state, and Nature meant man to be at his best sooner or later. It takes, as we have found, far longer to civilize and educate a nation like that of England, or a mixed people like that of the United States; the Greek citizen of the city-state was in some places (not in all) on a higher plane of intelligence, whether we look at art, poetry, history or philosophy, than the average Englishman or American, in spite of Boards of Education, public schools (both in the English and American sense), the newspapers, the cinema and the wireless; he was less essentially a Philistine; and this is a fact that we have to explain. The Persian, the barbarian generally (apart from savages in Russia and elsewhere), went in for a large state as we do; and, said the Greek, how much he missed of the highest things in life! And yet, as we have seen, the Persians did, and have done, more for mankind than some modern great nations. Greek thinkers were struck with this contrast, and tried to explain it. Do moderns see anything to explain?

One word more to end the chapter. How often in this

chapter, as in the previous one and the one that follows, has Herodotus been quoted by name? Yet much has been drawn from him without naming him. The fact is that, if a modern reader wishes to understand the Greeks, the simplest way is to read the *Odyssey* and follow it up with Herodotus, every word of him. It is better to read them in Greek, of course; but in any language they are great. There are several English translations of Herodotus, and (it is said) twenty-eight of the *Odyssey*.

A Persian Daric

Chapter V

WARS OF GREEKS AND PERSIANS

A. THE PERSIAN ADVANCE

It was of Destiny decreed,
  As now the years unfold,
Battle should be the Persian's deed;
  Yea, God ordained of old,
With troops of horse encompassing
He tower and town to earth should bring,
  And Empire be his meed.

So sang the Greek poet, heightening the glory of his country's victory over the universal conqueror. So, two generations earlier, said the Hebrew prophet, looking for the release of Israel from Babylon—"Thus saith the Lord to His anointed, to Cyrus, whose right hand I have holden, to subdue nations before him; and I will loose the loins of kings; I will go before thee; I will break in pieces the gates of brass, and cut in sunder the bars of iron; I will give thee the treasures of darkness and hidden riches". "Persians!" says Xerxes (in the history of Herodotus), "this is no new law of my bringing in and ordaining, but one which I have received, and which I will obey. For, as I have learnt from our elders, we have never been idle or inert, since Cyrus won our lordship from the Medes; but God ever leads us on, and betters our attempts"; and the addition of the Greeks "will make the land of Persia wide as the sky of Zeus. The sun shall see no land upon our borders, but I will traverse all Europe and make all lands to be one land".

Imperial destinies!—and the Greeks could not persuade themselves that any power could overthrow the splendid Croesus. In two battles it was done, and the Greeks had to face a new master. Miletus alone had had vision of what was coming; perhaps the great colonizing and manufacturing city knew the East better. The Spartans, we are told, sent envoys to Cyrus, forbidding him to hurt any city of Greece, for they would not overlook it. "And how many are the Spartans?" asked the King, and then to the envoys: "I never yet feared men of that sort, who have ground set apart in the midst of their city, where they gather and take oaths and cheat one another. These Spartans, if I keep my health, shall have, not the sufferings of the Ionians to talk about, but some of their own". The Persians, so the historian explains, are not men of the *agora* like the Greeks (see page 21). Cyrus marched off to the East and left a general to subdue the Greek cities of Asia; one by one they fought the Persian, Greek fashion, and one by one they were conquered, and their Carian neighbours too. The men of Phocaea alone would not submit, but forsook their city, and sailed to the far West.

Meantime in the far East, as we have seen, Cyrus conquered Babylon (about 538 B.C.); and there, as in Greek regions, he dealt gently with the religions of those he subdued. Then a last campaign against a people by the Caspian Sea, and Cyrus reached his end, about which many tales were told. He was buried in Persia, and two centuries later Alexander found that his tomb had been plundered, and ordered its restoration. It is still to be seen.

Cambyses, his son, reigned in his stead, and conquered Egypt. How shamefully he treated priest and god in

Egypt, the Greeks loved to tell; how he ripped out his dagger and stabbed the divine bull, Apis, and in due time was wounded in the same part of his own body, and died of the wound. The moral was obvious. But a fresh light was shed on the ancient conqueror's attitude to alien religions by the discovery, early in this century, of a papyrus written, about 407 B.C. by Jews in Egypt, telling how Cambyses had spared their temple at Yeb, which the Greeks called Elephantine (apparently the ivory-market).

Meanwhile the false Smerdis or Mardos, as the Greeks rendered Bardiya, though not a Persian, had usurped the throne; and the first task of Darius was to get rid of him, as he describes on the Rock of Behistun. Next came a rebellion in Egypt, which Darius had to suppress, and then he turned his mind to Europe. He made a famous but luckless expedition into Thrace, bridged the Danube, and tried to attack the Scythians. But they were nomads, and drove off, after stopping the wells; and at last sent a message, which consisted of a bird, a mouse, a frog and five arrows, which the herald said it was no business of his to explain to the king. But the Persian guessed what was meant, and retreated.

In 499 the Ionian cities of Asia Minor revolted, and it was five years before they were subdued. The story is confused enough, but two things or three appear. The Ionians won a big naval victory over the Phoenician fleet. The Athenians and Eretrians sent forces to support them which burnt Sardis, the old Lydian capital, now the Persian base in the West; and then Athens withdrew from the war. The Greeks were divided as usual; they quarrelled, and suffered a big naval defeat at Lade; and there was an end. The twenty ships the Athenians sent were "the beginning of many disasters for Greeks and for barbarians", says Herodotus. But moderns, in some perplexity, remark how long the Revolt lasted, how right Athens was to join in, how odd was her misconception of Persian strength, if she thought twenty ships enough, how futile her retirement; how each side was strong enough to hold the other in check, but neither for a long time strong enough to deal a decisive blow; how Persia had no large standing army, and had to operate over immense distances; and they incline to think that, failure as it was at last, the Revolt saved European Greece. Vengeance fell on the Greek cities of Asia, and Miletus was destroyed. Curiously, just as happened when the Turks sacked Smyrna in 1922, this meant an accession of the world's trade to Athens; and for this, and for other reasons, Miletus might better have been spared.

B. ATHENS

We have now to look at Athens. The sons of Pisistratus carried on his government not too badly, till one of them was murdered. It was, like so many of the murders that threw Greece into disorder, the outcome of private hate; it was not originally a political move, but the murderers became political heroes, as others have done elsewhere, and the theme of *scolia*, catches, or drinking songs; one of which may be rendered:

> Dearest Harmodius and Aristogeiton!
>   Glorious for ever shall ye be;
> Ye were the heroes twain that slew the tyrant,
>   And made our Athens free.

Strictly they were not liberators; for Hippias, the elder brother, held on gloomily for four years, when the

Spartans were fetched in to expel him. The attempt was all but a failure; but Hippias lost his nerve, and tried to smuggle his children out to the sea; the children were taken; and to save them Hippias gave up his tyranny and left Athens. The family went to the Troad, to carry on for twenty years making plots with the Persian in hope of a return. A Greek who loved his country was capable of doing it any mischief to regain it.

The twenty years that follow in Athenian history are confused enough. A revolution, a new constitution, the liberation of political ambition and rivalry, were not a combination to secure quiet. Some students have been strangely eager to write the political ups and downs of those years, but it is hardly possible. Political intrigue is hard enough to trace even when you are in fullest possession of the facts and the fictions; in this case we have not a tenth of them, and little is gained by guessing. One or two things stand out clearly. Athens made her neighbours understand definitely that things had changed; she displayed a spirit and a force in actual battle unknown in her citizens before;—"which shows that liberty is a good thing", is the ancient comment. A new constitution redistributed the people, broke up their old tribal attachments, and included in the citizen roll names of the alien Greeks, who, for two generations and more, had been migrating to Athens, and making it the new centre of trade and art and industry for Greece. Thirdly, and not least, the statesman Themistocles emerged, a man destined to save Greece from the Persians, a man of a "force of nature", of a "native intelligence", that made him "the shrewdest judge of the present and wisest at forecasting what should follow, with a gift for expounding what he had in hand and for hitting in an instant on the right expedient". He foresaw what was coming; and devoted his gifts to persuading Athens, in spite of opposition, to build herself a navy. Some Athenians thought the most serious enemy of Athens was Aegina, the island they could see from the Acropolis, the "eye-sore" of their city. They were slow to see the world as Themistocles saw it; still something was done, in spite of opposition, for by 489 Athens had some ninety ships.

For, meanwhile in 492, the Persians were getting a foothold in Europe as far as Macedonia. A great fleet accompanied the Persian conqueror on this expedition; but it was wrecked in a storm off Mt Athos. The Persians remained masters, however, of the shore-road along the North Aegaean. Orders were given for the building of a new navy for the King; and his heralds appeared in Greece, demanding "earth and water" from the city-states in token of submission. Aegina gave earth and water.

Day by day, the Greeks said, since Sardis was burned, his servant had been reminding Darius to "remember the Athenians"; and the family of Pisistratus sat at his elbow to embroil him still further with Athens. By 490 B.C. his new fleet was ready, six hundred ships, it was said. This time, with a new commander, the fleet avoided the Northern waters and sailed straight across the Aegaean, from island to island. At the holy isle of Delos, the Persian admiral took pains to conciliate the god with an immense gift of frankincense. He sailed on to the island of Euboea, and on the seventh day of the siege the town of Eretria was betrayed to him; its citizens had taken a share in the Athenian expedition that burnt Sardis, and those who now were caught were sold as slaves; the temples were plundered and burnt; and another old Greek port, famous in history, was destroyed. Only Athens was left, and her fleet was not in being. It was impossible now to misunderstand what was in store for her.

The Persian force moved on. The Athenian generals sent in haste to Sparta for help; but the Spartans, though resolved to help Athens, could not break their law; it was only the ninth day of the lunar month, they must wait till the moon was full. "So", says the historian with a hint of irony, "they delayed till it should be full moon." But on the Arcadian hills the Athenian runner, Pheidippides, saw the god Pan, who called to the man, and asked why the Athenians took no thought of him, who had often stood their friend and would yet again? That was all. The Persians put in on the Eastern shore of Attica; and on the field of Marathon the Athenians met them, and the famous battle was fought. There are difficulties about the story, things for which military critics find it hard to account; but some things stand out. Miltiades, the great opponent of Themistocles and his navy schemes, persuaded the Athenians to fight at once—a shrewd move. They fought and won a brilliant victory. But there was still the Persian fleet. It sailed round the headland of Sunium—men thought, in order to seize Athens before her troops could return to the city. It had only ninety miles to go. It anchored off one of the Athenian harbours, lay there a while, and then sailed back to Asia; and that was all. Athens was saved for the time being, and Miltiades was famous. More significant than all, the Persian army had sustained a conspicuous defeat in a land battle, for the first time in the West. The Greek *hoplite*, the man in armour, had shown himself to be the best of fighting men, equal to facing the conquerors of the world and beating them. For generations "the men who fought at Marathon", *Marathonomachoi*, were the great heroes of Athens, and were very conscious of it; and they deserved their renown.

But Themistocles had not changed his mind; the navy was needed. Several things helped him; Miltiades came to grief, and Aegina began to worry good Athenians; they must have ships to deal with Aegina. Above all an entirely unexpected discovery of a rich vein of silver in the Laureion mines—"a fountain of silver, a treasure hoard of Earth", as the Athenian poet called it—suddenly gave Athens the capital needed to build a fleet. The return of the Persians was delayed; Egypt revolted in 486; and next year the old King, Darius, died before Egypt was reconquered. He has been described as singularly able and enlightened, and (for his times) singularly humane, "the greatest Oriental that ever ruled in Western Asia". He was succeeded by his son, Xerxes, a man much less able and less energetic, even if the Greeks exaggerated his childishness and his beauty, as they may have. He had round him his father's captains; he had immense resources in gold and in man-power; and he failed; and at every point the chief source of Persian weakness seems to have been the fact that the man, who had at last to decide everything, was unequal to his task. The great difficulty of constitutional monarchy, said an English statesman, is the education of the heir apparent; and polygamy, a royal harem, if it offers a wider choice of heirs, does not better their education.

C. XERXES

It is commonly taken that epic must be in verse, but the History of Herodotus, written in prose, might well merit the name; an ancient critic aptly calls him "most Homeric of men". His theme is the conflict of Greece and Persia; but, as he says, "his story looks for digressions", and finds many; and every digression heightens the impression of the whole work. Slowly and discursively, with many a glance back into the history of the nations and cities concerned, and with ample leisure to portray the significant characters he meets, he moves onward with his task. Lands and their peoples, with their distinctive traditions, garbs, customs and diets he surveys, till at last the reader has seen the whole world, all of it, every race in greater or in less degree, involved in the Great War that Persia waged with the Greeks. Men in the past have called him garrulous and a liar, but his most hostile critic recognized his charm; and in modern days, as Archaeology has unveiled the past, and Anthropology has made us familiar with the ways and thoughts of less civilized races, it is more and more recognized what a pioneer Herodotus was, what truth and wisdom lie under his simplicity; and his charm is as potent as ever it was. He can be read again and again. It is the master-story of the Greek race. Even the tale of Troy hardly outdoes it.

Slowly the historian marshals the army of the Great King; it is a levy of nations; and one by one we inspect them in their national dress with their native arms, led by this or the other great captain or prince (not a few of them cadets of the Persian royal house). They gather, and make their way gradually down through Asia, and

The Persian Wars

reach the Hellespont, which has been bridged for them. They advance through Thrace and reach Doriscos, where Xerxes numbers his army. In two matters the great historian is weak; he will blunder in arithmetic, and use other men's chronologies and get them mixed at times; and he is not strictly a soldier nor a military historian. Yet from what he preserves, the expert gathers up the talk and comment of the camps, and, from a hint here and a hint there, makes out the plan of campaign and the course of events. Sometimes Herodotus seems not quite to understand some military movement, but he is not the shrewd narrator who covers his ignorance; and those of his readers who are more practised perhaps or more interested in military matters, see more than he tells them.

It is clear that the Persian plan of campaign was carefully thought out and prepared for; we are never told of anything failing on an emergency. At points in the route, food was laid up for the army, and fodder for the horses and mules on their long march; tackle and munitions were all thought of; a canal was cut across the isthmus of Mt Athos; and every main feature in the campaign was studied. (This is not to say the Persian War Office was superhuman.) Army and fleet were to act together, to move together (so far as land and sea allow); and the great secret of the campaign (on which Herodotus is not too clear) was that the Persian fleet, till it was beaten, was able again and again to turn the enemy's position. The Greeks had to fall back out of Thessaly, and, later on, to evacuate Thermopylae, not merely because the Persians found alternative routes, but because the Persian fleet could threaten their rear and their communications.

One point perhaps needs more explanation than it has received. More than once an exiled Greek, or the warrior Queen Artemisia herself, lays stress on the real weakness of the Greeks, their extreme reluctance to work together; why should not the King take them in detail, make a series of threatening moves that will break up the Greek forces, and send each contingent back in headlong haste to its own city or canton? This was in effect what Persia did in the days after the younger Cyrus, when the Peloponnesian War was over; she controlled the Greeks by playing upon this inability to unite, and subsidizing in turn one party against another. Such a control was easier than conquest—much easier and less expensive for the Persian, more harassing to the Greeks, than conquest and settled government would have been. But Xerxes would have nothing to say to such suggestions; he would crush his enemy once and for all.

Meanwhile Greece was in terror. The King was coming by land and sea with forces innumerable to attack Athens; that was the story, but in truth, all Greece was his aim; and taught by the fate of the Greek cities that would not surrender in time to Cyrus, and scared by the report of Xerxes' hosts, many of the Greek cities were for making peace with the Persian at once. An appeal was made to the Sicilian Gelon, tyrant of Syracuse, to help the Greeks; his turn would surely come, when the Persian was master of Greece. Gelon offered to send large forces, provided he should be in supreme command; but that was reserved for the Spartans. "Very well," said Gelon, "it looks as if you would have many to lead, and none to follow." After this Gelon temporized, waiting on events; and he had enough to do in Sicily, in coping with a Carthaginian invasion.

The Athenians consulted the god at Delphi, but the god evidently expected a Persian triumph. All he could offer was a warning to flee to the ends of the earth from a city doomed to destruction; "riding on a Syrian chariot comes Ares [the war-god], to give walls and temples to the fire". But someone advised them to try again; could the god not be coaxed to give some better answer for their country? This time the priestess told them that Pallas Athene, their national goddess, could not prevail upon Zeus of Olympus, for all her cunning; the land of Cecrops (Attica) must be taken; "yet doth Zeus grant to Athene a wooden wall that shall remain unsacked"; but the Athenian must not face the cavalry, the infantry, the mighty host from the mainland, but turn his back and go. And at the end came a sudden apostrophe: "O divine Salamis, thou too shalt destroy children of women, be it at seedtime or at harvest". What could it mean? Some were for putting a wooden wall to the Acropolis. Some thought wooden walls must be ships; but did not the words about Salamis imply disaster to the fleet as well? No, said Themistocles, in that case the god would have said "O *cruel* Salamis", and not "*divine*". He was, as he had been all along, for the fleet, for meeting the Persian on the sea, and was utterly opposed to the panic-stricken dream of a wholesale emigration and a settlement in some distant land.

The Peloponnesian plan was to fortify the isthmus of Corinth; to build a strong wall from sea to sea to keep the King's army out. They lived in the past and had no notion of navies. Soldiers rarely believe very much in fleets.

"Here", says Herodotus, "I am constrained of necessity to declare an opinion which most men will dislike, but none the less I will not refrain from saying what seems to me true. If the Athenians had surrendered to fear of the danger coming upon them and left their country; or if they had stayed in it and surrendered to Xerxes; none would have dared to withstand the King on the sea. And if none had withstood Xerxes on the sea, this, or something like it, is what would have come about on the land. Even though the Peloponnesians had strung many a wall, like so many shirts, across the Isthmus, the Spartans would have been left to themselves, betrayed by their allies,—not that the allies would have wished to betray them, but of necessity, as city after city was taken by the fleet of the barbarians; and, left thus alone, the Spartans would have done great deeds, and perished gloriously. Either that, or else, seeing all the Greeks Medizing [i.e. joining the Persians], they too would have come to terms with Xerxes; and so, either way, Greece would have been subdued by the Persians. For what was the use of walls put across the Isthmus, I cannot learn, when once the barbarian controlled the sea. But, as it is, if a man said the Athenians saved Greece, he would not miss the truth. For whichever way they turned, the balance would incline. They chose that Greece should remain free, and it was they who stirred up all the Greeks who had not Medized, and they who, under heaven, did in fact drive the King away."

And how much did they owe to Themistocles, who had talked them into building their fleet, who now talked them out of their fears about "divine Salamis", who by a trick made the King's admirals suspicious of the Ionian contingents in their fleet, who kept the Greek fleet from breaking up, bore with the folly and terror of his colleagues ("Strike but hear me!" was his famous word to one of them), and at last, by the most daring of all his manœuvres, brought on the battle of Salamis?

But, first, at the North end of the island of Euboea a furious gale destroyed some large part of the Persian fleet. The Persians set their priests to work; and the priests chanted to the wind for three days, and "stopped the storm,—unless it flagged of itself", an interesting afterthought. A second storm followed. "It was all done by God, to equalize things," says Herodotus, interested, as ever, in the question whether there are gods, and whether they concern themselves with human affairs. He is himself against the atheist view; he believes that the gods deal with wrong-doers, and that some oracles are genuine enough; and the salvation of Greece confirmed him.

But Xerxes was not yet really in Greece; Thermopylae lay in his path, and the Greeks held it. This pass between mountain and sea (running East and West, it should be noted) was so narrow that the immense Persian host was for the moment of no use; only so many could attack at once, and as many could hold them off. A traitor—if issues are to be judged from the universal Greek point of view, yes! But if a man must stand by his own state and not the general Greek world, ——? Epialtes the Malian showed the Persians a track over the mountains, and the Greek position at Thermopylae was turned. The fleet would sooner or later have made it untenable without his aid. Leonidas, the Spartan king, sent the allies away, and remained with three hundred Spartans, and some others, to fight it out. Some said it was because tradition made it unseemly for Spartans to desert a post they had come to defend; some that Leonidas saw here the chance of great glory, for he knew of an oracle that Sparta or its king must perish. So the Spartans combed their hair in peace, and made ready to die as befitted them. Sometimes a great leader, like Garibaldi at Calatafimi in 1860, sees that there can be too much running away, and that at all costs a battle is the only thing, even if everybody is killed. Garibaldi won his battle after all; Leonidas lost his; but they each achieved the same thing, each made a "demonstration" worth for the nation far more than the lives it cost. A great American, whom his friends wished to rescue, told them he "was worth far more to hang". So John Brown was hanged in due course, and became a battle song, and his name a watchword.

The Persians, at great cost, took Thermopylae; and in after days two lines of the poet Simonides told the story, with Greek "economy" and reticence. The Greeks, as Dean Inge has said, did not feel that there is something splendid in every superlative. What Simonides said, is, in the old familiar translation:

> Go, tell the Spartans thou, that passest by,
> That here obedient to their laws we lie.

Quiet enough these words; the name of the place says all that need be said; the world cannot forget Thermopylae.

Nothing now remained to delay Xerxes in his march on Athens, and he took the city, in spite of the wooden wall that some had built in reliance on their interpretation of the oracle. He destroyed the city, and sent a messenger to his far-distant capital to announce his triumph.

The Greek fleet lay between Salamis and the land, its commanders nervously eager to get away, to break up, to protect the Isthmus—to ruin everything, as Themistocles saw. It was now that he sent his famous message to Xerxes, telling him that the Greeks have lost heart and are for running away; with a hint to stop them, and make sure of another Persian triumph. At daybreak the

Greeks saw both their outlets blocked; a Persian detachment had sailed round the island and escape was hopeless; a battle was inevitable. The poet Aeschylus (who, it was said, fought in this battle as well as at Marathon), and Herodotus, briefly describe the battle,—a victory for hard fighting; there was no room for anything else.

The Greeks perhaps, even when the day was over, did not realize all that their victory meant. It had wrecked the central plan on which the Persian attack depended; there could now be no co-operation of army and fleet.

By the ruin of the war-ships was the land-host overthrown,

says Aeschylus. The Persian army would at once be face to face with the problem of food; for now that the Greeks controlled the sea, the Persian line of communication, which lay round the North of the Aegaean, might very well be cut. Xerxes, some suggest, lost his nerve. His staff may well have wished him off the scene, even before this. It is hinted to-day, that half the problem now might be to keep Western Asia quiet; rebellions were always possible. At all events, Xerxes went, and most of the army with him, or after him, or as best it could; and the retreat was full of disasters.

Mardonius was left with a much smaller army, but yet for those days an immense one. He wintered in Thessaly, and with the spring advanced again into Greece. But by now the Greeks could take some aggressive action themselves, and sent a fleet across to Asia Minor and the islands. On the same day, it was said, the two decisive battles were fought. Mardonius and his army were destroyed at Plataea in Boeotia, and a great naval victory was won by the Greeks at Mycale. The Spartans had the chief glory at Plataea; and yet, as we saw, "the Persians fell short of them neither in spirit nor strength; but they had no armour; they were no match for their adversaries in military skill, they would charge singly or ten together, in groups greater or smaller, hurling themselves on the Spartans and so perishing". It was once again the victory of the Greek *hoplite*, the victory of armour and discipline, which our own island has seen more than once. The battle of the Standard, Duplin, Halidon Hill, Flodden—one after the other shows that charges by unmailed clansmen could never vanquish men in armour, spearmen and archers. By land and by sea the Greeks had shown themselves the best fighting men in the world, and their freedom was secure—unless they sold it themselves.

For the moment, they were not for selling it; and out of the war there remained the Confederacy of Delos, a league to keep the Persian off the sea and to safeguard the freedom so gloriously won. Sparta threw over the leadership of the Greek world; she preferred, said the moralist long after, to have her citizens law-abiding, than to rule the world; but it may be that a modern explanation comes nearer the mark. With a serf-population fifteen times as large as the citizen-population—and those serfs not negro slaves but the remnant of a nation, that had fought bravely in the past, and were yet to prove themselves men after Leuctra (see page 158)—how could Sparta control the Greek world? She had not the numbers, even if she had had the imagination; and when, after the bad end of the Peloponnesian War (see page 148), she attempted empire, she failed for want of both. The headship of the Greek world passed to Athens; and Athens had fairly won it, and for fifty years or nearly she kept Greek waters clear of the Persians.

D. ATHENS AFTER THE PERSIAN WAR

Few who were on London streets at mid-morning 11 November 1918 will ever forget what they felt when the clocks chimed out eleven, and the maroons were exploded which told us that the armistice was signed and the war was over. As one went Northward through the streets, there were the people coming to their doors and hanging out flags; "it was over". And at night in those streets one looked at the gas-lamps now lit, and at the full moon, and realized there were to be no more zeppelins; "it was over". The world felt the same; "it was over", and a new age was to begin, very different from all we had known before. It had been much the same after Waterloo in 1815. A line in human experience had been crossed, and there was no returning possible; it was a new world. And so it was now for the Greeks.

Salamis and Plataea!—then the Persian menace was gone, and Greece could breathe again! The years that followed did not bring what was expected; there was no going back to that old world of which we read in Herodotus, the world of the sixth century, where islands and mainland cities lived their own lives, with collisions enough between the local tyrant and his enemies, or with the people of the next island or the next canton, but every city sovereign and independent, arbiter of its own policies. The Persian, like the Lydian before him, had reduced one city of the Asian shore after another; there had been no standing together; the Ionian revolt had fallen to pieces; after it, the Greek city-states of Europe had one by one despaired of resisting the Persian, and surrendered in detail, afraid of their neighbours, none trusting another nor ceding the lead to another. Only

at the last, with the utmost difficulty, had Athens con-
trived to keep Greeks together till the blunders of the
Persian could give a chance of victory. It was this
belated unity that saved one and all from being the slaves
of the barbarian, and nothing else could stop the barbarian from coming again, with wiser leaders. Away in
Asia, he could recover from his losses, amass fresh
treasure, assemble fresh armies, and, at his own time,
descend again on the Aegaean and take the Greek cities
once more in detail. The confederacy that saved Greeks
in the hour of peril was the only thing to keep them safe,
to prevent the peril returning. The old original plan of
each canton for itself was hopeless; but there was an
alternative way of life—federation.

From now onward all the quarrels of the Greeks (and
there were plenty) turn on this one issue—federation,
unity, a central control, or the old ideal of autonomy,
every city *autopolitan* as they called it, its citizens
"citizens of themselves"; and on the issue akin to it,
that must inevitably arise, who shall have the central
control—Athens, Sparta, Thebes, Macedon? It was with
extreme reluctance that Greek cities accepted even the
least diminution of absolute and extreme state-right
which any kind of co-operation involved. It has been
said that the Greek ambition was always for the smallest
form of association that was, humanly speaking, possible;
and, given that smallest form of association, the individual Greek wished "to live each as he pleases" with
the minimum amount of limitation from people next
door or in the city hall. The chief wars among Greeks
in the fifth century were revolts from the Confederacy
of Delos, though it was the only possible device to keep
a fleet together for the protection of all from the Persian.

Of these revolts we duly hear from historians; but neither historians, nor moralists, nor pacifists generally, trouble to make clear to us how much fighting and how many wars are prevented by the growth of the imperial state. Athenian control (for the Confederacy of Delos came to be that) must have saved endless waste of blood and treasure in the cities of the league; revolution was practically barred by the central control, markets were safe, the sea was safe, life was safe; but the "allies" were less grateful than they might have been. Where they bought themselves free of the necessity of building, equipping and manning ships for the confederate fleet, they hated to have to pay the price—the "tribute" as they called it, to make it odious. But worse than the tribute, they hated the control.

Meanwhile Athens was rapidly gaining a position in the world's trade and industry not less significant than her political supremacy as head of the Confederacy. Miletus and Eretria were destroyed; the policy of Solon and Pisistratus, and (we may add) Themistocles, in encouraging the settlement in Athens of people with crafts and trades and brains generally, was bearing fruit. Athens was fast becoming the centre of the world's commerce and manufacture. The Peiraieus was geographically somewhere near the centre of the world's waters, and thither came the world's merchants. It was an *emporion*, as the Greeks called it, a centre to which came *emporoi*, merchants, bringing their goods in bulk, where they made their bargains and took away new cargoes; a centre of distribution, as we call it. Many of the chief industries, too, of Greece were centred in Athens. Without steam or electric power, there was of course no factory system such as we know; but factories there were, in which slaves by dozens were employed in turning out goods for sale in lands about the Aegaean, and beyond it. It seems likely, too, that much, or most, of the carrying trade of the Greek world was in Athenian hands; they owned the ships that carried the goods which the merchants of other cities brought or took away. The building, equipment and manning of the big fleets which had to be afloat every summer (as well as the ordinary building of merchant-vessels) must have meant endless employment about the Peiraieus, bringing in skilled labour from everywhere. In all sorts of references we find hints of the large numbers of "alien residents" (*metics*), generally Greeks, but not always, who lived in Athens and the Peiraieus and never meant to live anywhere else. Trade, contract, association, banking, all were free in Athens; capacity there had its highest reward.

All this employment meant in the long run a heightening of democracy. It was *Demos*, men said, who had won the war, who safeguarded the peace. The "men who fought at Marathon" were a legend, but the seafaring men of the fleet had won Salamis; it was they who still kept out the Persian and held the allies in hand; they were the people; and one by one the old traditions were changed, and Athens became the standard democracy of the world, and of all time.

An Athenian coin

Chapter VI

THE GREEK CITY

A. THE CITY-STATE

ANCIENT life was in many ways very different from modern. Probably most people who read this book will be citizens of a great nation, or of a great empire. To us it seems natural that one people should inhabit one land, or, like the British, should spread over many lands. We forget that England, France and Germany, like Italy in more modern times, were only slowly united as we see them to-day; and that such unions have very generally only been possible in great level countries of plainland, without mountains to make barriers. In ancient Greece no such thing happened; the mountains and the sea worked in with the Greek temper; and from first to last the centre of life was the city-state, each of them quite independent of the city across the mountains or ten miles away.

In Great Britain laws are made by a Parliament in London, to which every city and county send so many members according to the number of people. Greece had no Parliament; it was not a nation, though it was a race. Each city governed itself, made its own laws, had its own revolutions, fought this neighbour and made peace with that, and then reversed its hatreds and friendships. The city-state was the regular thing; indeed, men came to think of it as the only natural way of government, as if tribes and lands and empires, as we know them in history, were unnatural—as if modern

England, with its unity of nation and of land, were really a violation of nature, a mutilation of human character. Your British subject, the Greek might say, as soon as he has elected his Member of Parliament, has abdicated. He has no more to say in international questions; even in his own city, he does not count, when once he has elected a Town Council. As a result, the Greek would go on to say, he loses interest in half the things that really make a man; he leaves it to Parliament to frame the laws; to the King or the prime minister to decide on war and peace; to the judges to decide cases in the law-courts; to old aldermen to arrange market dues and street-cleaning, and the height of buildings. What has the Englishman left for him to do? The Englishman's life, according to the Greek, is the merest broken arc of the full circle of man's life, and the Englishman, as a result, ends by being a mere decimal of a man, a vulgar fraction, a negation of nature. Yes, there is something unnatural, the Greek would say, about this whole scheme of dele-gating powers; you English are barbarians; you are really not free, but subjects; hence your undeveloped, yes! your atrophied minds. The Greek idea was to be free; and for a time he managed it in a city, great or small, with a little territory around it, and, when fortune favoured him, with a harbour.

Let us look at the little city, the city that teaches the man, as we saw. To most modern eyes, it would have seemed a mean little town; the streets were narrow, dirty and crowded; the houses did not stand in gardens, with windows looking upon the street. It is only in modern lands, in the great united countries where there is no fear of invasion, nor of brigands, that it has been safe for houses to have windows looking out on street or country.

The ancient was more apt to build his house as some sort
of a square, with all the windows looking inward, like
an Indian *busti*. If it were a small house, this made it
dark; and small houses they mostly were. In the later
days of Greece, when great kings were founding new
cities, they gave them wide and straight streets, not
as wide as we should wish them, but wide in comparison with the old cities; and the cross streets
they set at right-angles to the main streets. They
admired this chessboard pattern for a city, which the
English oddly enough think rather dull. When St John
had his vision of the Heavenly Jerusalem, he conceived
it to lie foursquare, that is, all the streets at right-angles.
But in the old Greek cities, as in our own, the streets went
every kind of way, following the lines of the old cattle
tracks, perhaps; and they were far dirtier than any slum
in an Anglo-Saxon land. There were no sewers; as in
modern Madras, refuse was supposed to be carried away
by men set to the task.

Generally, all the shops that sold the same kind of
thing were in the same street; very commonly, the man
who sold the things, also made them; and the idler might
wander from street to street, and watch a dozen crafts at
work. Somewhere in the city was the *Agora* or market-
place, where the citizens gathered early in the morning—
"to chatter" as their enemies said. In the docks lay the
shipping, and dockyard hands were loading or unloading
the cargoes, while their captains were across the street
in the little inns (like the queer little cafés in a modern
Greek port), chattering with dealers who might want to
buy the goods they brought or might want to take
passage to some other port with goods of their own. All
sorts of dialects would be heard; to-day the attentive ear

can tell the Yorkshireman from the East Anglian and the Somerset man. The great national divisions had then, as they have now, their different dialects and intonations. To this day broad Scots is affectionately called "Doric" after the dialect of one great division of the Greek people. In some towns there was a more or less fortified hill, which, in the oldest days, would have been a refuge, if the town was raided. In later days, there might be a temple on top of it, or a tyrant might hold it with a garrison. As long as the tyrant held the citadel and kept his children safe there, he could do very much what he liked with the town; and he might not need a very large garrison; but, in process of time, all, or nearly all, the tyrants were driven out. The Athenians claimed to be the friends of the people, and helped to secure them against being ruled by tyrants. In the long run, Athens became, in many ways, the model city of Greece, and most people, when they think of a Greek city, think of Athens.

The model city!—how would you imagine it? What would you expect to find in the model city? The great Athenian political leader, Pericles, has described, in an immortal speech, what he thinks the model city to be, and what it ought to do. In the first place, it is a free city, a government of the people by the people, democracy. The administration is in the hands of the many, and not of the few. There is no electing Members of Parliament; and Parliament, Town Council, and Law Courts, are, at bottom, one and the same thing, an assemblage of all free citizens. They meet in one place to be Parliament, in another place to be Law Court; but, as not every law-suit is important enough to need the whole people to judge of it, they have an arrangement for drawing lots to select (say) two to five hundred to hear the case. Our law, Pericles continues, secures equal justice to all alike. Poverty is no bar, but a man may serve his country, however poor and obscure his origin. We recognize merit wherever we see it. There is no exclusiveness in our public life. We like to do as we please, and we are glad to see our neighbour do as he pleases. Sour looks are not pleasant, even if they are harmless, when we do not see eye to eye with another. There is a spirit of reverence in our public life, a great respect for the authority of the magistrates and for the laws, especially for those laws which protect the injured, and for the unwritten laws, to break which means admitted shame. In no other city is such provision made for relaxation from toil. We have regular games and festivals; home life is refined; our daily delight is to banish melancholy; our city is great and open, and all the pleasures of earth flow in upon us and make life pleasant and rich. We do not expel foreigners; any foreigner may come and go as he will; and the more he learns, the better, for our city is admirable alike in peace and war, and, in a word, is the model city. It is the education of all Greeks. Look, then, at the type of man we breed. We do not brutalize our youth, to make them physically strong. We mean them to be all-round men. We wish them to love the beautiful, but to remain simple in their tastes; to cultivate their minds without loss of manliness. We expect a man to take an interest in public affairs; and, if he does not, we think him useless. We expect him to grow up to be a sound judge of what the nation ought to do or ought not to do. We expect him to take an intelligent interest in all that goes on in Greece, so that he may be able to serve his country with accurate knowledge of the facts of the world, and right judgment upon their significance. Some people think that men are courageous from ignorance, and that when they reflect they begin to hesitate. Our view is different; we count those men brave, who calculate in the clearest way both the pains and pleasures of life, who take the measure of the danger, and then face the risk. In short, Athens is the school of · Greece, and what I urge, he concludes, is that you should love Athens;—and he uses the strongest word for love, a word that means a passion that forgets self, a passion that will make men live for Athens and die for Athens.

This speech is famous. It represents the ideal of popular government. Pericles recognizes that democracy, the government of the people by the people, requires the highest development of which every single citizen is capable. Too often in our modern states citizens dismiss matters from their minds. "The Government will attend to that", they say; in plain words, they abdicate. In Athens, says Pericles, there is no abdication. The same man will, sooner or later, have to contribute his knowledge to help the city to decide on a policy; to listen to alternative policies being proposed and argued; to judge between the arguments set forth on both sides, and to give his vote honestly and intelligently for the policy which will be best for the city. What is more, when the policy is determined, the citizen will have to help to carry it out; he must bear arms, or he must take a part in the rowing of the ship, or perhaps in navigating it. He must be ready to row; to steer; to fight; to give orders, or to obey them. When the war, if there is a war, is over, he may have a farm to cultivate, or a workshop in which to make and sell goods.

In some parts of the world, town people think farmers

are the stupid class; the farmers rejoin by thinking the smart people of the streets stupider than they suppose. In Athens, says Pericles, all of them are gifted with minds capable of the highest form of intellectual pleasure. This is a large claim; but year by year the Athenians had festivals, at which were performed famous plays by great poets; and they knew that these were great plays—they got the great words by heart. They knew the great music, and could sing it themselves. When one thinks of the trashy amusements of England and America—the flicks and talkies and music-hall songs—and realizes what songs and what poetry the Athenian carried in his heart, we may wonder whether we have progressed as far as we suppose.

B. THE ARTS

Let us take one Athenian play and look at it—a very simple one, and not an outstanding one, *The Trojan Women* of Euripides. The play begins with a scene in which a god and goddess talk to each other. They have quarrelled, but now they make friends; and the god of the sea agrees to wreck dozens of Greek ships as they sail home from Troy; the island shores of Euboea will be strewn with wrecks and corpses. Why? Because one of the victorious Greeks has annoyed the goddess Athena. And then these horrible gods vanish.

All the time that they have been speaking, on the ground some feet beneath them, a woman has been lying in the dust. She is a slave. She had been a queen, and a great queen. The king, her husband, has been killed. Her sons have fallen in battle. Her city has been burned with fire. She and her daughters are going into slavery in a strange land. Everything that can go wrong with

a human being has befallen Hecuba. But all through
the play, the poet shows that she is a woman of great soul.
She rises above herself to inspire hope and courage in her
fellow sufferers. Contrasted with her, are the conqueror,
Menelaus, and his wife Queen Helen (see page 36).
What is left for the poor Trojans? Nothing—unless it is
the hope that the little boy, Hector's son, may be spared
to build Troy again; and, just as Hecuba suggests this,
in comes a messenger from the Greeks to say the baby
must be thrown from the rocks and be killed. He does
not wish to deliver this message, but the Greeks have
realized the danger of the child growing up, of his
building Troy again, and the risk of a second Trojan
war. So, with broken hopes, the utter failure of everything, the play ends, and the queen and her daughters
go into slavery.

What does the poet mean by drawing such a scene?
people have asked, and they may well ask. It is a mere
succession of painful episodes.

> But things like this we know must be
> In every famous victory.

Then, the poet seems to ask, is victory worth the price?
And when all goes wrong with human life, what is right?
His answer is: the great spirit of Hecuba is right; it is the
greatest thing that human life can show—this victory of
the human heart over the most dreadful conditions. The
play forces the spectator to search his heart; to ask
whether he himself has put the right values on things;
does he wish to be like Menelaus, happy and glorious,
and be no better a creature than Menelaus is? Would
it not be better to be like Hecuba, in spite of her mis-
fortunes? Then does not that mean that the real life,
the real great thing, lies in the spirit?

This is one Athenian play; and in many and many another, one poet or another explores life, makes you realize the terms on which human beings have to live—that we shall not have it all our own way—that the other man, with whom our quarrel is so just, is also right—that the real tragedy is the division of good against good. These are not simple ideas, but it is in grasping them that we realize what life is. And these wonderful poets brought questions of this kind—problems as great as these—into their plays; and these plays were performed before popular audiences; and the Athenian people loved to have it so. And their comedies imply and ask for brains, as none did in human history till the age of *As You Like It*. No wonder Pericles could boast that his people had intellectual enjoyments. No wonder the Greeks quoted the old poet, and said that "the city was the education of the man". A city that takes pleasures of that kind is an education, at once to the boy and girl who grow up in it, and to the stranger within its gates, who should go back to his own country and tell them what a city might be. It is because we think of a city like this that we believe it is worth while to study ancient history.

But the drama was not the only sphere of art in which the Greek of the great period found his education. While Sophocles and Euripides were producing their masterpieces, Pheidias the sculptor was busy with his. His statue of Athene was set up in Athens in 438/7 B.C., an epoch-making piece of work. It has not come down to us; statues of bronze and of marble have been destroyed for all sorts of baser uses, the latter even to make lime; but this Athene of ivory and gold is only represented by one or two diminutive and dull copies, and by devices on coins. What art criticism there may have been in that

day, has not survived; but we have, as it happens, a
number of later comments on the other famous statue
of Pheidias, the Zeus at Olympia, which show how art
entered into the lives of Greeks, and of some Romans;
and after all, if we do not know what was *said* of the
sculpture of Pheidias in his own day, we know it was
made, and made not for private persons to adorn their
houses, but for national purposes.

Pheidias, we are told, was asked what model he would
use in making his Zeus, and he said he was going to use
three lines of Homer:

> Zeus spake, and speaking his dark brows inclined;
> The ambrosial locks from that immortal head
> Streamed, and he made the great Olympus shake.

And the Roman conqueror, Aemilius Paullus, said that
Pheidias had embodied the conception of Homer, and
none but he had done it. There is nothing more perfect
among statues than those of Pheidias, wrote Cicero; he
had no model to copy; in his own mind he had a conception of beauty beyond all other men, and intent upon
this he devoted art and hand to reproduce it. So too said
the philosopher Plotinus; Pheidias looked to nothing
visible, but he pictured to himself what Zeus would be,
if he wished to appear before our eyes. Dio Chrysostom,
a generation or so younger than St Paul, wrote that he
thought a man heavy-laden, who had drained the cup
of misfortune and sorrow, if he were to stand and gaze
at this statue, would forget the heavy and the weary
weight of all this unintelligible world. The Roman
Quintilian held that the beauty of the image added
something to religion, so truly did the majesty of the
image represent God. Perhaps to-day the best repre-
sentation of Pheidias' statue is the head found at Jerash
in Syria, about which there has been some question as

to whether it represents Aesculapius or Christ. There
appears to be little doubt that the sculptor of it was
inspired by Pheidias.

But the whole Acropolis, and the Parthenon itself,
were ever before the eyes of the Athenian. It might be
that

> Imagination slept,
> And yet not utterly. I could not print
> Ground where the grass had yielded to the steps
> Of generations of illustrious men,
> Unmoved. I could not always lightly pass
> Through the same gateways, sleep where they had slept,
> Wake where they waked, range that inclosure old,
> That garden of great intellects, undisturbed.

Unlike Wordsworth's Cambridge, fifth-century Athens
had her illustrious men still with her, an unexampled
series, in art, literature, war and statecraft. The city
might well, as Simonides said, teach the man. Modern
cities are all far too big, with their monotonous suburbs
(London or America, it is all one), their characterless
comfort and squalor, their imitation of one another; no
city in the world can boast such a family of living sons,
such concentrated intellect and creative power; and no
city is a sovereign state; St James', Whitehall, Washington
control them, and in themselves are nothing, mere places
of assembly. Athens was at once a city in a scene of
unforgettable beauty, looking out on sea and mountain
and island, an imperial city, a garden of great intellects
—everything in short that could touch the imagination
and make the heart beat. "Be *lovers* of your city", said
Pericles, and he knew that they were; and men of other
cities and other races caught the same passion.

Some reader, perhaps, will say, "And so speaks every
provincial from Sheffield to Vermont and Venezuela".

Plate II

Athens

No doubt; the Master has to pray to be delivered from his disciples, and the parody is all the tribute that some have for the masterpiece.

C. BOY AND YOUTH

If the city teaches the man, and gives him his outlooks and his ideals, or, if in Plato's caustic rendering of the same idea, Demos is the sophist who corrupts us all, still something should perhaps be said of the home. Perhaps the home-life was too dull, the mother too apt to be stupid, too like a woman in an Indian zenana. Greece paid horribly for not training her women to the level of the men. Yet childhood is much the same the world over. The Greek baby had a rattle, the "admirable invention" of a philosopher, Archytas, "which people give to their children to amuse them and prevent them from breaking anything in the house; for a young thing cannot be quiet". Their toys are still found, models of things like those that English children play with—dolls, tables, cooking pots, carts and boats. Ball play was universal, but not with a rubber ball; that we owe to Mexico. There was the swing, the hoop, blind man's buff. A Greek picture shows us something like hockey.

On the island of Rhodes they had Swallow songs and Swallow games. In the month of *Boedromion* (and what that was, the song will tell) the children went round the houses, like Scottish boys of old days at Hallowe'en, and sang:

Come again has the swallow,
    He brings you the spring;
Glad seasons shall follow,
    Glad years does he bring.
His breast and his back,
One is white and one black.

Some fruit from your store!
    Whatever you please—
For you are not so poor;
    Give us wine, give us cheese,
Wheat-cake or pulse-bread,
    Whatever you choose,
The swallow will take it,
    He will not refuse.

But if nothing you give us,
    Don't think we will go!
We'll take your house-door
And the lintel—and more!
There's your little wife sitting,—
So, when we go flitting,
We'll easily carry her off as we go.
So open the door
To the swallow once more;
We're just little children,
Not men of fourscore.

As lads grew older and stronger, there were athletics,
but not quite those we know. England owes more health
and happiness to her grass than we realize, and something more to her team games. The team had too small
a part in Greek athletics—as in Greek politics; and perhaps the one helps to explain the other. There was no
cricket in Greece, no boat-race. Young Greeks boxed
and ran; if they were very rich, they drove chariots,
especially after the Cyrenians gave them the new kind
of horse; each played his own game "on his own". There
was indeed the torch race, in which the lighted torch was
passed on and carried by one after another. The successful athlete shed a glory on his state, we are told, which
even an international footballer hardly beats. Every
four years at Olympia, oftener in other places, there were

great gatherings for Games. Of course, they were
religious festivals; but, as you watched the race, you
forgot everything else. "Run to win!" said St Paul,
who, Jew as he was and a Pharisee at that, had evidently
watched the athletes at Tarsus; it is not his only reference
to Greek athletics; they come into his mind and his
language oftener than one might have expected. Greeks
differed as to the Games; some thought them overdone;
and, as the centuries passed, though the Games continued, they declined in meaning, and ceased to be
national events. The Roman peace was over the world,
and the truce of the god, which meant much intercourse,
in science and in trade, in earlier days, counted less.
But in those early days the Games inspired a poetry,
which, in its kind, the world has never seen equalled.
"Strong-winged imperial Pindar, voice divine", stood
in the front rank of the poets of Greece, and he knew it,
and said so. He is not of universal appeal to-day; but
he is sensitive to beauty in many forms—in the human
frame and in human energy, in the colours of nature, in
the music and colour of words, in legend and myth; and
to those who love such things and feel how fugitive they
may be, he speaks as few others have ever done.

D. SLAVERY

After the statues of Hermes were mutilated in Athens in
416 B.C. (see page 146), the men who were alleged to
have done it were brought to trial for their impiety, and
a number of them were condemned. An inscription
preserves the record of the sale of their confiscated
property. From the house of Cephisodorus in the
Peiraieus his slaves were sold, and their prices are given.

A drachma was in purchasing power roughly equal to
a dollar. Here is the list, which needs little comment.

A Thracian woman	165 Dr.
A Thracian woman	135
A Thracian [man]	170
A Syrian	240
A Carian	105
An Illyrian	180
A Thracian woman	220
A Thracian	115
A Scythian	140
An Illyrian	121
A Colchian	153
A Carian boy	124
A little Carian boy	72
A Syrian	301
A Melittenian [man or woman?]	151
A Lydian woman	170

What we call "domestic service" to-day, was constantly the work of the Thracian woman slave; *Thratta*
is the Athenian slang equivalent of "slavey". For a
slave was commonly given no special name but was
called by his race. The police of Athens, such as they
were, the "bowmen", were apt to be Scythians, pur-
chased for the purpose by the state. Perhaps some of the
men slaves in the list given were employed in manufacture. The largest number we hear of in any one factory
is said to be about 160. The Athenian historian tells us
that, when the Spartans occupied a fort in Attica in the
Peloponnesian war, artisan slaves ran away from Athens;
he tells us that the runaways numbered some 20,000;
and he is famous for his carefulness about figures. Thus,
there is justification for those critics, who say that the
splendid democracy of Pericles rested on slave labour.

There is abundant evidence also for the practice in Greek warfare of selling the surviving population of a captured city wholesale into slavery (see page 148). In time sentiment changed, and Greeks began to feel that it was not right to sell or to enslave Greeks; foreigners stood on a different footing; and philosophers conjectured that barbarians perhaps were "slaves by nature", which would of course justify their enslavement. Later on the Stoics said outright that "Nature" recognized no such thing as a slave; all men were born to be free; slavery was not natural but contrary to Nature (see page 286).

Slavery under the Romans seems to have been horrible by law and in practice. At Athens we hear a different story. "There is," says an Athenian oligarch, one of the severest critics of their democracy, "there is the greatest ill-behaviour at Athens among slaves and resident aliens; and it is not permitted there to hit a slave, nor will a slave stand out of your way. The reason why this is the custom of the place, I will set forth; if it were legal for a slave, or a resident alien, or a freedman, to be struck by a free man, one would often strike an Athenian citizen under the impression that he was a slave; for the people there are in no way better dressed or better looking than the slaves and resident aliens". He goes on to explain why slaves are allowed so much freedom; it is partly due to the need of them in the navy, partly to their being allowed to acquire property; there are "rich slaves". So the "equality of intercourse between slave and free" is not quite unreasonable, he says, though he clearly dislikes it. In Sparta another man's slave will fear you.

Perhaps the strangest phase of slavery is found in the

circles of the Athenian bankers. A banker would buy his clerks in the slave-market. They might very well be educated Greeks, sold from a captured city; but there were some famous head-clerks who had little of the Greek about them, in speech or look or movement. Athenian law allowed a litigant to challenge his opponent to produce his slaves for torture. It was supposed that slaves could not otherwise be relied on to give true evidence. In such a case the banker might hurriedly set his chief clerk free, to save the man from this horrible risk. In one famous instance, a great banker, who had once been a slave himself, emancipated his chief clerk, and at last left to him by will his business and his widow; this was not without parallel, and it excited little remark.

The flight of 20,000 slaves is evidence enough that men were not content to be slaves in Athens. Escape was harder for women. But, at the worst, it must be admitted that slavery at Athens, bad as it was for master and slave, and bad economically, does not show the horrors of Roman slavery, or of American. No negro slave in New York or New Orleans is known to have inherited his master's widow along with a bank.

E. THE GODS

The reader of Homer is left in no doubt about the gods of Greece. They are as well known to him as the heroes; their personal aspect and their characters become quite familiar. Grey-eyed Athene plays a large part in the *Odyssey*, and enjoys the many wiles of Odysseus as much as the reader. Apollo, angered by the wrong done to his priest, descends from above, and the arrows rattle in his quiver as he comes down in wrath. Zeus, it must be

confessed, is a dim, almost a confused, figure; at times
he is as compact of human nature as his wife Hera, or
Athene his daughter—terribly human, a later age felt;
but at other times he seems to melt into Fate or Destiny,
the factor hard to guess or to know (as later Greeks put
it), but inevitable as the future itself. Herodotus is right
in saying that Homer gave its character to Greek religion.
Whatever Homer's own thought of the gods, and whatever the thought of men or tribes around him, his poems
fixed the tradition as he gave it. No doubt, as poets do,
he selected for his own purposes what he wanted, with
little thought of being a religious reformer at all; but
what a great poet rejects may be as significant as what
he accepts; and so it proved. In some phases of Greek
religion Homer was clearly not interested; and wherever
his poems were read (and they were read everywhere),
men thought of the gods as he pictured them, no doubt
with proper reservations and respect for local gods, but
with less and less interest in them. Homer's Olympians
became universal gods, Panhellenic, a common èlement
in the thinking of all Greeks, while the local cults of
parochial gods (if we may call them so) were rarely
known ten miles from the parish.

In the mid-nineteenth century there was a desire to
turn into sun-myths as much as possible of Homer's
Olympus and its inhabitants. Scholars have ceased,
however, to unlock every mystery with a sunbeam.
Anthropologists have risen who believe as fervently in
corn-spirits and year-demons and the like, as their
predecessors did in the sun-myths. They point out
strange survivals in the religious practices of historical
Greece, things far more "primitive" than Homer—odd,
homely and sometimes disgusting rites performed in

honour of dim and lowly gods or goddesses, powers of
vegetation or of the underworld or of the regions of the
dead. Some of these powers were half-animal, or perhaps
had once been whole animals; some interpreters have
insisted that even Demeter had once been a pig. In any
case, after the "Homeric" hymn to Demeter was written,
such hateful ideas were forgotten in Greece; she was a
goddess indeed, with a human heart. Thus, whatever
might be the squalid local traditions, Greeks tended to
link the local cult with Homer's religion of all Greeks,
or to transform it, if possible; they would give their local
god one of the great names—as do Hindus to-day, to get
some cohesion and order into their pantheon. The local
god had often a local wife; and, when he became an
Olympian who visited the neighbourhood, the fame of
the goddess fell as his rose; and later ages were embar-
rassed by the number of local wives that a universal god
might have.

While this Panhellenic movement was re-shaping
Greek ideas, another universal religion swept over
Greece. The god Dionysus appears from India or, at all
events, from Asia and Thrace. Strange things were to
be seen wherever he or his legend came; women became
possessed, fled their homes and sought the forests; they
grew conscious of new strength, and it was said they tore
living animals to pieces, as pagan Arabs once did to
living camels, and more recently the Indians of British
Columbia have done to living dogs. It all seemed in-
explicable, unless you said a god did it, that he came
into the women and gave them his strength. So Dionysus
was admitted to Delphi as Apollo's younger brother.
Regular festivals in his honour were set up in Athens and
elsewhere, and the distressing proofs of his deity ceased

to be conspicuous. After him came Orpheus, who has been variously explained as a god, a singer, a fox-totem, or a personified ideal. Whatever Orpheus was, Orphic priests play a large part after this with their rites and legends and the "poems of Orpheus"; they taught in some form a doctrine of a future life, and, for money payments, would prepare men for it with ceremonies and initiations, which were apt to turn into jollifications. Meantime at Eleusis rites of Demeter also promised life after death. Men and women went through rituals, and "were put into frames of mind", as a great Greek critic said; they felt, and they supposed that they had learnt.

Little or no moral impulse came from any of these movements. The moral growth of Greece is due to the thinkers, not to the priests and devotees. There was negative criticism of divine legends, in plenty. Of what *colour* are the gods? asked one thinker, who had seen black gods in North Africa. Pindar, the most orthodox of all really great poets, rejected repulsive legends; "I stand aloof", he said; but he kept much that later on seemed wrong. Aeschylus, the great tragic poet, who fought at Marathon (as he says in his epitaph), did not reject the gods; but, wrestling with the problems of Right and Wrong (and finding it a hard enough struggle), he found moral law ruling the universe, and linked it somehow with the Olympians. Herodotus, a generation later, is an open-minded but sympathetic inquirer; he collects all the evidence he can find as to gods and oracles, divine justice and a moral order; he weighs it carefully, and, with some waverings, decides for the gods as forces making for the moral order. Euripides and Plato reject the legends. Euripides (see page 124) sets the gods of legend alongside of human sorrow and the moral grandeur of common men and women. Plato will sweep Homer and Olympus, gods and all, out of his ideal Republic; "we must never speak of God but as He is".

Thus tradition and the thinkers looked different ways; and common people made the best of it, doubting where convenient, plunging on any alarm into wild superstition, and ready enough to gather up any and every idea about the gods, Greek notions and foreign, sceptical or pious, into impossible combinations, which they could always re-arrange. Later on Egypt and Phrygia and Persia supplied universal gods, when Alexander's influence made something of the kind seem likely or desirable. The Stoics tried hard to develop the Homeric Zeus into the One God behind all creation; but the legends were too many for the dogma. It must never be forgotten that Greek religion had no creed and no dogma, nothing standardized, and, if plenty of priests, no episcopate.

F. SPARTA

There was one Greek state conspicuously unlike the rest. Many legends grew up or were invented to explain why Sparta should be so different in all her institutions from all other Greeks, with perhaps some likeness (men said) to some of the Cretans. Elsewhere in Greece men remarked the wearing down of old clan usages; Sparta was a place of strange survivals. The growth of cities and of overseas trade on a large scale, the planting of colonies, the resulting intercourse with foreigners, the spread of philosophic questioning, the rise of art and of literature, all meant the freedom of the individual man to shape his own course in the world, to find his own aptitudes and pleasures, in a word (to quote a Greek thinker) "to live as he pleases". But Greeks remarked that everything they took to be progress was forbidden in Sparta. Nothing that we think distinctively Greek—art, athletics, literature or philosophy—was of any interest to Spartans. You could hardly call the place a city; it had no buildings of any note; it was little more than five villages. Spartans had nothing to do with trade or even with farming; there were subject populations round them, the *Perioikoi* who manufactured and sold some iron, and *Helots* who tilled the ground. One colony had gone from Sparta, but there were peculiar circumstances about it which were not very clearly explained. Foreigners visited Sparta from time to time, but they were apt to be ordered to leave and not return. The Spartans were a race of soldiers— not as to-day we might apply the name to a country where all the men are compulsorily trained for some period in the army, but because they were bred to be soldiers, were trained to be soldiers, and were nothing but soldiers, the steadiest and most invincible in the Greek world, but, after all, mere soldiers, and, as a rule, neither generals, strategists nor administrators. What one of their ablest men said of another—"that he did not know how to rule free men"—was true of most of them; they were unendurable masters.

They had a number of very curious customs. When a boy was born in Sparta, the baby was submitted (men said) to the state authorities, who should decide whether he should be brought up or at once exposed to perish. If he was to live, they assigned him a farm or estate, tilled by *helots*, and on the produce of this he was to live till he died; he might not sell the farm nor the *helot* serfs; they were not his to sell, they belonged to the state, which would want them for the next Spartan boy born after his death. From childhood the boy was under discipline;

he went barefoot, he had but one garment; his food was scanty—but he was allowed (almost encouraged) to steal food, if he were too hungry. They thought that judicious thefts would train the boy for stratagems in war; and, to make sure that he stole cannily, he was well whipped, if he was caught. The Spartan legislator, Lycurgus, it was said, noticed that at thirteen or fourteen boys develop a certain independence or uppishness, as you may prefer to call it; so he piled on extra discipline, extra tasks, and drilled into them a respect for their elders nowhere else to be found in Greece. A Spartan boy, meeting a grown man, must put his hands inside his clothes, look at the ground, and pass on in silence; Spartan boys, someone said, were as silent as statues and as modest as girls. There was endless drill for them, in the gymnasium and in the open, hunting game, and (a little later on) killing *helots* on the order of the magistrates. The public whipping contest was famous, at which boys were sometimes whipped to death without a murmur. Men and women did not eat together; there were men's meal-clubs, some fifteen in a group, and the nastiness of the food became a proverb, almost a national boast. All was regulated by the laws and controlled by the magistrates; nowhere, men said, were men more obedient to authority than in Sparta. (It is true that Pericles said men were more law-abiding in Athens; fifty years later Plato was quite sure they were not;—it is an advantage to find our informants disagreeing. It was disagreement in opinion that made Athens so interesting a place, while its absence made Sparta so dull.) Precise rules and long practice made the Spartan soldiers, in their red coats, almost invincible for generations. One of their kings led them on all campaigns.

For, when it came to government, Greeks looked with
fresh wonder at Sparta. All over Greece kings had been
abolished, except for religious rites; the name *king* was
kept, because the gods were used to it, and certain
sacrifices could be performed only by kings; so kings
continued, but were very minor magistrates. But Sparta
kept kings for much more important purposes, and had
two at a time. There were two royal houses (which
generally disliked each other), descended, so ran the
story, from the twin sons of the Achaean prince who
conquered the land afterwards Spartan, when the Dorian
invaders brought back the exiled sons (or great-grand-
sons) of Herakles. The mother of the twins wished both
to be kings; so, as there was no telling which was the
elder, the people adopted both. It has to be said, however, that elsewhere in the world there were joint-rulers
or war-chiefs without this explanation about twins. The
Iroquois in old New York State had two war leaders (of
the Seneca tribe); the Romans and other Italians had
two consuls, or praetors, as they might be called in
various tribes at various times. So the story about the
twins may have been made up; at any rate the Spartans
told it, and kept two royal families for centuries.

Every year they elected five magistrates called *ephors*.
Elections can be held in various ways; modern elections
need paper and pencils; a hundred years ago in England
voters publicly declared their votes; in Athens at certain
periods they chose certain magistrates, and even an
important financial administrator, by lot. In Sparta it
was election by shouting—"and a very silly plan, too",
said a great Greek thinker. They locked up the returning
officer as it were in a telephone box on the market; and
the names were called, and he was fetched out to say

which shouts had been loudest—as it might be, numbers 2, 3, 4, 7 and 10; and those persons were elected. Such is the story told by a responsible writer; but, however elected, the ephors ruled. On entering office, they made a proclamation that every Spartan must obey the laws and shave his moustache; they also proclaimed war on the *helots*, so that it might be quite a pious and holy act to kill them. Once they found the *helots* rather unsettled; so they announced that every *helot* who had done the state good service might declare what it was, and, if it were good enough, he should be set free. Two thousand were incautious enough to accept the offer; there was a great festival, but before very long the whole two thousand had been put out of sight—a rather grim phrase.

A council of twenty-eight men aged sixty was supposed to advise the kings; and there was an assembly of full-grown Spartan men, but it was not quite sovereign. It might vote this or that, as put to it by the ephors, but there was a proviso that if the assembly voted "aslant", the kings and elders should "put things straight again".

At first, and for long, Sparta was only a minor power in the Peloponnese, overshadowed by Argos and engaged in wars with the Arcadians who controlled the mountain passes. But she had in her army a force in the long run unequalled by her enemies. She took a large part of the Argive land, and many were the stories of their wars. Once three hundred champions on each side fought it out till three only were left alive, two Argives and one Spartan. As there seemed to be no one left to fight them, the two Argives marched home as conquerors; the Spartan stayed on the field; which had won? So it came to a general battle, and an Argive defeat; and from that day the Argives wore their hair short till they should recover the lost lands (which they never did), and the Spartans ever after wore long hair. People outside, who wanted to ape the Spartans, began by growing their hair long. The fights with the Arcadians of Tegea were never successful till a clever man guessed a riddle. Why the Spartans always failed, they could not understand, but they consulted the god at Delphi. He told them they must bring home first the bones of Orestes, son of Agamemnon; and the bones were

> Where blow two winds of strong necessity,
> And stroke meets stroke, and woe on woe is laid.

This was not very clear. But in time a Spartan herald stood in a Tegean smithy and chatted with the smith, who told him of a giant's bones below the shop; and he reflected upon bellows and anvil, and on iron, a "woe" to mankind. So Orestes was dug up and taken to Sparta, and Sparta became supreme.

Supreme she was for long in the Peloponnese. Not all her neighbours liked her, nor willingly allowed the supremacy; but no power in that country could stand against her terrible soldiers. So they obeyed, and sent her contingents when she wanted to make war. Corinth, the great commercial town on the isthmus between Peloponnese and the mainland of Greece, had perhaps most influence. She stopped one expedition of the Spartans to restore the tyrants to Athens, and eighty years later she manœuvred the Spartans into engaging in the long and disastrous Peloponnesian war to break up the Empire of Athens. This was achieved, but it is not clear that it did Corinth any good. The next worst thing, men say, to being defeated in a war is to win it; and the Peloponnesian war did nobody any good; all its effects were disastrous. It weakened Greece all round, and took the hopefulness out of Greek life.

Chapter VII

THE DIVIDED GREEK WORLD

A. THE PELOPONNESIAN WAR

ASK any intelligent person what was the cause of the great European war of 1914 to 1918, and you may get a more or less reasonable answer; but take a second opinion and a third, and you may be confused; take two or three dozen, and the chances are that you will end by not believing any of them. You will be tempted to conclude that it was quite inevitable yet the merest accident; that it could have been most easily averted but for the action of a few people, though who these few people were, you may not be able to say very certainly. Men feel and remember differently, says the historian of the Peloponnesian war; they listen to what they chance to hear, and do not test it; "so little trouble do men take in the search after truth; so readily do they accept whatever comes first to hand".

But he suggests further a distinction between causes, occasions and pretexts; and here we may remember the sentence already quoted, "a hidden cause is better than an obvious one" (see page 69). When the Spartans had resolved on war with Athens, they were not ready; so, while they prepared, they made time by sending embassies to Athens, and making one demand or another, the refusal of which might make their reasons for fighting look better. The crowning stroke was the message: "*We* wish to maintain peace; and peace is only possible if *you*, the Athenians, will let the Greeks govern themselves (*auto-*

nomv)". They asked Athens to dissolve the Confederacy of Delos, and be done with allies and subjects—very much as if some foreign power offered to allow Britain to enjoy peace, if she would consent to Scotland, Newfoundland, the Isle of Wight, India and Jamaica, and perhaps other conquered tribes, becoming independent republics. The one was as likely to be conceded to a threat as the other. There was this difference, however; many of the allies of Athens wished to be quit of her. How little it all meant, and what was the real value of all this negotiation, was seen when peace was made in 421. Sparta forgot her zeal for Megarian trade and for Greek freedom, as Mr Madison, the American President, forgot, when he made peace in 1815, why he had gone to war with Britain in 1812. So much for pretexts; as for causes, "the Spartans were influenced, not so much by the speeches of their allies [the Corinthians] *as by the fear of the Athenians and of their increasing power*; for they saw the greater part of Greece already subject to them". The cause, "the real but unavowed" cause, which Thucydides here lays bare, would explain many another war, whatever the contemporary politicians explained, while they manœuvred for position.

Pericles struck the right note at once; Do not give way to the Spartans, whatever they ask; you will not really be going to war for a trifle. No, yield one thing because it does not matter, and they will raise another issue. Make up your minds that you will yield nothing. When war begins, there are three watchwords to remember; keep a firm hold on your allies; count Athens and the Peiraieus inside their Long Walls as an island, and let your farms and country houses go; make no additions to your empire. His advice was right in every particular,

though there was a loud outcry when the enemy raided
the farms. But Pericles would risk no battle on land
against the Spartans; let them burn haystacks.

Three or four events are all we need note here in the
first ten years of the war. The famous plague broke out
in Athens, which the historian describes with minute
care, from personal experience. It cost many lives and
made deep depression. A little later Pericles died. In
425 a lucky storm drove an Athenian fleet into Pylos—
Navarino bay on the West coast of the Peloponnese
(famous for the naval battle that set modern Greece
free); and, for something to do, the sailors took to putting
up a fortification on Spartan territory. This fetched the
Spartans very quickly out of Attica; but luck was against
them, a Spartan force was cut off, high and dry, on the
island in the bay, and was forced to surrender. To recover
these men, and because she was sick of the war, Sparta
made peace in 421.

It was an uneasy peace; and it really ended, when in
415 the Athenians sent out the great expedition to conquer Syracuse. Why they did so, historians debate; it
seems to moderns a folly, even if it was feasible, as seems
just possible. Thucydides says it was a "passion" (*eros*),
like that of a man in love with a girl, neither springing
from reason nor to be overcome by reason. Others
explain it otherwise; Athens had great trade interests
in Sicily, and Syracuse was growing too strong to be safe;
Athens had allies in Sicily by whom she must stand or
all her hold upon the Western Mediterranean would be
lost; and so forth. The expedition sailed, splendid beyond
anything attempted before by any single Greek city;
but it was a curious and unlucky thing that, just before
it sailed, in one night, nearly all the statues of Hermes

at the doors of temples and houses were mutilated; uncanny too that, on the day of sailing, the women were wailing for Adonis, the lost lover. What was more unfortunate was that Alcibiades was accused of the mutilation, and was recalled from command of the fleet, and it was left in charge of Nicias, a wealthy and respectable man, but middle-aged, afraid of the Athenian people, superstitious, and already ill with a disease very likely to be fatal. He got the fleet into Syracuse harbour, fumbled everything, and, when it was clear he ought to abandon the siege, was scared by an eclipse of the moon, stayed on too long; and the result—"of all Greek actions", says Thucydides, "this was the greatest, the most glorious to the victors, the most ruinous to the vanquished; for they were utterly and at all points defeated; and their sufferings were prodigious. Fleet and army perished from the face of the earth; nothing was saved, and of the many that went forth few returned home. Thus ended the Sicilian expedition".

Great emperors have gone to Moscow with like result; such things have happened, said the Greeks, and in all human probability will happen again. But what is less likely to happen is told by Plutarch, a luminous story. Some of the Athenians, prisoners and fugitives, were saved for the sake of Euripides. For the Sicilians, it would seem, more than any other Greeks outside Greece had a yearning fondness for his poetry, for ever learning by heart any fragments and morsels of it that people chanced to bring, and teaching them to one another with delight. And at this time, the story goes, many of those who reached Athens at last, greeted Euripides with affection, and told him, some how they had been set free from slavery when they had taught all they remembered of his poems, and others how, as they wandered after the battle, they were given food and water for singing his songs.

The war went on, Athens unspeakably weaker, her enemies stronger and exultant; but victory was not so near as they thought. For nine years the Athenians held out, in spite of a short but bloody revolution (soon reversed) at home, in spite of the brilliant young Persian prince Cyrus backing Sparta with fresh subsidies and new fleets, in spite of their own reconciliation and fresh quarrel with Alcibiades—till at length their last fleet was destroyed, and the Dardanelles, the route by which their food came, was in Spartan hands. "It was at night", says Xenophon, "that the ship came in [to the Peiraieus] which brought the news of the disaster; and a sound of wailing passed up from the Peiraieus between the Long Walls to the city, as one told another. That night none slept. They wept not only for the dead, but far more for themselves, for they looked to suffer what they had done to the Melians, when they reduced them by siege, to the people of Histiaea, of Scione, of Torone, of Aegina, and many other Greeks." They had sold them for slaves. We will not follow the agonies of the siege, the triumph of Sparta, the destruction of the Long Walls to the sound of flutes on "the first day of Greek freedom"—which it was not. The war was over; and the empire of Athens, her confederacy—it was all "Troy town", all a thing of the past.

But it was a great past, and nothing like it was ever to be seen again in Greek seas. Athens with her allies had driven the Persian from Greek waters, and laid down a line in the Eastern Mediterranean which the Great King's fleet was not to cross. The menace of an autocrat from the East was gone; the Greek cities of Asia Minor, of Ionia "the mother-land of culture", were free; if they paid "tribute" to keep up the fleet, without which the coastline towns could not be independent of the *Hinterland*, they were safe from Persian satraps, from Greek tyrants and oligarchies. If the story of the confederacy seems to be full of wars, like the story of the empires that followed Alexander's, like the story of Rome, it must never be forgotten that again and again the great empires have meant peace among their elements. A sentence in Thucydides records a day in Sicily, when the men of Naxos and their barbarian allies slew a thousand men of Messene, an unthinkable disaster to a small town; it must have been a large proportion of the adult men, and it is told in a sentence and passed over, a day's battle among Greek neighbours; and how many like it are unrecorded? While Athens ruled, there was to be no revolution in the streets of a little town and the victims carried out next day packed criss-cross on carts.

Whatever hopes of autonomy Sparta held out to her allies, she gave them none; there were *harmosts* (governors) in the European Greek towns, satraps in the Asian, murder in the Laconian countryside, the break-up of the Arcadian town into villages, the overthrow of the confederacy of Olynthus—all for the good of Spartan men, trained by Lycurgus in nothing but the strength of the brute and the discipline of the drill sergeant;—and for the ultimate benefit of the foreigner, the Macedonian.

B. THE ANABASIS

Xenophon's *Anabasis* is the one book about which everybody who has done even a little Greek knows something. For many it is a dismal memory, with its *parasangs* and its repeated phrase: "Thence he marches". But for anyone who likes a good story that carries one along, a first-hand tale of real adventure, there are few to match it. You must, of course, know the language in which you read it, and picture the scene. The weary *parasangs* gain an interest, when you learn that a *parasang* appears to be an hour's march; and you see at once that, at different times of the year, and over different ground, *parasangs* will vary a good deal. A bad mountain road, snow or swamp, will shorten the distance covered, and eight *parasangs* may be a heavy day's marching and not take you very far. Realize this, and begin to note what marches the army makes, and other questions arise. You think of camping grounds and the need for abundant water; you wonder why some days are so long, and some so short, and see at last why, after a number of long heavy days, the army halts; the men are tired out and no good for fighting. Once begin to watch and question, and the marches have a new interest, and you realize that this is a living story; and, as you again think it over, you see how it made History.

Darius II, king of Persia, died leaving two sons, of whom Artaxerxes II was his successor. Whisperers told the new king that his brother Cyrus was plotting against him. This was not incredible; it was common enough in Eastern monarchies; and whether the charge was true or not, the best way of escaping the accusation was to do the thing and to do it successfully. So Cyrus set about raising troops. He knew there were no troops to beat Greek *hoplites*, Greeks in armour. So he began to gather them on the quiet, some enlisted here, some there, and engaged in small wars with which he seemed to have nothing to do. When he was ready, he assembled them at Sardis in Asia Minor, and marched up-country, spreading a tale that he hoped would mislead his brother; he had a private war with another Persian governor. An old enemy of his, Tissaphernes, thought his preparations rather too large for this, and posted off to the king. The Greek soldiers were not quite sure of the prince's real purpose, and, when they reached Tarsus, their suspicions led to a mutiny; they would not go into the interior of Asia; they had not been hired to fight the Great King. It looked awkward for the prince; but they were wheedled into going on, with a promise of higher pay. There was another mutiny when they reached the Euphrates; but a Thessalian captain spoiled it. He persuaded his company to cross the river; this would mean extra bounties from Cyrus, and they could always go back. The rest followed. There was no going back when once across; and the Greeks in their thousands marched down the river, fairly committed to fighting Artaxerxes.

"But will he fight?" "By Zeus," said Cyrus, "if he is the son of *my* parents, he will." And if Cyrus wins— "Men!" he cried, "the empire of my father reaches South to where men cannot live for the heat, and North to where they cannot live for the cold; all between, my brother's friends rule; and, if we conquer, my friends will rule". Meantime there were alleviations. They had some good hunting, chasing ostriches and wild asses, though the ostriches beat them; and they learnt how much better dates could be than anybody knew in Greece. Once in a review, they scared the Cilician queen out of her wits, when they charged; and they laughed to see the barbarians run. They were impressed, too, to see Persian nobles, gay with necklaces and bracelets, throw off their scarlet cloaks and put their shoulders to the wheel, when Cyrus found his waggons stuck in the mud.

At last the two armies met; and the victory was already won, when Cyrus caught sight of his brother, dashed at him in rage to kill him, and was cut down there and then. The victory was won, but the expedition had failed; and there were the Greeks in the middle of the Persian Empire, far from the sea, on the wrong side of the Euphrates, and surrounded by enemies, a thousand miles from Greece. Their leaders were trapped and killed; they had only their arms. No, said an Athenian, they would not surrender their arms; their arms were all they had; they would use them. "Young man," said the King's envoy, "you seem quite a philosopher, and you talk charmingly; but know this—you are a fool, if you think your valour can overcome the King's power." The young man was perhaps Xenophon, and on him above all fell the task of getting the Ten Thousand out of the Persian Empire.

Xenophon tells us how he got the soldiers to rally from their depression, and then how they pursued their long march to the sea, first with the Persians hovering about them, and then outside the country which the Persians cared to control, among mountain defiles, whose savage natives rolled boulders upon them. They had no cavalry, and they had to do their best with newly mounted infantry to keep off attacks on their line of march. Ten or twelve thousand armed men (originally more) with camp followers—it was the population of a city to be guided to the sea and to be fed, as they made their way among the mountains of Armenia. They met strange people, who lived in underground houses, and offered them barley wine in bowls. They found honey for themselves which made them ill, as if drunk or mad—a honey still known in those regions. They had to march in driving snow which fell till it was six foot deep, and their rawleather shoes grew sodden and froze to their feet at night. When the storm left off, snow-blindness began. Through it all Xenophon had to think of their welfare, and at times even to use violence to make a dejected man get up and march, to save him from frostbite and death.

At last, after dragging on interminably, day after day, Xenophon with the rear-guard heard a wild shouting from the van. The country was all aflame and the natives were on the move; was this another sudden onslaught? The shouting grew louder, as more and more men reached the ridge. Xenophon at last, in some anxiety, galloped to the rescue, and as he rode caught the words: " *The Sea! The Sea!* " They all gathered on the ridge, and in great excitement fell to embracing one another with tears; generals, captains and all. The sea was the Greek's element, and now, after the long and dreadful march, it would be plain sailing, as the phrase goes.

But it was not; for where were the ships for twelve thousand men? At Trapezus, a famous Greek city on the shore—the Trebizond of legend—they held a great celebration of their escape; and Xenophon describes some of the national dances. Thracians in full armour danced to the flute, leaping lightly in the air and using their swords; one struck another and he fell (with great art, Xenophon says; and the natives cried out); the victor spoiled the fallen man, and, chanting the glories of his king at home, went away; and the others carried off the dead man, who had not been hurt. Other Greeks danced the *Karpeia*; one of them laid aside his arms, and pretended to sow and to drive a yoke of oxen, often looking round in fear; in dances a robber, and they fall to fighting, in rhythm with the flute; and the victor binds the other and drives off the oxen. Other dances followed —an interlude among adventures, and both tell us about the Greeks; and so does the whole story.

Once free of Persian satraps and savage mountaineers, once on the sea, the story might seem to be over; and so some of the Ten Thousand thought, and took the first chance of getting away from the rest. But Xenophon had to lead them back to Greece; and he did, while they mutinied and threatened to stone him, and made friends again, and then suspected him of wishing to found a new colony on the Black Sea and never to let them see the Peloponnese again. He got them somehow to Byzantium; and there fresh troubles followed. The Spartan governor did not want them (who would want such an army?) and some of them he sold for slaves—a fact to be noted; such was Spartan government. A large number Xeno- phon took away up-country into Thrace, where they met another sort of barbarian nearer home; and he describes a great uproarious primitive feast, at which King Seuthes threw the meat about to his guests, and there was plenty of drink, and the chiefs brought presents, a white horse, a slave, costly clothes; and all Xenophon had to offer was his army. Seuthes jumped up in delight and did a war dance; and after that clowns and jesters came in. But Thrace was not as savage as some might think; they had fixed rules and boundary posts to regulate the looting of wrecked ships, "honour among thieves". King Seuthes had not, alas! the money to pay his Greek troops. But deliverance came; for King Agesilaus of Sparta had resolved on war with Persia; he too would try to capture

Artaxerxes; and the Ten Thousand, or what was left of them, were the men to do it. So they found a paymaster and fresh fighting for a while, till "ten thousand archers", as the king said, drove the Spartans out of Asia—not men, but archers stamped on gold coins, the Persian *darics*. There lay the strength of Persia; her weakness had been shown to the world by the march of Cyrus and the retreat of the Ten Thousand, and the world did not forget it.

Xenophon had had enough of fighting, and the rest of his life he seems to have given to writing books and hunting and bringing up his twin sons in the country.

C. SPARTAN ASCENDENCY

Athens was utterly ruined by the Peloponnesian war, her empire passed to Sparta, her walls were digged down, her democracy was overthrown and a board of thirty set up in its place. Within a couple of years the democracy was restored, and the "Thirty Tyrants" were gone; within twelve the walls were rebuilt with Persian money; within thirty a new confederacy was formed with Athens as its centre; and thirty-three years after the fall of Athens, Sparta suffered on the field of Leuctra a defeat that set free her age-long subjects and surrounded her with eager and triumphant enemies, a blow that deprived her of a large proportion of her citizen soldiers and of all her prestige, a disaster from which she never recovered. All the world hated her, and she could not replace her dead sons, nor persuade the world that she was invincible— the Sparta that had promised freedom to all the Greeks and had given them over to *harmost* and satrap. Empire (*arché*), to quote the pun of an Athenian orator, was to Sparta the beginning (*arché*) of misfortune.

The government of "the Thirty" in Athens was atrocious. "To be able to use the city as they pleased", they got the Spartans to send a garrison. One of their own leaders protested that it was unwise to kill men regarded by the people, men who might have done their party no harm; but "there is always loss of life with a change of constitution", said his rival; and the killing went on. Refugees from the city crowded to Megara and Thebes. Suddenly on the heights of Phyle, fifteen miles from the city, and well in sight of it, 2500 ft. above the sea, appeared a band of seventy exiles headed by Thrasybulus. Troops were sent to clear them out; but a sudden snowstorm drove the troops back, and the exiles fell on them as they retreated. It was a ray of hope, and men who hated the new regime rallied to Thrasybulus, till he had 700. How this number was fed, we are not told; but the people were with them, and the tide turned. In the spring Thrasybulus swooped down upon the Peiraieus, and took it, and held it. Lysander, the Spartan general, had the Peiraieus blockaded and besieged; but the Spartan king Pausanias was jealous of him; did he want to make Athens his private property? The Boeotians and Corinthians, too, had no wish to see Athens in Spartan hands, very intelligibly. A battle followed in which Thrasybulus' party was lucky enough to be beaten by Pausanias, who was for peace. And peace was made. The "tyrants" were to go; otherwise Thrasybulus pled for amnesty, and in a short time Athens resumed her old constitution; "and they swore oaths that they would not remember evil one against another; and to this day they live together as fellow-citizens, and *Demos* abides by his oaths". So says Xenophon, writing, it would seem, long afterwards, but giving in vivid detail all the moments and movements of the great deliverance which he had witnessed in his youth; Xenophon can always tell a story, and here he had a theme indeed.

So Athens was free, but in what a plight! The empire and all foreign possessions, public and private, were lost; all the state treasure was gone, and a hundred talents were owing to Sparta; no one had any money; trade was at a standstill; the fleet was lost, the walls and the docks destroyed. But in eight years she was on her feet again. For one thing the oligarchical party had wrecked themselves, and for eighty years no attempt was made to change the constitution; and the Peiraieus was still the familiar harbour, the centre of distribution for all Greece, and very fairly in the middle of the world of trade. When trade began to revive and ships to find freights, where else could they take them? And the merchants began to haunt the familiar wharves and streets, bringing money and fresh spirit and revival. Sparta fell out with the Persians, and the Athenian admiral of a Persian fleet won a great victory off Cnidos over the Spartans. He told his satrap what was quite true, and indeed obvious, that nothing would more effectually hamper Sparta than the restoration of the Long Walls that linked Athens to the sea; the Spartans were notoriously ineffectual in siege operations, and Athens, once safe from them, would counter-balance Spartan power. So the Walls were rebuilt.

The Spartans abused their power; the interest of Sparta was the one thing to be considered, their king insisted; and Spartans had little political sense, and took short views. Their violence undid them, for their outrages upon their allies in time of peace (such as the sudden seizure of the Theban citadel) turned the world against them. They broke up the confederacy of small towns gathered round Olynthus in the Northern Aegaean; every city was to be isolated; they could bully a divided Greece. Sparta made a new treaty with the Persian King, conceding his claim that the Greek cities of Asia Minor should be his, and securing his sanction that every Greek city should be "autonomous"—in other words, that no league of cities should stand in Sparta's way (387 B.C.). All the same, Athens was able to start a new confederacy in 377; and in 371 Sparta fell out with the Thebans on the central issue of league or town. The Thebans claimed to speak as Boeotians, and the Spartans said they should not. The battle of Leuctra followed; and Epameinondas led the Thebans to "the most glorious victory that Greeks ever won over Greeks", and "utterly beyond all hope or belief". Four hundred Spartan citizens, an enormous proportion of them, were killed; and Sparta's great days were over. Year by year the Thebans invaded the Peloponnese; the Messenians, after being *helots* for four hundred years, were free, and a nation once more; and the Arcadians were independent again. At the battle of Mantineia in 362, Epameinondas was killed. "After the battle", writes Xenophon, ending his *History* and laying down his pen, "confusion and disorder were greater than ever in Greece. For me, let me have written so far; what follows shall perhaps concern another."

D. SOCRATES AND DEMOS

In Athens the restored democracy made one supreme blunder that has never been forgiven. Many Athenians perhaps forgot it, but Plato remembered; and the world has looked at the Athens of the fourth century through the eyes of Plato. Once again the man of genius, who writes, shapes the judgments of posterity. Athens made Socrates drink the hemlock on the charge of corrupting youth. To later generations this has been almost unintelligible. But History is of little value if it brings no perplexities; it remains outside us; it is when we realize how hard it is to judge the men and the issues of the past, that we profit from History. The killing of Socrates involved no political issue, no constitutional change; it did not affect international relations; but it is far more significant than any of the things over which historians are apt to linger.

The man had long been a familiar figure in Athens, with his ugly face, ugly as a half-burlesque old god, yes, but within there was a god indeed! Like Dr Johnson, he was physically immensely strong; and, like Dr Johnson, he was the friend and inspirer of young men, witty, charming, incisive, great in conversation, in argument, in challenge; he made a man think. One of the best modern definitions of the work of a university is that "it breaks up men's dogmatism", teaches them that they do not *know* what they thought they knew, and "sets them at a universal point of view". Plato said much the same long ago; the real man must be "the spectator of all time and all being". What the university is supposed to do, Socrates did for men; and they loved him.

But there were those who hated him, which also is very intelligible. He made young men carry their heads so high; he taught them to doubt everything, to cross-examine their seniors; and he left them with no beliefs; and you could see what followed. The two most disastrous names in Athenian history were Alcibiades and Critias, the latter the arch-villain of "the Thirty", and both had been pupils of Socrates; that was what they learnt from him. How can a state be secure without belief or tradition? It is, after all, rather absurd to say that men of experience, long trained in affairs of state and commerce, loyal to the state and grown old in its service, such men as Pericles pictures, are really fools because they cannot analyse their experiences and reply to the clever quips of an undergraduate. There are, as Wordsworth wrote in his *Ode to Duty*, those

> Without reproach or blot,
> Who do thy work and know it not.

Anytus, one of the accusers in the famous trial, which ended with the sentence of the hemlock, is a speaker in one of Plato's Dialogues. He is discussing things with Socrates. A decent, reasonable man, not unkindly, but conventional, Anytus thinks that after all the best education for a young man is association with men of experience, with good citizens who have done the state some service. Socrates cross-examines him, makes unmerciful fun of him before spectators, and leaves him confused and humiliated. Yet in Plato's *Republic* the same idea is advanced; association with the best types of men is the best training for the young—"not of whom you are bred, but with whom you have fed", as Sancho Panza's proverb puts it. Most people would prefer the men Anytus had in mind, with all their errors and limitations, to the infallible officials invented by Plato. But all that is by the way; a man is judged by his influence on his friends, and that literally killed Socrates. But Demos had made a huge mistake.

The Funeral Speech of Pericles, from which sentences were drawn in Chapter VI to describe the typical citizen of Athens, is through and through full of idealism. Athens after the war and "the Thirty" is realist; everything comes down to fact. The aim is not to educate the rest of Greece, but to have a really comfortable Athens—commerce, of course, and comfort for the largest number of citizens, at the expense—now that there were no longer allies—of the stranger within the gates and, above all, of the rich. A pamphlet survives in which the author says that the real hope of Athens lies in the Peiraieus; it is a centre of distribution for all the world; merchants come there from everywhere, and bring us prosperity; we ought to have better hotels for them. Contrast this with Pericles. But, it will be rejoined, Athens still had her festivals and her theatre, as of old, but not the men of genius, who of old wrote the plays for those festivals. The festivals however come into politics now; they should be free for all citizens; the well-to-do can pay for the theatre—and for the navy, and for everything else; capital can always be taxed. *Eisphora* is the name of the significant tax, a tax not on income but on property—something in the nature of a capital levy; but it did not bring prosperity. As for national glory and empire—look back over the Peloponnesian War; how much better to have an Athens pleasant for tourists and students and residents! And now that the rule of the few is for ever discredited, liberty has full swing; a man may "live as he pleases", may act as he pleases, may talk as he pleases; and if he offends the better-bred—people ought not to be better-bred in a democracy, all should be equal there.

Yes, wrote Isocrates, the great educator of those days, there are two sorts of equality—the equality of the equal, and the equality of the unequal. But Athens paid no heed to such talk. Is not the city full of freedom and frankness, says Plato, the very asses equal, and the bitch as good as her mistress? Any man can do as he likes, hold office or avoid it, go to the wars or stay at home; the whole thing is a sort of bazaar where everybody can pick what he pleases—who cares? And anybody can train his sons as he likes; and Demos is so genial that he forgives anybody who says he is the friend of Demos, if he says it loud enough. The citizen bred in such a place is its natural product; he catches the spirit of the city: his mind is a democracy in itself, a popular assembly of inclinations, impulses, fancies, desires, one as good as another, all alike deserving indulgence; and he lives from day to day indulging the humour of the moment, whatever comes into his head. As for the ideas of law, discipline, self-control, principle, he packs them off, like bad citizens, into exile; it is a jolly life, he "lives as he likes". And out of such constitutions, and such habits of the individual mind, comes the wrecking of the state, and after that the Tyrant again. In the nineteenth century this seemed quite like Ancient History, and very obsolete: we forgot the Napoleons; but to-day we are less certain that History will not repeat itself.

It is hard to say that Plato was wrong in all this. There is, however, something to be said on the other side. In Athens, even in his period, life seems to have been safer than elsewhere; there was less of violence and murder. In spite of the hemlock cup given to Socrates, thinkers were free, free even to criticize democracy, and it has seldom had so merciless a critic as Plato, to whom no hemlock was given. But, of course, in ancient days talking was more dangerous than writing; even now Demos misses the significance of books. There was a good

deal of socialist or communist talk, enough to make it
worth while for Aristophanes to make fun of it in his
comedies played before the people; this of itself marks
a change—he attacks ideas, in earlier days he attacked
politicians. It is a question whether the Athenian people,
unlike the British, did not rather enjoy having its ideas
and its heroes laughed at on certain occasions; so that
we cannot be quite certain how widely people really
welcomed talk of re-distribution of property and state-
control of everything, to enable everybody to live as he
likes. The Athenian at all events seems not to have had
"a single-track mind", but rather enjoyed to see contradictory ideas yoked up, if it was done with enough
comic spirit. Of the comic spirit there was less in this
age, and there was less poetry; the war and national ruin
left most men intent on practical matters—on national
recovery first, and then on quiet and comfort as far as
they were possible. We see the same feeling to-day,
touched perhaps with a deeper motive. Morals seem to
have been neither much better nor much worse than in
the previous generation. There was more Rhetoric, less
sophistry; for Rhetoric now really meant what we call
a liberal education; Isocrates invented it and Oxford
inherits it. There were also philosophers, and above all
Plato, whose chief interest it was to find an intellectual
basis for the moral life, some Laws of Nature (as later
on the Stoics called them) by which a man might
shape his conduct for his own happiness and the good
of the state. If Socrates had to drink hemlock, and
Euripides was dead and gone, Plato must be credited
to Athens; with all his savage criticism of his country,
of the people who had killed his master, he was an
Athenian; and no Greek has so deeply influenced the

6-2

thinking of mankind. Other moral teachers gathered there, thinkers whose influence affected Greeks for generations, and later on profoundly helped to shape the better mind of Rome. Philosophy rather than tragedy, prose rather than poetry—and Athens excelled in philosophy and in prose as she had in the others before. Every man who writes a lucid and interesting prose to-day owes something to Isocrates, who lived through all this period and taught up to a great age, grumbling at Athens, but never deserting her. Nor did Art die; methods and ideas changed; the portrait bust and the unclad goddess were more to the mind of sculptors than the traditions of Pheidias— once more realism and the leaning to fact, and not without significance in the history of Art.

To sum up, there is a great change in Athens. Much as the eighteenth century in England with its philosophers, its practical people and its men of sense, differs from the mad ideals of church and state in the seventeenth, this fourth-century Athens is practical, sensible and matter-of-fact. It is of no use for a city to try to rule the world; Athens failed at it before the war, Sparta after. Local patriotism declines; but Greeks are still Greeks, and perhaps (the city and its politics apart) more apt to recognize it. Xenophon's Ten Thousand taught Greece something of this; but all round there is a growth of feeling for Greece as a whole and a slight loss of interest in the native place, at least in any imperial dreams for it. The bitter cry of Demosthenes is that Greece seems willing to accept even Philip of Macedon as a Greek and as a leader.

E. PHILIP OF MACEDON

In 359 Philip of Macedon became king, over a people divided between primitive clan ideals and the beginnings of Greek culture, uncertain of their future, and uncertain also to which of several pretenders to the throne to give their allegiance.

Perhaps the Macedonians were described as happily as is possible with brevity, when they were called Greeks still at the Homeric stage. There are tribes and chiefs and nobles; and, if there is a would-be Agamemnon, it is all he can do to hold his own, and he is very apt to be murdered. A prince of Macedon (Alexander by name) figures largely in the story of the Persian invasion, a spirited young man, whose sympathies are with the Greeks; or so Herodotus learnt, presumably at or near his court, a generation later. When he became king, he aimed at expanding his kingdom to include the rich lands of the river Strymon (Struma to-day) and the gold mine region of Pangaion in Thrace, territory washed by the Aegaean. Persian suzerainty was ended for him, too, by the battle of Plataea; but the Athenian Confederacy held his coasts. The next outstanding figure on the Macedonian stage was the usurper Archelaus, over whom Socrates in Plato's dialogue shakes his head; but in such a country, at such a period, legitimacy is his who wins, and Archelaus won. He aimed at consolidating his tribes into a real kingdom and getting control of Thessaly to the South. He also, like a good Macedonian prince, had a friendly feeling for Greek culture; Euripides left Athens, and found a new freedom for a while in Macedon, and wrote his *Bacchae* there. After fourteen years of kingship, Archelaus was murdered; and the old game of pretenders began again, and did not long stop till Philip made himself autocrat.

Philip is overshadowed by his son, but there were those who very pointedly let that son know that his father was a great man. Philip was at once a military genius who created a great military power, and a political genius who made a more or less united nation out of divided tribes and factions. Outside Macedon he was hampered by his own cleverness. He had the statesman's outlook and used the politician's methods. He saw that Greece must be united if she was to recover her life and prosperity; and he seems to have seen that the real enemy was the Persian foreign office, with its subsidies of gold "archers", constantly promoting war in Greek lands and Greek waters. The Persian Empire saved itself by paying its enemies to quarrel. To achieve his ends, Philip, Greeks tell us, stuck at nothing—bribery, trickery, adroitness of every kind. But permanent victories are not won by trickery, as Alexander saw later on; there is nothing convincing about a conqueror who has tricked you. Men tried again, and Philip had at times to do the same work twice over. But a large part of his work he did once for all.

We need not here follow all the dodges and manœuvres by which he secured his throne, humbugged the Athenians, and became master of his own coasts in the first few years of his reign. But that was one of his first aims; and, along with this control of the seaboard, he had to secure his Northern frontiers against barbarian Thracians and Illyrians. Sum up this earlier work as the consolidation of an independent kingdom, safe from invasion landward and seaward; after that comes expansion, first southward and then eastward. Thessaly was divided against itself, no new thing indeed there;

and one party called in Philip from the North, and the other invited the Phocians from the South. The Phocians had not been of great consequence in earlier times; but now they had risen under an effective leader, and possessed themselves of great wealth by capturing the oracle and shrine of Delphi, and looting its treasures. It was some years before Philip achieved all he wanted, but by 353 he had overthrown the Thessalian prince, and was master of the Thessalian harbour on the gulf of Pagasae, which brought him a long way nearer Greece. He made an attempt to take the pass of Thermopylae, but for once Athens was too quick for him, and that had to wait. After some fighting with barbarians in Thrace, Philip dealt finally with the confederacy of Greek towns of the Chalcidic peninsula centred in Olynthus, the luckless group which Sparta once, and now Philip, broke up. He was now master of the Northern shore of the Aegaean, of his own ports and of Pagasae. A peace was made in 346, which enabled him to crush the Phocians finally, to become liberator (i.e. something like master) of Delphi, and then to conduct the Pythian games, which enabled him to pose (at least to himself) as an entirely genuine Greek. Macedonians were sensitive on that point; were they or were they not really Greeks? Their kings must have been Greeks; descendants of Achilles could not be anything else; still it was worth establishing a little more. The point may not seem to us of much importance; but history is made by the ideals of great men, by their fancies, too, and their sentiments; and if Philip is to be understood, this feeling for Greece has to be recognized, and the lurking doubt that hung about it.

The years of "peace" enabled Philip to attend to his neighbours in the North, and to set on foot various intrigues in Greece; and it became so clear that his ambition was not satisfied, that in self-defence Athens made overtures to Persia. In 340 war began again, if it had really left off very much; and Philip besieged Byzantium. Anyone who has gone by sea to Constantinople, as Byzantium has been called for sixteen centuries, will realize what the two straits mean, the Dardanelles and the Bosphorus. The chief food of Athens, the wheat and dried fish, had to come that way from South Russia; and Philip meant to hold the straits and control the food-supply of Athens—the manœuvre by which Sparta had crushed Athens sixty years before. It was a famous siege, but it failed; and the Byzantines attributed their escape to their goddess, Hecate, and took her symbol, the crescent moon, for their emblem. The symbol has had a curious history, pagan down to Constantine, and after him Christian till the Turks took the city in 1453, and still to be seen as a Turkish device, even on packets of tobacco; and all the time the crescent has remained on Christian churches for the sake of old memories and in the faith that (as a Christian prophet wrote) "the South wind will some day cease blowing". So History is linked together, and the past never quite dies.

It was not long before there was some more foolish trouble about Delphi, and Philip seized his chance, flew to the aid of the outraged god, and in the fervour of his piety swept through Thermopylae and held Elateia on the Greek side of it. The troubles of the god were forgotten, and Athens and Thebes leagued themselves to save Greece; but it was too late. Philip won two great victories, one on the shore of the Corinthian gulf which gave him a naval base there, and one at Chaeronea (August or September 338), the most famous of his triumphs, a battle that marks a new period in history, as Hastings and Waterloo have done since. He could now (with a little diplomacy) dictate terms to Greece. He put garrisons into the citadels of Thebes, Corinth and Chalcis. He had been in his youth a hostage at Thebes and did not like the people; but Athens represented one of his own ideals, and by friendliness to Athens he could let the Greeks see once more that he too was a Greek, and of the best type, a believer in art and letters and culture and all the best things for which Greece stood. By now, Isocrates said, it is the mind, not the blood, that makes a man Greek; and Philip had reasons, practical as well as sentimental, for proving his title both ways. He was going to gather up all Greece in one Hellenic league and deal with Persia. But before he could do this, a private enemy, for some reason of his own, saw fit to murder the king.

From the story of his reign certain things were evident to thoughtful people. On the one side was Athens, floundering about, as Demosthenes faithfully pointed out, with irresponsible demagogues and mercenary generals. The generals were at heart afraid of the Assembly of their employers; and the mercenary soldiers, ill-paid and ill-behaved, were a source of dread to the allies. The popular leaders often had no real knowledge of foreign affairs and no policy; and, when they had a policy at all, they must discuss it in public, and then, with infinite delays, try to carry out a policy about which they had warned their enemy! Philip was an autocrat, master of a race, not orator to an assembly; he knew his world; he could form his own plans without opposition or public discussion, carry them out in his own time—and be inside Thermopylae before the Greeks knew he was starting. So much was plain; and Demosthenes makes it yet plainer in words that still live. No one, however, could have been certain that Philip would be so abruptly murdered; and, if they had foreseen it, they would have been certain that history would repeat itself and that the Macedonian danger would be over. No one could foresee Alexander.

So it was not then realized, as we see well enough now, that Chaeronea was "the end of an old song", the end of Greek political freedom, the end of the city state. Not quite the end; institutions and traditions take an unconscionable time in dying; but a new epoch had begun, in which it did not matter how long they took to die; something else was alive now and ruling the world. The prince, the hereditary monarch, dominated the world; the Greek was to rule no more—unless you re-think your standards. Greek assemblies and Greek demagogues were to have less and less to say about the making of the world's history; but Chaeronea, the end of political independence, was in truth the beginning of a new empire for the Greek mind; and Greece became, first for the nearer East, and then for the West, what Athens had been to Greece—an "Education", an inspiration, an ideal. East and West looked more and more to Greece to learn what are the things that matter to the human soul, thought, truth, beauty, creation, the mind. Captive Greece captured her conqueror, once and again, and Hellenized the ancient world, and is in process (slowly enough) to do the same for the modern world—

First fruit and best of all our western world;
Whate'er we hold of beauty, half is hers.

Philip had done more than he dreamed of doing, builded wiser than he knew.

F. GREEK WARFARE

At this point, on the eve of new movements of great significance in the history of the world, we may pause to recapitulate and sum up, if only in outline, the changes in the art of war since Homeric times. It will quickly be realized how closely they bear upon the social structure of Greece.

We cannot read far in Homer without remarking two things. Every hero but one (see p. 237) wears bronze armour—helmet, cuirass, and greaves—and carries a bronze spear and sword; and it is only the heroes who count in battle; common men with their dog-skin caps and leather shields hardly matter. That age passed; and the blacksmith (as we call him) was one of the chief causes of its passing. Iron is not unknown to Homer; but, when iron replaced bronze in common use and in the manufacture of armour and weapons, a new order rose. Nobles replaced kings; and then, as metallurgy advanced and weapons grew cheaper, democracy began, with the heavy-armed commons, very much as after the Middle Ages gunpowder ended chivalry and brought in a new age.

At this stage the Persian prince, Mardonius, made an interesting comment on Greek war; the opposing forces, he said, looked for some level ground, and there hacked one another to pieces. Yes, says the modern commentator, Mardonius thought of Persian armies operating over great distances; but on that level ground grew the food of the Greek towns; the enemy's one strategy was to destroy the crops, and the heavy-armed turned out to stop them. There was no manœuvring; it was weight against weight—doubtless with more spirit on one side or the other; but the fight was a straightforward massacre. In a battle in 425 the Sicilian Naxians and their allies killed more than a thousand men of Messene, and then most of the fugitives on the roads. Accumulated fury lies behind such a day's doings; and in the warfare of Greek town with town there was apt to be plenty of it.

On the other hand, where the fight was not immediately before the people's eyes and obviously for the next winter's food, or where acute hatred of a neighbouring or rival city was not involved, it is noticed that Greek generals, elected by popular vote, were shy of risking any heavy loss of life. They might hear of it again, and be brought to trial for it; Nicias says as much to his Athenians at Syracuse; they will change their tune when they get home. Hence there is little venturesomeness in their tactics; and there was another reason for this, in the men.

The iron armour was very heavy; and while the *hoplite* (the Greek in heavy armour) could stand so far against any troops that might be brought against him, there were drawbacks. Only one-fifth of Greece is level ground, and the *hoplite* found hills impossible; and muddy or swampy land was almost as bad. Let an Englishman experiment with heavy suitcases hung in front of him and behind him, and after some hours of it he may find, not indeed his courage reduced, but his energy somewhat flagging, his *élan* evaporated. Greek soldiers, again, resented fighting in the lunch hour.

In the Peloponnesian War Greeks discovered what the modern world learnt when Braddock and his force perished in July 1755, that light-armed troops in forest regions can be far more effective than heavy regulars.

But the light-armed needed a far more elaborate training than citizen soldiers, the *hoplites*, would endure; so they must almost always be professionals. As a rule, then, they were mercenaries, hired very generally from Thrace. In 393 the Athenian general, Iphicrates, made an immense sensation in Greece, by destroying a Spartan *mora* (regiment) with light-armed troops. The Spartan heavy-armed were reputed invincible. Iphicrates attacked them on the march, showered javelins on them, ran off unhurt when they turned on him, and came back with more javelins; and each time this happened, it was with rising spirit on the Athenian side and flagging on the Spartan, as they grew "ever fewer and fainter of heart".

When the Peloponnesian War was at last over, Greece found herself with ruined industries and a superabundance of men who had no trade but soldiering. Cyrus the Younger, as we saw, hired thirteen thousand of them. From this time onward, more than ever, Greek wars could be, and were, waged with mercenary troops; and this made everything unstable. A Persian subsidy made war so easy; a good citizen could vote for it, with perhaps very little risk of personal service; the Persian government understood this, and kept Greece divided. Mercenaries, moreover, irregularly paid, would desert, or would pillage from anybody; and neither those who hired them, nor those against whom they were hired, nor neutral towns and villages, could guess what they would do or would not do. The strain was intolerable. Philip thoroughly realized the position; he and his son saw that there could be no quiet in Greece till the Persian paymaster was dealt with. We are not informed as to any diplomatic relations he had with Persia; but

it became known that in 341 Athens made overtures to
the Great King, and this could only have one meaning.
Meanwhile it is easy to see how much stronger and more
reliable was the national army which Philip had developed than the loose congeries of hirelings (soldiers
and generals) that his Greek opponents must put against
him. This is not to say that they did not fight; but the
hereditary monarch, with a policy and a people behind
him, beat them, as the Romans two generations later
with native Italian troops beat the mercenaries of Pyrrhus, no easy task indeed but achieved. It was no doubt
some relief to Greece that Persian satraps and the
Persian King were hiring Greek mercenaries too; the
Persians, says Plato, in spite of myriads of nationals,
think their salvation lies in mercenaries and foreigners.
Artaxerxes reconquered Egypt with Greek troops. When
Alexander crossed to Asia, we are told there were tens
of thousands of Greek soldiers in Persian service.

By this time war was far from being the simple matter
it had been. Trained troops and differentiated troops
made new movements, new combinations, new manœuvres possible, and a new type of strategic capacity
necessary. The "generals" that Greek democracies had
elected were often little better than amateurs, like the
politician consuls that Rome sometimes sent against her
enemies. To handle two types, or three types, of troops
is not merely twice or three times as difficult as to handle
one type; it is a different art. The story of Alexander
shows how a man of genius understood and used the
new tools ready to his hands, and how he co-ordinated
them. *Hoplites*, light-armed, cavalry (in which the
Greeks had always been weak), the *phalanx*, the immensely long Macedonian spear (the *sarissa*), the new

siege-engines (a great feature in the next generation)—
put all these together, and something is done to explain
the age of the Successors of Alexander. Who but Kings,
with their immense resources, could hire the new
armies? And who else could use them, or find the men
and the means to control them?

Fresh developments followed. War changed its character. Mercenaries were hired to fight, not to die; and
they took care not to die. Massacre gave place to manœuvre; and it became the recognized thing that, when
troops were clearly out-manœuvred, and were going to
be beaten, they would surrender; the battle was over,
there was no good in going on; they held their *sarissas*
erect, and fighting stopped. Sometimes with strange
results; the king or prince who had hired them was
done for, and they might go over in a body to his conqueror; why not? Or take the case of Pergamum; there,
in a strong fortress, King Lysimachus kept his treasure;
the warden of it was nobody, a Paphlagonian, the son
of a flute girl, a eunuch, men said. The king perished;
and the warden held on to the treasure, and hired troops;
he was strong enough to make useful alliances, and he
left a stable dynasty of sensible nephews behind him, a
dynasty of which we shall hear later on (see p. 245).
Or again, in 255, when the fortunes of Carthage were
at a low ebb in her war with the Romans, a mercenary
general appeared, a Spartan, Xanthippos; he served
Carthage for one year, and did wonders. "One man
and one brain", says Polybius, "laid low the forces that
had seemed invincible, and restored to confidence a city
obviously and utterly ruined." The Roman army was
destroyed and Regulus captured; and then the Spartan
took ship and went home, very wisely, men say.

Armour and training, men with no trade but soldier-ing, and kings with treasure—we can see how they shaped and re-shaped political and social life. But twice over in the ancient Mediterranean world it was the power, that fought with its own nationals, that tri-umphed; blood sometimes means more than gold reserves.

Bronze statuette of a hoplite

Chapter VIII

THE EARLY ROMAN WORLD

A. ITALY AND ITS RACES

ITALY, the central one of the three great peninsulas of Southern Europe, in spite of ancient story, is utterly different from Greece. The two lands have been associated in the minds of men for ages, but Nature built them on different plans, and sent into them races of different make. Greece is a land of mountains, with a much broken coastline; indeed, as we saw, it would not be absurd to say (if just a little contradictory) that a large part of Greece is not peninsula at all, but a mass of islands. Mainland and island Greece is well furnished with bays and creeks and harbours. Italy consists roughly of two parts—the peninsula (six hundred miles long) with the great Appennine range as a spine, and the valley-land of the river Po, surrounded on East, North and West by the Alps. The coast is not broken like that of Greece, and you can count on the fingers of one hand the important harbours—Tarentum, the bay of Naples and its towns, the mouth of the Tiber. Venice and Genoa are medieval creations. Brindisi is a port because men insisted on a short sea passage to Greece; Dover is not one of the chief ports of England, but we all insist that it shall have harbour walls and piers of some sort. The Eastern shore of Italy was inhospitable; the Western has always been more inviting. The Adriatic Sea was disliked in antiquity; it was stormy and cold, the climate rainy, the Balkan shore without much arable land; but from the beginning

Western Italy has charmed those who know it; "see Naples and die" runs the proverb. A big mountain range with spurs may harbour tribes hard to control, but the geography of Italy did not so effectively bar all hope of unity as did the broken surface of Greece. Italy again, though exposed to the Scirocco from Africa, is not threshed by the North Wind from Russia. The region of the Po lends itself to cultivation, and the Po is not the only navigable river. There was a good deal more trade carried on in boats and floats on the Tiber than we sometimes think; it was one of the best ways into the country.

Population has come to Italy from the North and from the South. Saracens in the Middle Ages and Greeks in ancient days came to Italy by sea. For our present purposes we may neglect the Saracens, and the Greeks must yield place for the moment to the peoples they met in the country. There were the Aborigines, as they were called by a Greek historian. We need not spend time in guessing about them any more than about the Picts. It seems agreed that throughout the Mediterranean lands there were races of men of one type, not very tall, dark-skinned, black-haired, with a distinctive shape of skull, and small hands (a palm $2\frac{1}{2}$ inches across). They were in France long before the Franks came, and even before the Gauls; and to this day the type can be recognized. The Aborigines, whoever they were, and whatever their numbers, being assumed, three outstanding races invaded the land, of whom the Italians are the chief. Just as the Celtic inhabitants of Britain (leaving out the Picts) were of two strains, the Gaels and the Britons, the Italians consisted of Latins and Oscans, with some differences of language. They spread over the country, and then others followed. An Indian poet has a curious simile to describe such tribal invasions; he pictures the tribes as poured over the country like sugar-cane juice over a flat surface; one outpouring follows another and the hardening sugar lies in uneven layers. So in Italy, pouring over the Aborigines, come the Italians, not exactly overlaying them as sugar does sugar, but taking their lands and overpowering them, and gradually absorbing them.

The second of the invading races and the least numerous was the Etruscan. They arrived in Italy after the Italians but long before the Gauls, and scholars are still arguing as to where they came from; the ancients said from Asia Minor. They settled in the Po country, and especially to the South of it, in the region still called after them Tuscany, and in a scattered way in various spots still further South and beyond the river Tiber, as far as the Bay of Naples. They lived in towns, and had a peculiar art and language of their own; they borrowed the Greek alphabet, but they were long the enemies of the Greek upon the sea, and the friends of the Carthaginian. Legend, here supported by what excavators and archaeologists tell us, says they held Rome for some time; perhaps for some generations, and again perhaps (for it is a guess though probable) with intervals. But in time their numbers declined, while those of the Gauls and the Italians increased continually; and by the time of the Empire there were very few of them. One place still knew them, Mantua the home of Virgil, a town almost inaccessible among lagoons, defended by water and mosquitoes, though the poet says the strength of the place is its Etruscan blood.

These then were the peoples whom the Greek settlers found in the land, when they came swarming like bees for a new hive. One town and another in Greece, as we saw, sent out its colonies; and some of these colonies have had long and important histories which are not finished yet. Marseilles was founded by Greeks about 600 B.C., and is still a great port. The Greeks came in such numbers that Southern Italy was known as "Greater Greece", and there and in Sicily they found natives, and Etruscans, and Carthaginians; and though they never could drive the Carthaginians out of their fortresses at the Western end of Sicily—fortresses which even the Romans could not capture, but which were only evacuated by treaty after a long war—they made the new lands their own. True to their nature, they fought one another, but they brought with them a civilization beyond any known there before. Syracuse, their chief city in Sicily, had a very mixed population and a great trade. The original settlers were largely from a village near Corinth, perhaps not of very noble origin; but noble their descendants claimed to be, when they had the luck to hold on to their lands. The stories of farms on Manhattan Island, making families rich in later centuries, illustrate how the *Gamoroi* (land-owners) of Syracuse came to be so important. But the luck was not always with them; and Syracuse, like other Greek towns in the old land, was from time to time ruled by "tyrants", men very often of great ability, fine soldiers, shrewd statesmen, and genial patrons of the arts and of artists—as long as you kept on the right side of them. One of these, Hiero, is famous for his patronage of the poet Pindar and for a brilliant naval victory over the Etruscans (474 B.C.). A helmet, dedicated to commemorate this victory, was found at Olympia in 1817; it bears a short inscription, telling the story in the Greek way—few words but enough, and very

Plate III

explicit: "Hiero, son of Deinomenes, and the Syracusans, to Zeus, Etruscan things, from Cume".

Some centuries after the Italians came another race over the Northern mountains, in fresh hordes and great numbers, from time to time, some into Italy, some into Greece, and some right into the centre of Asia Minor— the Gauls. They shocked the Greeks very much, when they burst in on them, about a generation after the death of Alexander—they were so tall and so beautiful ("the most beautiful people on earth", says the Greek historian Polybius; and if you have seen a shapely Highlander you will believe it), but so strange and uncivilized. They were "mad for fighting"; and it disturbed the settled habits of Greek and Roman soldiers to have to stand the charge of huge, howling, naked savages, beautiful as they might be; for the Gaul threw off his clothing and dashed yelling into battle with nothing but his shield and his long sword, and perhaps a gold chain round his neck. Look at the statue of the dying Gaul, big and beautiful and shock-headed, naked but for the necklet, a noble and pathetic figure, and own cousin to the Highlander who fought at the Battle of the Standard, at Pinkie and Flodden, much in the same way and as disastrously. But there were plenty of them; Gaul (France) was full of them, they overflowed into Britain, and they flooded North Italy, over Italian, aboriginal and all, and became masters of the rich and fertile plain of the Po river. Cattle and gold were all their wealth, and there they spread, living in unwalled villages, with very little furniture, feeding mostly on meat (later on, it was pigs that they kept by the thousand); and as they had no other arts or sciences, says the Greek, their business was farming and fighting.

B. ROMAN KINGS

Macaulay's *Lays of Ancient Rome*, if nothing else, have brought Romulus and Remus into English literature. "Every schoolboy knows" (as Lord Macaulay used to say) how King Amulius ordered the children to the Tiber, and the mother to the tomb; and how the she-wolf mothered the twins, till a shepherd found them; and how they grew up in the country and at last avenged their mother; how they built Rome, after watching for eagles, and then quarrelled. It is a famous story, but not the only one; for in ancient books we read the names of a good half-dozen other people, who founded Rome, or after whom Rome was called. The stories are so many, and so different, that it is clear people were guessing. To guess once more, perhaps the city was called after the river. Tiber is its name these many centuries; once it was *Albula*, Virgil says, "white-ish", from the mud it carried down; and perhaps before that it was *Rumon*, because (men guessed) the river gnawed its banks away. But, in legend and in guess, we have touched the river; and if, as we saw (page 11), the River is one of the keys to history, we can believe it. Where the shore-road crosses the up-country road at the ford, there we have learnt to expect to find the town; and there, in fact, we find Rome. A river, a ford and a fortress are the beginnings of Rome, in a place of abundant springs, and out of the pestilent air of the swamps to the South, the Campagna as it is now called.

Learned men in ancient days calculated the date of Rome's founding; so many consuls or other magistrates, year by year, would give the date at which kings were expelled and the republic began; before that, if thirty or forty years were allowed to a reign for each of seven kings (legend said they were seven), the date of the foundation would be reached; and they fixed it at last at what we call 754 B.C. Let that stand, for all Roman dates are reckoned from it; a fixed era, even if badly calculated (like the birth of Christ with us), saves a lot of trouble. To reckon that such and such an event fell in the last year of the reign of William IV, even if it is added "in the first year of van Buren's presidency", would leave most people vague. Romans generally gave the consuls of the year to indicate a date; *Consule Manlio*, says Horace, to give the year of his birth (65 B.C.). Historians, however, kept a firm hold of the year of the foundation, once it was calculated.

754 B.C. then. But moving about in a region of fairy tales, of fairy lovers and she-wolf mothers, miraculous eagles, and so on, we drift away from the historic shores of Italy to a sort of fairyland. Yet Italy and Sicily were no fairyland. Carthaginians and Etruscans, yes, and early Greeks were already sailing up and down the shores. We are told that Syracuse was founded in Sicily in 734; and long before the Roman Republic began, there were Greek towns in Italy, and Marseilles in Gaul. The date of Rome's foundation may be uncertain; but the dates of Greek colonies, planted deliberately by commercial communities familiar with settled governments, and presumably with methods for reckoning years, are much more likely to be remembered. No one can guess the year when York was founded; but New York and Montreal were not founded by primitive men, and the dates are certain. We may take it that there were Greek cities along Italian shores long before the story was told how

Brutus had driven the Tarquin kings from Rome. But what is the bearing of all this?

Simply this; Italy was not fairyland, the land that Ovid and Livy picture; it was a land of men, of tribes half civilized, with a fringe of cultured towns along its shores, and trading ships going up and down; and, where bay, creek or river offered, the traders put in to sell their wares, but, as we saw, they would not go further up than the ford. But above the ford, as we learn later, there was a great deal of traffic in smaller boats on the Tiber and its tributaries; and up in the country, just as Kolaios found at Cadiz, there were plenty of people ready to buy Greek goods, and to pay high for them—woollens and fancy slippers from Miletus, pottery (wheel-made and glazed) from Samos, and anything else that a clever dealer might push. Rome, like other towns on fords in primitive lands, was a centre of distribution; and men from up-country came down there to buy the overseas goods. A commercial city, says the great German scholar Mommsen, and indebted for the beginning of its importance to international intercourse.

So we have two stories—one of kings, full of legends and wars among neighbours, of victories and invasions and speeches, of the foundation of religious rites and traditions and ceremonies, a story told us by the ancients in splendid verse and prose; and another humbler story, not told in full by anybody, but gathered in hints, traced in broken pottery which people find throughout Italy, in graves and in masons' marks, and confirmed by what we know of what happens when roads cross rivers, and ships come up to be tied to wharves, with goods to sell inland, and sometimes sailors who run away from their ships. First let us look at the early Rome of legend, of accepted legend, saying nothing about the competing legends which failed to capture the great writers.

After Romulus came Numa Pompilius, the king, who, the Romans said, invented their religion for them; and a very good religion, too, they pointed out, for it was very simple and very inexpensive. Modern writers hold that much of this religion must have been there long before Numa. After this reign of quiet and piety, Tullus Hostilius enlivened things with wars and conquests; his second name suggested as much with its hints of hostilities. Next came Ancus Martius, a crafty king, men said; chiefly interesting perhaps, because, just as Englishmen talk of Queen Anne being dead, the Roman poet Horace used this king's name—

> *Ire tamen restat Numa quo devenit et Ancus*
> Where Numa went and Ancus, we must go.

Then came a real change—three kings of Etruscan origin, Tarquinius Priscus, Servius Tullius and Tarquinius Superbus; and plenty of legends commemorated them. The first was the son, they said, of a Greek exile who settled in an Etruscan town; and his wife, Tanaquil, was very ambitious, and urged her husband to leave the Etruscan town, where people looked down on him as a sort of foreigner, and to go to Rome, a new place, where, among a new people of mixed origins, his worth might tell. They set off; and just as they reached Rome, an eagle swooped down upon their waggon, swept away the man's cap, flew off, flew back, put his cap on again, and was gone. This could only be a prophecy of future glory, his wife said (all Etruscans were supposed to understand omens, and she did); and of course it came true. Servius Tullius, men said, must be the son of a slave-girl (*servus* meaning slave); but they tell us that he invented the Roman constitution, divided the people up into "centuries", according to their property, an arrangement which lasted long after he was gone, and, beginning by being a military scheme, was the basis of Rome's political structure. In the ancient world, everything, it was thought, must have a beginning, and somebody must begin it; so to Servius was assigned a distribution of the people which was the foundation of Rome's political security and much else. But not everybody is equally sure of all this to-day. Servius may have done something of the kind, but perhaps more likely to be true is the tale of his death. We have already discussed folk-memory in telling the story of Periander and the women's clothes (see page 61). Servius had a wicked daughter who married the last Tarquin, and they or their servants killed the old man. His body lay in the street, where she was driving; there was no room to pass it; "drive over it", she said; and the street was known as Guilty Street ever after. The reign of this Tarquin matched its beginning; the king and his sons were odious to the Romans, who rose in rebellion and drove them out. And that was the end of Etruscan rule in Rome.

Archaeologists have said that great building remains in Rome must date from the period of the Etruscan kings; others have said they must be later; it belongs to experts to differ. But it is easy enough to believe that there was an Etruscan period in early Rome, very possibly several Etruscan periods. The town on the ford meant, as we have seen, control of the coast road, control of the market and the centre of distribution, control of all goods going up-country, and (what is more) freedom for Etruscans, if they held it, to ravage Latium, or for Latins to invade Etruria. A significant place, which would be fought for; but we need not suppose that, when it was captured, all the beaten party went out. The common people would stay, whoever ruled the city; nobody would want to kill them, if they would go on working and keep quiet. Let us suppose (it is not proved at all) that once and again Etruscans and Latins gain, lose, and regain the place; each time fresh people come in, and, if some go out, more stay; each capture makes the place more important, and tends to mix the population still more. The first Tarquin's father was a Greek, we were told; and it is the way of big ports and of centres of distribution to draw together and to keep a pretty mixed population. When New York was twenty years old, eighteen languages were spoken on its streets; like Rome, it lay at the place where sea-going ships and the river trade of a great *hinterland* met. For a long time both in Rome and New York the aristocracy (so far as there was one) consisted of the people who owned land in and about the city; and they are more easily remembered by historians than traders or dockside labourers, stevedores or middlemen. If it is still urged, as once it was, that trade so important as we imply could not develop without coinage, all the history of the New World is against such a criticism; the story of Quebec, Montreal and the Hudson Bay Company proves that there can be immense trade without money, trade enough to set Europe by the ears in a Seven Years' War. Trade and a mixture of races —both things quicken the life of a community; both mean new thoughts, contradictions, new views, and the habit of considering what other people have to say; and the last can be noted among the Romans, wherever you take them. Plenty of the Romans were stupid enough, as their poets tell us; but it is better not to judge a race by its stupid people, or at least not exclusively.

C. EARLY YEARS OF REPUBLICAN ROME

The early history of republican Rome, as given by the historians, consists of struggles in the city between Patricians and Plebeians, and of fights with neighbouring tribes which ended in great extensions of Roman territory. We are given a great deal of detail, but much of it is unreliable; after all the movements are of more importance than the details or episodes. There are episodes in History that make epochs; but those of which we hear in early Roman history are of no great consequence, even if we were sure of them.

But struggle there was, we may be sure, between Patricians and Plebeians; and if we ask who they were, there is a margin of doubt. They had different customs, different cults, we are told, and they used different armour; their marriage rites were quite distinct; perhaps they disposed of their dead in different ways; all of which points to their being of different races. One or two links connect the Patricians with the Sabines; their chief gods were the same; and a story was current in Roman histories that a Sabine chief emigrated to Rome with five thousand followers, which looks very like capturing Rome, but to call him an immigrant softens the blow. The poet Juvenal says that the original aristocracy of Rome were shepherds or thieves; but he was a satirist. The indications show a body of people, very conscious of race; they would not intermarry with the Plebs.

The Plebeians were probably of many sorts; some of them perhaps "aborigines", whatever they were; some, traders and runaway sailors of various races, Greeks probably included; many were probably captives from villages and towns destroyed in war, who were forcibly settled in Rome, as was done as lately as fifty years ago by the Khalifa in the Sudan. Since the Khalifa was overthrown, escaped slaves drift to the towns, unable to find their way back to their tribes, or perhaps unwilling; they make mixed marriages of some sort, and they show a readiness for new ideas; they understand coinage better than the tribes did from which they were stolen; and they realize the attractions of private property, which is easier kept when it consists of modern coin and not of primitive cattle. All this means the wearing down of tribal distinctions, a blending at last of stocks; and that is what we surmise among the Roman plebeians. Probably enough in early days, as certainly in later, fugitive slaves resorted to Rome, and broken men of all sorts, who had lost home and tribe, and adventurous spirits. It must not be supposed that these very mixed people were intellectually inferior to the Patricians; they were probably at least as good or better, in variety of mind and in experience of a wider and less settled world—the sea, trade, sacks of cities, personal danger and resourcefulness. But, to begin, they had no rights.

The City was ruled by Consuls, as they were at last called; and behind the Consuls sat a Senate, a body which grew steadily in power, as we shall see. No Plebeian could be a Consul; and there (they say) the fight began, which ended after long struggles in the equalization of the orders. Patricians and Plebeians are to be one political body, and one race, with free intermarriage. The strangest survival of the long wrestle was the tribunate, a special magistracy invented to protect the Plebeians from injustice and oppression, but which in time gained the power to block state business and veto the acts of Consuls and Senate. The *Plebs*, the body of Plebeians, was treated almost like a foreign state in the city which was the home of all; and its magistrates were secured not so much by law as by treaty. By the time the struggle was over, the whole government was deeply changed, though it was not supposed to be. Before, the Consuls were supreme, and took the advice of the Senate; after, the Senate was really supreme, and the Consuls were only two among a number of magistrates. The business of government could no longer be done by two magistrates; it was complicated by the growth of trade and of population and by the extension of the territory. It must always be remembered that, if population doubles in fifty years, at the end of a hundred years it is fourfold what it was at the beginning, and at the end of two hundred years sixteen times as much. We have no figures to go by; but, even if this calculation is too rapid, as it well may be, there must have been many more people to govern, and far more business, far more law suits. The long struggle meant years of argument about political ideas and principles, and developed a political instinct which has stood the world in good stead.

In the two hundred and thirty years between the expulsion of the Tarquins and the coming of Pyrrhus, we watch the growth of Rome, and the consequences of it. First she slowly amalgamated neighbouring tribes a few miles away; then she had to fight larger tribes of much greater strength a long way off, Northward and Southward. In the middle of this period there was a great raid of Gauls, who overthrew the Romans in battle, chased them to the city, and captured it, but could not take the Capitol (387 B.C.). The stories are famous of the Senate sitting to await their arrival, and their wonder at the grand old men, till one of the old men hit a too presuming Gaul; of the Capitol being saved by the cackling of geese; of the Romans trying to buy the departure of the Gauls, and of Brennus throwing his sword into the scale. The great beautiful men at last roamed off, but Italy was in dread of them for many a year; they might at any time surge out of the Po valley and sweep all before them. It was a relief to many, not least to the Etruscans, that Rome developed a military power equal to coping with the Gauls. Whatever land in Italy the Romans gained, they cemented their Empire with military colonies and long roads. These were not the roads of early man, but carefully planned straight hard roads, not Macadamized like ours, but built of fitted stones clamped together, built to last for eternity. What they meant in enabling legions to move quickly over the country, can easily be seen; for trade they must have been a godsend, and it will be noted that all roads led to Rome, and naturally made her more than ever a centre of trade. The roads tied Italy together, as in modern days the Canadian Pacific Railway has done for Canada and the Trans-Siberian for Russia.

It was all done at the cost of fighting; and the tribes whom the Romans had to fight were largely of their own blood, as steady fighters as themselves. But, once the fighting was over, the fact that they were of one blood made union of some kind the easier in Italy, as it did in England. It was not easily achieved; but later on, when foreigners invaded Italy, the Italians showed that they preferred union of some sort with Rome to "liberty" given them by foreigners. *Timeo Danaos et dona ferentes,* says a man in Virgil; he fears the Greeks even when they offer gifts; so did the Italians, and they were more doubtful still when a Carthaginian proposed to set them free. The British dominions have not hankered after liberty offered either by Germans or by Americans; they know where they are. When we find the same thing in Italy, it is plain that from the first Rome understood the art of governing. Perhaps the struggles in her streets between men of different blood were her first lessons in handling difficult problems of race and usage. It is important to note her skill in this; for the scandals of the bad days of the break-up of the Republic suggest that Rome's government was bad. It was good—better, in any case, than anything it replaced in one land and another; and in many ways good, even compared with modern attempts at government; it aimed, not always, but generally, at sense, moderation and conciliation. The Roman did not theorize so much about government, about right and wrong, as some people of more modern times; he cared little for theory, but built upon experience.

D. EARLY ROMAN SOCIETY

Unless we are thinking about savages, it is difficult to describe a state of society, for society is always moving. The most conservative people will change; if nothing else changes them, a rise in wealth will. But, if with due watchfulness for movement, we try to make a picture of Roman society in these first two centuries of the Republic, certain things grow clear. Rome in countless ways lagged behind contemporary Athens, far behind; she has no drama (of any moment), no literature, no philosophy. It is a narrow world of practical people, busy with political argument, trade, farming and the conquest of their neighbours—narrow, but destined to widen.

Meanwhile there is a gradual movement from a rather primitive poverty to something a little easier. The houses are still simple, square-built, with the windows inward upon a small courtyard, called the *impluvium*, apparently because the roofs sent the rain into it to lie stagnant and breed mosquitoes. But as the malaria did not come till Hannibal's soldiers brought it, the water and the flies were not yet at their worst. The rooms were small, and must have been dark. The walls, as for long in Greece, were of sun-dried bricks which needed projecting roofs to keep them from being washed away by the rain. The roofs were of thatch or shingles. The streets were crooked, and probably very dirty.

As for food, spelt (*far*) was a grain already beginning to go out of use for men; but it was long offered, even in Horace's time, to the gods, who were supposed to prefer old habits. Oats were given to animals. The grain for human use, generally wheat, was roughly ground, or crushed, in handmills by the women, or pounded; and it was cooked into a sort of porridge. There were no public bakers till about 170 B.C. Of vegetables garlic was most popular, and long remained so. Figs, grapes, apples, and to some extent olives, were used. They ate the pig and the goose; Italy and Rome in early days were peculiarly associated with the pig; "and no animal", wrote Pliny the Naturalist long afterwards, "offers more to the palate; it has nearly fifty flavours, while other creatures have only one each". The sheep was kept for its wool and its milk; the cow had to do the ploughing. Cheese was made, but not butter. There was of course no sugar in the Mediterranean till after the Arab conquests in the Middle Ages; honey had to take its place. The bees fairly earned the poem that Virgil wrote for them. Fish was not cared for; and the Romans had in earlier days little interest in hunting.

Dress was simple. Men and women wore at first very much the same, the *toga* with its loose but ample folds, but women were beginning to use instead of it a long gown (*stola*). In thinking of early dress in Rome, it is well to remember that there, as in Greece, needles, buttons and scissors were not cheap and obvious tools; scissors seem to have reached Rome from Sicily only about 300 B.C. Without them dress-making must have been awkward, and simple designs, or none beyond the whole cloth, would be inevitable. In India to-day garments often consist of one broad and very long strip of cloth wound round the person; the famous Roman *toga* was not essentially different. The wool was spun and woven by the women. Women altogether seem to have been more really useful in these early times than progress now permits them to be. Soap was unknown till about the Christian era; razors were an early invention; but we learn that Scipio Africanus was the first notable Roman to practise the daily shave.

There was no means of telling the hour except by the sun in these two centuries. *Horologium* hardly means clock in our sense; indeed the clocks we know are a medieval invention, and watches (that will keep time with any accuracy) far more modern still, scarcely two centuries old. A Roman household would send out a slave to watch for the shadow of a certain gable falling on a particular stone; when he came back, they knew it was noon.

When foreigners began to come, changes as ever

followed; ancient thinkers were suspicious of the sea and of people who came over it; they upset old customs. The first physician who practised in Rome was Archagathus, apparently a Greek, in Hannibal's time. But Greek masons and artisans had come long before, as masons' marks on building stones reveal, and the hints we get of better buildings. Roman coinage began only about 350 B.C.; no doubt, as at Montreal in the old fur-trading days, there was foreign money of various kinds. A national coinage means that the nation has accumulated some store of metal. Italy had no silver mines. The first Roman coin was a sort of brick of bronze weighing a pound. It will easily be understood that retail shopping and small purchases would be difficult when there was no "change". We have already noticed that by 280 B.C. Roman roads reached great distances in Italy. It is always interesting to ask how much a road costs, how much does it cost to build a foot or a mile of road, uphill or down dale, who finds the money, who pays the workmen, where the stone is hewn and how it is carted. These questions are important, but they are not easy to answer. All that can be said here is that the money was found, and that the Senate or its agents administered it; and that will help to explain why the Senate grew in power. To be in charge of great works or to be handling other people's money on a large scale, always means power; and honesty in these matters is a good thing; and in these early days the Senate was honest. The Appian Way was begun in 312 B.C.—"the queen of roads", a poet called it long afterwards. There are also problems of engineering as significant; whence came the skill that mapped and built the roads?—and the imagination that conceived them? The last is the most wonderful.

E. THE TWELVE TABLES

As often in human history, the most significant thing done by the Romans in these two hundred years, was done with little realization of what it would mean. Law and custom in primitive communities are much the same thing, as the Greek word *nomos* shows us; and neither law nor custom changes easily. It is long in the story of any race before custom quite clearly grows into law, longer still before *laws* are *made*, and longer again before law is written down. But the time comes when men demand that law shall be written, that they may have a chance, before they break the laws, to know what the laws are. To reduce a law to writing means re-thinking it; and when once deliberate thought upon laws, or law, begins, there is always a feeling that improvements are possible; and a new era of legislation follows. In the middle of the fifth century B.C. the existing laws of Rome were reduced to a code by ten men chosen for the purpose (*Decemviri*); there were perhaps alterations to meet the needs of the day, and some of the changes may have been borrowed from Greek cities—survivals, simplifications, borrowings, they have been called. The "Twelve Tables", in which they were drawn up, mark an epoch; their publication was the birthday of modern law.

From that day to this, wherever in the Western world men think about law or legislation, they think along Roman lines; there must be trial, evidence, proof; there must be no making of new laws by the judge, he is there to interpret and administer laws made by the sovereign, whether people, parliament or king, laws deliberately made with principles of justice at the core of them; there shall be no fear, favour, or terrorism in the court, no suggestion of bribery; proceedings at law are to be as decent and dignified as the State in its highest moments can be in the eyes of thoughtful men. The court represents the State. To this day in England at the assize sermon His Majesty's Judge comes into the church greeted, like the King, with the national anthem, "God save the King"—a symbolic act, to suggest whom he represents, and the majesty of King and people, who have made the law which he administers. Nothing perhaps can show how much we owe to Rome better than a story, which a Greek historian tells of a Persian king, who learnt that a judge had been taking bribes; he had him killed at once, his skin dressed and made the covering of a cushion for the judgment seat. The judge perhaps deserved his fate; and perhaps his son who succeeded him on that seat might be the better for the reminder. But that is not law, in any sense; it lacks the very elements that make law—it is unthought-out, it is caprice, the fancy of an individual, not the considered judgment and will of a community; there is no telling what will come next, and it invites reprisals—the constant dangers when a despot can make up the laws as he goes along.

From this time onward Roman law grew in range and dignity, and, many people will add, in simplicity and justice. The foundations were laid, and men could safely build on them; the principle is clear that justice is the ideal of law. This has not always been attained; judges have been foolish and corrupt; nations and parliaments have lost their heads as badly as any tyrant; but in the main, taking centuries together, the growth and development of law owes nearly everything to the Romans. The two chief dangers in law-making are reluctance to change and too great readiness to change; the Egyptians show the first and the Greeks and Americans the second. The Romans avoided both perils.

But the Twelve Tables did more than lay foundations for the law of the civilized world far in the future. They there and then became part of Roman education. Cicero says that he learnt them by heart at school, three centuries later. Put this alongside of the Greek boy learning *Iliad* and *Odyssey* by heart, and the Scottish child learning the *Shorter Catechism*. The first things you learn may shape your mind for ever; it is not so much the things themselves as the way in which you are brought by them to think of everything you may afterwards meet. Consider this Roman education—no Greek dramas, no Greek philosophy, no Greek art (or very little), hardly any books, no science or mathematics, next to nothing to train the imagination, but law, law, law. Whenever a Roman thought seriously, he must think along legal lines, drive for some legal principle, and see how it bears on the case. No wonder they governed the world so well; no wonder they did so much for the world! But they did not do everything for the world, and this amazing education left out too much. When times changed, as we shall see they did, the Roman people were not ready intellectually for the changes; the Roman lawyers were ready, and did greater and better work than ever, but the common Roman was unprepared. He had not been properly trained to think, and he lost his bearings, and ruined himself and then the Republic. An education too closely concerned with the practical proved fatal; and it wakes a certain wonder whether the so-called "scientific" education of to-day may not in like manner be leaving the mind and imagination unfitted for the work of living in a world which is not chiefly chemical.

Chapter IX

THE JEWS

A. THE DIFFICULTIES RAISED BY JEWISH HISTORY

No ancient people of the East has had a stranger history than the Jews, but the earlier parts of that history no one can read with very much conviction. Research and excavation have revealed with a startling exactitude the history of Assyria, Babylon, Persia and Egypt; but archaeology unsettled Jewish history, and fresh discoveries make new uncertainties, which remain difficult to explain. Some ancient tablets have been found, which can be dated securely, and they seem to suggest that some of the Israelite tribes were in Palestine long before Joshua; or at least their names were there, and were perhaps half-divine. The walls of Jericho, it is now realized, did fall down; an earthquake overthrew them very near the date at which we wanted them overthrown. Clean against the Law, as given in Deuteronomy, there was a Jewish temple at Yeb in Egypt about the time when Cyrus let the Jews return to Palestine. Abraham, Moses and David had long been assumed to be as historical as Queen Victoria, and their lives and minds as well known; in the nineteenth century they were transformed—Abraham ceased to be a sheikh and became a tribe personified; Moses became a myth; and David was no longer the writer of the Psalms. Once again there was change, and Moses was given a grudging permission to have existed. The fact appears to be that

Jewish history was written over and over again by the Jews, always for a purpose, and always with some carelessness that left loopholes to allow glimpses of contradictory matter. The Philistine Goliath is killed by two different people; and, if it is explained that the hero who killed him had two names, or changed his name, such explanations are too easy. We remember that the son of Aeneas had two names, and Romulus two, and Pallas Athene—which is very well when we are mixing legends; history is not made that way.

But the history of no ancient people should be so valuable, if we could only recover it and understand it. Its history explains a nation, and here is a people, far more conscious of its race to-day than ever it was under the Jewish kings. No longer a nation, they are scattered all over the world, eager everywhere to take on a local colour, but everywhere conscious that nobody believes in this local colour; they are an alien race wherever they are. Foreigners and Orientals still, they intermarry only among themselves; they maintain tribal customs and ceremonies, which their fathers practised in the days when Pericles guided Athens; for they know that the continuance of their race depends on nothing but the maintenance of rite and taboo and the refusal of Gentile marriage. No other race of the nearer East survives so stubbornly or so distinctively. It is all so familiar that it takes thought to realize how singular it is; and its explanation lies in a remote and half-hidden past.

Stranger still, the ancient religion of the Jews survives, when all the religions of every ancient race of the pre-Christian world have disappeared, save for a small remnant of Zoroastrians (Parsis) in India, and a few of them at Yazd in Persia. No church and no creed is "ever the same", whatever their adherents claim; interpretation varies from age to age and permits strange changes, not of belief of course, but of attitude to belief—which is after all the same thing. To believe the same dogma but to count it of little importance means that a man does *not* believe as his grandfather did. Judaism shows many colours from age to age, but fewer changes than the Christian faith; there has been no Reformation to change every emphasis alike for reformers and anti-reformers. It is the unchanging religion that has preserved the race. Once let a liberal or reformed Judaism prevail, and the race will disappear, by process of intermarriage.

Again, it is strange that the living religions of the world all build on religious ideas derived from the Jews; Protestantism, Catholicism, Islam, all have creeds in which One God is central. The other great systems, Hinduism and Buddhism, have no creeds at all; they are curious amalgams of philosophic speculations and popular superstitions, with nothing universally held and universally required of all believers.

This then is the problem offered by the Jews to the historian; and once more the sentence already quoted from Polybius recurs; the great matter is not, "What happened?" but "Why did it happen?" In the preceding paragraphs, "What has happened" has been set forth in a very rough and ready way; there is little difficulty there; but when one comes to ask why the Jews developed as they did, no satisfactory answer is given. "Now the Lord had said unto Abraham, Get thee out of thy country." It is almost as abrupt as Homer. "And the Lord said unto Moses"—but if Moses is not a historical person? Somehow or other, God, the One God, comes into Jewish history, and all the other gods go out and finally dissolve into sheer nothingness, mere fancies of the ignorant. Israel becomes growingly conscious of the One God, until after the exile all Jewish life is modelled on the basis of a belief which astonished the rest of mankind, it was so abstract, so contrary to all tradition, so obviously unintelligible and unacceptable to every tribe and nation known. "The maker and father of all it is difficult to discover; and, when found, it is impossible to declare him to all men", said Plato. "It would sound odd for a man to say he *loved* a god", wrote Aristotle. "I love the Lord", sang the Jewish psalmist, and it was true. Mankind, East and West, Christian and Moslem, accepted the Jewish conviction that there is only One God; to-day it is polytheism that is so difficult to understand, that is so unthinkable. But still it remains the historian's hardest task to explain why or how Israel came to the central belief in One God. If Moses be gone, is it a whit easier to believe that "the word of the Lord came to Jeremiah, saying, Before I formed thee in the womb, I knew thee"? Whatever guesses are made about Abraham and Moses, Jeremiah was a thoroughly historical character, as intimately to be known from his writings as Charles Lamb. He was a contemporary of Kolaios, as we saw, and of Nebuchadnezzar. The New Testament itself is so named after a phrase of his. He has to be explained; and here as so often is the case with genius, the man is more intelligible than the commentators, even when they agree.

Not to prolong this introduction, there stands the Jew, ancient and modern, to be explained. His continuance needs some explanation; and Polybius' question makes it harder still. Why does the race continue? Why does Judaism live? How did it really begin? These questions

will not be answered here; all that can be given will be
an outline of what happened; but the reader will waste
his time, unless at each stage he address to himself the
question of Polybius, Why did it come out so?

B. HEROES, KINGS AND PROPHETS

However the re-writers of Jewish history went to work,
however careful they were about dogma and framework
and Moses' laws and dates (to which indeed they assign
at least enough space), they had a mass of stories to draw
upon, told with the utmost life and vividness. One has
only to recall from among many others, the adventures
of Joseph with his brethren, in the pit, in Potiphar's
house; of David with his harp and his slingstones, David
cutting off the skirt of Saul's garment, and lamenting
Absalom; of Elijah, on Carmel, on Horeb, in Naboth's
vineyard; of Ahab, generally sinful and always interesting.

Moses is of them all the most re-written, so remodelled
to the standards of the latest Jewish revisers some centuries before Christ, that it is hard to associate any traits
of character with him. It is like a face reproduced in
a newspaper from a dim print of a photograph taken in
a bad light; it has been through too many processes; but
the chief thing to remember is that there was originally
a human face and a strong personality. Two things stand
out in the story of Moses, never obscured; he brought
Israel out of Egypt; he did not enter the Promised Land.
That he gave Israel the Law is abundantly emphasized;
but in ancient story all institutions and laws tend to be
assigned to a great national hero, real or legendary, to
Solon at Athens, to Lycurgus at Sparta, to Numa

Pompilius at Rome. A generation ago these men, with the exception of Solon, but with Moses included, were reckoned legendary. It was supposed that the figure of a great lawgiver was invented to hang the laws upon. To-day more attention is paid to "Folk-Memory" (as we saw in the case of Periander burning the women's clothes, page 61); and it begins to be felt that at the centre of a great national movement there is generally a great personality. Garibaldi was the figure in nineteenth-century Italy; he had only to speak, and young men would follow "the voice speaking like a spirit inside him" —to speak of Italy, and they realized Italy, and she became an ideal. He was the force that drove and inspired them; in him, fallible, simple, impulsive, sometimes foolish, but true, was embodied the movement that really *made* Italy. In our own days we have seen men who incarnated in themselves ideas, which have changed the course of nations, from Abraham Lincoln to Hitler. It would be arrogant to assert it is *unlikely* that a personality was the centre of the Israelite movement; from Mohammed himself to Ibn Saud, the Semite has responded to such men.

We have to ask what were his ideas; and we can only answer by asking other questions. Those were not the days of economic leadership, nor did men of letters mould Israel till centuries later. But how old is the idea of the "covenant" between Israel and Israel's God—Shaddai, Jahweh, Adonai, Jehovah, however he is named? That Israel left Egypt as monotheistic as the Jews of modern Poland, and then relapsed again and again into paganism, is not likely. But it does not seem incredible that the national leader was a man conscious of a mission; such men generally are. Solon claimed no divine inspiration;

in his outlook only common sense was needed. But all through Jewish history, the leaders are conscious, or say they are conscious, of divine guidance, which may come from Baal or Jehovah, as in Moab from Chemosh. It is, then, not absurd to associate Moses with a distinctive religious belief: but this is not to say that it is proven, or to claim that we clearly know what it was. The "Ten Commandments", it is agreed by scholars, can hardly be primitive. At all events, Polybius, to quote him again, gave us a sound canon, when he said that "to invent all is not convincing nor Homeric", implying that, however much a great story may be developed or embellished, there is generally somewhere in it a solid nucleus of fact.

Of the other national heroes, some look more real, some more legendary. Joshua leads the tribes into Canaan, to make the great change from nomad life to agriculture. Samson is a sort of Hebrew Hercules, heroic, friendly, rather stupid, with a comic streak in him. He carries off the gates, he asks riddles, he amuses himself with Delilah's questions. He is a tragic figure, too, as Milton saw and reminds us, more tragic than Hercules. But there is always a question whether his name is not too like the Semitic word for *sun* (Shemsha) for him to be quite historic. No doubt, there are historic features in him, as in Robin Hood; and the stories of both are good reading. But David is on another footing; and here we can see quickly the difference between the older and the later stories—the later (in *Chronicles*) giving us a choirmaster king, an Edward the Confessor, the earlier something more like the "uxorious bandit" of a once famous sermon. The truth probably lay between these stories. But once again the historian must ask, Round what sort of person do stories gather? and the answer always is, Round somebody really interesting; and till the Chronicler gets a hold of him, David is always interesting, whatever he is doing. He replaces the royal house of Saul; he unites the Israelite tribes in an insecure union; he captures Jerusalem and makes it the national capital; he puts the Philistines out of history for most people; he is driven out by a son's rebellion; he returns to Jerusalem; he has hates and loves like the best and worst of men; and, right or wrong, he interests, and the reader (if human) cannot help liking him. His son was historically something of a tyrant and a good deal of a squanderer, but he too impressed himself on mankind—oddly enough, as a sage. David writes psalms: Solomon invents or collects proverbs (very homely and middle-class proverbs, too, that suggest a shop-keeping Hellenistic age); and the historian asks, What was the string (so to speak) round which such reputations crystallized? To say that most of the Psalms belong to a later age than David, may be quite true; but why should anybody have thought of saying that David of all men wrote them? Our answers may be various; but if all are guesswork, all will hint at a personality again, and a lover of song.

After Solomon the kingdom is divided into two, with capitals at Jerusalem and Samaria. Of the kings in general, perhaps their subjects, and certainly most readers, might incline to say what the Chronicler says of Jehoram: "he reigned [so many] years, and departed without being desired". Kings are common to all lands in ancient story; more distinctive of Israel are the prophets, and the Jewish historians find more interest in them than in the royal houses. Elijah is an outstanding if mysterious figure; there is nobody like him in his courage, his gloom and darkness, his fierce indignation, his zeal for Jehovah and for the rights of men against Ahab and Jezebel the foreign queen. His successor Elisha is a less impressive person in the books, but he seems to have had influence. Round both gathered legends and tales of miracle. A generation later Amos lives in an atmosphere of economics and international politics, like a modern clergyman, with a keen sense of justice and injustice, denouncing luxury, and prophesying. But it is curious to note that he is silent about the "calves" worshipped, or at least symbolizing the god, at Samaria, which the historians of a later date constantly denounce. Far more interesting, as men of more range and insight and higher literary gifts, are Isaiah (represented by most of the first thirty-nine chapters of *Isaiah*) and Jeremiah. Of Jeremiah we have an intimate knowledge beyond what we have of anyone in the ancient world of his date or centuries after. His writings reveal a man of many thoughts and many moods, sensitive beyond the guess of the men he had to encounter, and far stronger in purpose and character than the careless reader of to-day realizes. Once again, the real interest of old Jewish history, apart from David and Elijah and a few other dynamic characters, lies in the prolonged warfare carried on by the champions of the national god against the "gods of the nations", against the Baal of Tyre, against the Baalim and other objects of worship round which the older agricultural tribes of Canaan had performed fertility ceremonies, survivals of an age of magic and disgusting enough. It was very long before Jews became convinced that these "other gods" did not exist; and it is commonly to be observed, where men and women believe there are more gods than one, that from prudence or fear they take care to be on good terms with as many as possible. As a brilliant French scholar put it, "polytheism knows no false gods". There lay the uniqueness of the Jews; they outgrew all temptation to recognize "other gods".

C. BABYLON

The one effective road between Mesopotamia and Egypt lies up and down Palestine. Before Israel invaded the country or the walls of Jericho fell, the Egyptians had controlled the land; and we are told that it was in one of the recurring intervals of weakness in Egyptian history that the Israelites were able to enter and take possession of a land long more familiar than themselves with civilization. But as the powers of Mesopotamia pressed Westward to the Mediterranean, the small kingdoms of Syria and Palestine were exposed to a double menace. It was in vain, as a rule, that shrewd observers like Isaiah would tell the king of Judah to keep out of quarrels that did not concern him; his city was rather aside from the direct route; "in quietness and confidence shall be your strength". Shishak, king of Egypt, spoils Solomon's temple in Rehoboam's reign; Josiah long after is defeated and killed by Necho of Egypt (the Nekos of Herodotus). "The Assyrian came down like the wolf on the fold"; and pestilence laid low the army of Sennacherib, as both the Bible and Herodotus tell us. The mouse in the Egyptian god's hand, which Herodotus describes, is the symbol of plague, as it was with the Philistines, when they returned the Ark to Israel after Eli's death. A Greek geographer tells us of plague spreading from field mice to an army in Spain; and everybody knows to-day that plague is carried by the fleas of the rat, and in America by those of the ground-squirrel.

But when Nebuchadnezzar succeeded his father (a usurper, it is true) on the throne of Babylon, the hour had struck for the breakdown of the kingdom of Judah. The dynasty of David, like so many Eastern dynasties, had fallen away from its founder; the kings were puppets or fumblers, who lacked the sense not to meddle, who would not face facts, but started rebellions which were bound to fail. The Babylonian king solved his difficulties with the wretched little kingdom, as the Assyrian had done with the Northern half of the people; he carried away to Babylonia nearly everyone who might be a leader, but "left of the poor of the land to be vinedressers and husbandmen". The city he sacked and the temple he destroyed. The 137th Psalm tingles with the emotions of the deported exile: "By the waters of Babylon, there we sat down; yea, we wept when we remembered Zion. ... How shall we sing the Lord's song in a strange land? If I forget thee, O Jerusalem, let my right hand forget her cunning". The curse at the end of the psalm shocks careless readers, of commonplace benevolence, who do not realize what the poet had seen, and what he ever saw again in imagination; the accent falls on the pronoun "*thy*" and all is clear—"Happy shall he be that taketh and dasheth thy little ones against the stones". This was the way of Babylonian conquerors and of the Catholic soldiers of Cortés in Mexico.

Much has been made of these captivities. The "Lost Ten Tribes" have been sought far and wide; even the Saxons have been made into "Isaac's sons". But one or two things have to be proved first. How far did *Ten* tribes survive, and go into exile as Ten tribes? It would seem that a good deal of the Northern population remained in Palestine, as later on of the Southern, though foreigners were planted by the Assyrians in the Northern country. Nothing is known, it is all guess work, as to what became of the people removed by the Assyrians. The Southern exiles, however, though restless enough at first, at last followed the line suggested by Jeremiah in his letter, and settled down in Babylonia; and many of their descendants never went back to Palestine. They have rather moved East, and the Bagdadi Jews, the Bene Israel and certain other Jews of India may be their descendants. At all events they learned "to sing the Lord's song in a strange land". Babylon fell to Cyrus, without a battle, as we saw; and the Jews were given leave to return to Judaea. It has been put, epigrammatically but not untruly, that "Israel went into captivity a nation and returned a church". The whole character of the race seems changed, not so much transformed as intensified. The false gods and village cults, stone pillars "under every green tree" (still familiar in Southern India), no longer attract the Jew; in psalm after psalm he speaks his contempt for them—"mouths have they, but they speak not". The national life centres in Jehovah.

Few books have deserved a better fate, or found a worse, than the memoirs of Nehemiah. They have been ruthlessly cut up by an ancient editor, and bound in with a prosaic record called after Ezra. Nehemiah was a contemporary of Pericles, a man of the Persian court of Artaxerxes, with a spiritual life that finds expression in sudden ejaculations of prayer. He gave up the career of a courtier to devote himself to building up Jerusalem and inspiriting his people. Every page he writes presents

a man, battling with problems, danger without, apathy
and treachery within, bent on keeping the Jewish race
pure from admixture of alien blood, and its religion as
pure from alien ideas. No doubt he did not work wholly
alone; others followed him; and, though there are huge
gaps in the history, the Jewish people emerge very much
what Nehemiah had wished to make them. After him
comes a dim period of a century or more.

D. HELLENISM

The battle of Issus (333 B.C.) opened for Alexander
Syria and Egypt; and, after taking Tyre and Gaza by
siege, the king went to Egypt and to the oracle of Ammon.
On his way, says a Jewish legend, he visited Jerusalem.
The High Priest, warned by a vision, robed himself in
the full splendour of his sacred vestments, and, accompanied by a great crowd in white garments, met the
conqueror, who drew near alone and worshipped the
Sacred Name engraved on the gold plate upon the High
Priest's breast. So says legend, but History knows nothing
of it. But Jews were soon to be found in large numbers
at Alexandria, the Conqueror's great foundation.

The great moment for Judaism in the Hellenistic
period was not the victory of Alexander but the reign
of Antiochus Epiphanes (175-164 B.C.). "King Antiochus", says the Roman historian, "tried to destroy
superstition and to introduce the Greek way of life, but
was prevented by his war with the Parthians from
improving this most dreadful race." He was a king with
a hint or two of genius, but more of the charlatan, and
was nicknamed *Epimanes* by his Greek subjects. (*Epiphanes*
means "magnificent"; the nickname, with the change

of one letter, "rather mad".) He had been a hostage
in Rome for thirteen years, and liked Romans, but,
looking on himself as a successor of Alexander the Great,
he conceived it his mission to spread Greek culture. The
Jewish priesthood did not represent the highest spiritual
life of Judaism; their office was hereditary; they were
descendants of Zadok, Sadducees, and their name has
become a proverb for low ideals. They were ready to
compromise with the king, and the Temple was quickly
"Hellenized"—"polluted", said good Jews. For if the
priesthood cared little for the religion of their fathers,
the common people cared for it much, and the land
flamed with rebellion. The family of the Maccabees led
the rebels; and, whether we put all down to the Parthian
war, or allow a little to a treaty made between Judas
Maccabaeus and the Romans (described in the eighth
chapter of *First Maccabees*), or whether we attribute
something to Providence, Judaism was saved, and
regenerated. Perhaps the book of *Ecclesiasticus* in the
Apocrypha represents fairly what a Jew cultured and
liberal, but moderate if orthodox, might be; he believes
in One God but not in immortality, in the glory of the
Law, but also in this world and its goods; he is pious,
no doubt, but very canny and prudential. After the
national crisis, more is asked of God—some explanation
of history, of the evil in the world, of the destiny of man
and of individual men. God has much to explain; but
the writers of the books and psalms that survive believe
that it can be explained, and will in time be all clear;
meanwhile a good Jew must be loyal to his race and to
his God. Some of them bluntly supposed that the
Gentiles were created to be destroyed; others felt this
too harsh—if Gentiles acted aright and lived good lives,

ought not God to allow the good life to outweigh the unfortunate pedigree? Others again felt the whole problem of the Gentile too complicated to decide; they had better let it alone.

There is no doubt that the Greeks had a very great influence on the Jews. The attempt of Epiphanes failed; it was crude and harsh; but, meeting Greeks daily in the cities of Egypt and Asia, the Jews could not escape their questioning, as the Christian could not later on. There was a great deal that was attractive in Greek ways of life—literature, the theatre, athletics; and, after all, Greek philosophy, with all its vagaries, was at bottom an attempt to reach truth. So the Jew argued with the Greek, and really learnt more from him than the Greek learnt from the Jew. A new Jewish literature sprang up, written in Greek, like the Greek "tragedy" on the Exodus written by a man called Ezekiel (*not* the Ezekiel of the Bible). Still more significant, the Jew began to think somewhat like the Greek. When the writer of *Wisdom* calls God "the first author of beauty", when he says that "the cosmos is champion of the righteous", he is expressing ideas not wholly new to the Jew, but he is giving them a new turn, more suggestive of the Stoics than of Isaiah. The Old Testament was translated into Greek, and many legends grew up about it. Seventy elders made the translation, from whom it is called the *Septuagint*, and miracles hailed the glad day when it appeared. Later on, the miracles were changed to dreadful portents, when the Jews made up their mind to break for ever with everything Greek, as they did in the second century A.D. But perhaps there was no day on which the translation appeared; it seems that, as we should really have expected, the translating took years and was only very gradually finished. In the same period (dating it very loosely and roughly) books were written in Greek professing to give accounts of Egyptian and Babylonian religion; but, from all that is known of them, it is clear, in the light of modern discovery, that they were very inaccurate. But the Septuagint is a more interesting book, and, though the Jews rejected it after about A.D. 150, it became the Christian Bible. It was the Bible, too, that St Paul read long before he was converted. If later on Judaism renounced and excommunicated Greek culture, it remains as evidence of the appeal of Greek culture, that 3000 words of foreign origin, mostly Greek, are found in the Talmud, the body of writings of the Jewish rabbis.

E. THE ROMANS AND THE HERODS

In the year 66 B.C. the law proposed to the Roman people by an obscure politician, called Manilius, transferred the command in the war against Mithradates from Lucullus to Pompey. In the course of the next few years Pompey did far more than conquer Mithradates. He swept through the East—the nearer East—like another Alexander, and became Pompeius Magnus, Pompey the Great, while flatterers even discovered some facial resemblance between the two conquerors. The significance of his achievements belongs to another chapter (ch. XIV).

A civil war in Palestine led to Pompey being called in. His advance through the country was unopposed, the chief fortresses surrendered to him, and Jerusalem was his for marching in. But not the temple. Its fortifications were strong; siege-engines were required, and for three months the siege went on, till the temple fell to an assault amid a great massacre. A contemporary

Plate IV

Jerusalem, by J. M. W. Turner

Jewish psalmist (whose psalms are attributed to King Solomon) says, "he poured out the blood of the dwellers in Jerusalem like the water of uncleanness". "He was an alien," says another of these psalms; "the adversary wrought insolence, and all things whatsoever he did in Jerusalem, he did even as do the Gentiles in their cities unto their gods." This is obscure; but another psalm is not obscure: "I delayed not until God showed to me that insolent one, lying pierced on the high places of Egypt, made of less account than him that is least on earth and sea; even his dead body lying corrupted upon the waves in great contempt; and there was none to bury him....He said: I will be lord of earth and sea; and perceived not that it is God who is great". What had Pompey done? "By right of conquest", writes the Roman historian, "he entered the temple. Thence it became common knowledge that there was no image of a god within, the shrine was vacant, the mysteries empty." English readers may have to think twice to realize that this was an epigram. A temple is the house in which an idol is kept. Here was one of the most famous temples in the world, the most jealously guarded; and when Pompey enters it, he finds in it—nothing! A temple like Mother Hubbard's cupboard—after all this mystery!

It is hardly necessary to do more than glance at the history of the Jews for the next century and a half. Herod "the Great" stands out, great as compared with his family, not one of the world's great men, the founder of Caesarea, the name of which might atone for his relations with Brutus and Cassius, the re-builder of the temple at Jerusalem. He was an Edomite, the Jews said; and he murdered his wife Mariamne of the Maccabee stock and so many more of his family, that the Emperor Augustus is credited with a Greek pun to the effect that he would feel safer as Herod's swine (*hys*) than as his son (*hyios*). It is to this Herod that the massacre of the Innocents has been attributed. We read by and by that "Archelaus did reign in Judea in the room of his father Herod", and then Scripture is silent about him; for the Roman government had to draw the line somewhere, and cleared out Archelaus. But other Herods had their turn, over sections of Palestine. They were only one among various minor dynasties, to whom Rome conceded small princedoms which sometimes had to be revoked. The situation is described vividly in the parable of the Pounds in St Luke (ch. xix). A certain nobleman went into a far country (i.e. to Rome) to receive for himself a kingdom and to return. But his citizens (his fellow-citizens or nationals) hated him, and sent envoys to follow him, with the message (to the Imperial Court) that it would be unwelcome to them to have this man as king over them. That is very intelligible. What happens at Rome is not told; it does not bear on the point of the parable, but it is fairly clear. The nobleman and the envoys bribe and counter-bribe Imperial chamberlains and secretaries— or, in blunter language, the freedmen of the Emperor who had at least enough power under Tiberius and some later Emperors. At last the Herod, or whoever he is, comes back king; and two tasks await him at once; he needs a staff, viziers or what you will, to "administer" his kingdom—in English, to get out of it all they can, and to know ahead of the time whether any rebellion is planned, and to crush it before it reaches a head; the other task is, in the words of the Gospel—"those mine enemies, that would not that I should reign over them, bring hither, and slay them before me".

Such princes alternated with a poor type of Roman governor, like Pontius Pilate, who mingled the blood of Galilaeans with their sacrifices, and, to avert a riot, ordered the Crucifixion. Felix and Porcius Festus, before whom St Paul was brought, were not very much better. Religious extremists were unfamiliar figures in the Greco-Roman world; they were not unfamiliar among the Jews. It is noteworthy however that many Jews of sense, not merely time-servers, had no quarrel with the Roman government; bad as an occasional weak governor like Pilate might be, Rome in general was less terrible than the Herods. But there was an irreconcilable element; and it came to rebellion, to furious fighting and the utter destruction of Jerusalem, city and temple, by Titus in A.D. 70.

That year is a landmark to be noted in the history of Judaism and of the Christian church, both of which have moulded the history of us all. The temple was gone, and with it went the whole priestly system of the Jews; there could be now no more sacrifices. The Roman hoped it would be the end of Judaism, but he reckoned without the synagogue. All over the world, wherever Jews were, twelve Jews might form a synagogue. It was not a temple; far from it; it had no altar, it could have no sacrifice; it was more like a private prayer meeting of familiar friends. They read the Old Testament together, sometimes expounded it in a sort of sermon, they sang the Psalms, they recited prayers. To us this hardly sounds novel or epoch-making; but it was both. Ancient religion rested on idol, altar, sacrifice and priest; it was unthinkable without them. Here however was a religion intimate and held with passion, that had none of these aids, and fiercely refused them. The destruction of the temple was really the end of the Jewish compromise between traditional and spiritual religion; altar and temple, and all the old associations, many of them magical, went overboard; and the Jews found that a spiritual religion sufficed, and proved to be a far more real and uniting thing.

The fall of Jerusalem meant also the final cleavage between Jews and Christians. We read that Titus knew about Christianity; the Christians were a Jewish sect, rooted in the temple; he knew that the two religions were hostile; but he thought that he was uprooting both at once. But the Christian church was the stronger for the breaking of the tie.

Fifty or sixty years later the Jews rebelled again, led by a man, called the Son of a Star (Barcochebas), a prophet who breathed flames. It was a serious revolt, and was only crushed after furious fighting and great massacres. Judaism settled down to a sullen acquiescence in the hated Roman rule, and avenged itself by washing its hands for ever of Hellenism; the Greek Bible, Greek culture, literature and philosophy, Greek everything, were one and all damnable. As a modern Jewish writer has put it, as "Judaism became more thoroughly Judaized, Christianity was more and more Hellenized". The Jews who still felt the Greek influence found their way into the Christian church.

Chapter X

ALEXANDER

A. THE OVERTHROW OF PERSIA

OF all the heroes, warriors and statesmen of the ancient world, none, not even Caesar himself, stands out like Alexander; none changed so profoundly the ideas of men whether they thought of the government of states or the government of the universe, of peoples, men, Nature or God; none influenced more strongly the imagination of those who came after him, whether princes or thinkers, writers or the tellers of legend. The first thing is to realize how great were the changes he made and how he made them; and then comes the far harder question, what sort of man was he who did all this? It is not enough to make a list of his qualities, good or bad, as if in a schoolboy's report; for when you have added together all the good qualities you find in such a man, what are you to do with his defects? Are they to be added in or subtracted? Is it not plain that the great men of History did not achieve what they did because they were so like us common people—because they lied or coveted, because they had their stupid moments like us, because they drank too much or neglected duty? The more faults you find in the great man and the more obvious his weaknesses, the more earnestly you have to look for the real power which enabled him to achieve what he did. But perhaps when all is said, we have to confess that we do not know what genius is; and it is the genius in a man that does most.

We can recognize it, and sometimes see that even his faults spring from it and help him to that strange unity with men, which makes them believe in him and turns them into ready helpers of his great designs.

Alexander, then, succeeded about the age of twenty to his father's throne in 336 B.C. If History always repeated itself, his Macedonian kingdom would have broken up into tribes and civil war; but it did not. He held it together; he made it clear North and South that he was king as Philip had been king. Then he crossed into Asia and never returned. In 323 he died of a fever, still a young man, at Babylon; and in the meantime he had changed the face of the world and given a new current and new motives to all the thoughts of men. We have to look more closely at the stages of his progress, and try to discover what was in his mind. We have to distinguish between the policy of the moment and his deeper and greater designs. His life is all made up of battles—yes! but also of campaigns; and a general thinks in one way for a battle, but for a campaign in quite another way. But Alexander's life was not all made up of campaigns; the campaigns were steps to an end, which we have to make out; but yet what led him to work for that end and what it was to do for the world, if achieved, and how his mind shaped his course as it did, we have to guess as best we can, and perhaps to confess that, even with the whole story before us, the life completed, and the great ideas working on after the man was gone, we are not big enough to fathom the mind of genius or to register its workings. It moves in a mysterious way, like the Source from which it comes.

Philip, then, was murdered in 336 B.C.; and his son Alexander succeeded him. Several things had to be done in Europe before he could launch out on his great life-work. There was a congress of Greeks in the Peloponnese, an expedition against barbarians in the North, and then the revolt of Thebes. Alexander marched swiftly South-ward, swept suddenly through the pass of Thermopylae, and was at the gates of Thebes. He attacked, and the city fell, and he destroyed it, but, as Milton tells us,

> The great Emathian conqueror bade spare
> The house of Pindarus, when temple and tower
> Went to the ground.

The whole thing was symbolic; Thebes was betraying the cause of Greece, which the king represented; Pindar was the great Greek lyric poet. Napoleon maintained that Alexander's political sagacity was shown most clearly in the skill with which he appealed to the imagina-tion of men. It is the comment of one great leader of men, the creator of a new age, upon another of his own kind. There should be no more Greek rebellions; Greece should be united; and Alexander should be recognized as the representative of all Greece, as in other fields Pindar had been a figure recognized by all Greece. He loved a symbol, and a symbolic action.

In April 334 B.C. Alexander crossed into Asia—to con-quer first the Persian King, and then the world; and he never returned. One of his first acts in Asia was to visit Troy. He had been brought up on Homer—the noblest education for a prince. But he not only read and loved Homer; he was descended, he believed, lineally from Achilles; he liked to think so, as anybody might, and he never forgot it; he would copy his great ancestor, bravest of Greeks, but he would not forget that he was also descended from Andromache in her tragic captivity.

Some would call this a romantic fancy; but it means something real to a man to have a hero's blood in his veins.

Three great victories over the Persians mark his onward course, and mark epochs in the history of mankind. The victory on the river Granicus in the Troy country made him master of Asia Minor (334 B.C.). In the course of a few centuries this land was thoroughly Hellenized—that is to say, Greek education, Greek habits of life, Greek ways of thought spread nearly all over Asia Minor. In this Greek land St Paul founded churches; the ancient races came together and were merged in one another by Greek culture and Christian faith. Christian Asia Minor was a large part of the Empire of Constantinople, and it was till the eleventh century A.D. one of the bulwarks of Europe against the invading Moslems. After centuries of endurance of Mohammedan rule, the "Greeks" (the Christians) of "Turkey in Asia" were transplanted bodily, a million and more of them, to European Greece in 1922. It is a curious reflexion that there were never so few Greeks in Asia Minor as now since the great migration (see page 74), nor so few Christians since St Paul went home to preach in Cilicia. But the Hellenization of Asia Minor was in its time an immense contribution to human progress. Alexander's second great victory at Issus (333 B.C.) gave him Syria, Palestine and Egypt, lands which first Macedonian kings and then Roman Emperors ruled for a thousand years. He had great fights at Tyre and Gaza before he conquered these famous old towns (332 B.C.). He had to be master of the sea if he was to rule the world, and he mastered the Mediterranean by becoming master of its shores. The Persians had a fleet in the Mediterranean, but by conquering the ports and harbours, Alexander freed himself from all danger from it. He then went on to Egypt.

In Egypt he founded what was for ages one of the greatest of all Greek cities, Alexandria (331 B.C.); and next to it in significance comes the Syrian Antioch on the Orontes of which we read so much in the New Testament, which was founded by one of his successors. Palestine became partly Greek, though not wholly; the Jews remained Jews, but they took on a great deal of Greek culture. How much the world owes to men of Jewish faith and Greek education, it is impossible to compute; but the debt is great. The great mark of real development is, as Antigone puts it in the play of Sophocles, "not to join in hating, but to join in loving", to love things that disagree at first sight and clash with one another—just as Plato once said that "there is an ancient quarrel between poetry and philosophy", though it is quite clear that he loved both. In the practical world Alexander is the great uniter of thoughts that clash, and perhaps that is as good an explanation as any of his making a new world, or making the old world over again, which is the same thing; indeed the latter phrase brings out better the difficulty as well as the value of his achievement.

From the time of its foundation all the thoughts of men were moulded by what was thought and written in Alexandria. The Bible was translated into Greek for the Alexandrine Jews. There, too, the Greeks got their knowledge of Egyptian religion, and began to worship Isis, as if she were queen of all the gods, which Hera (Juno) had been in Homer. In Alexandria there taught some of the greatest of Christian teachers, as everybody remembers who thinks about the Athanasian Creed, which bears the name of a great Christian of Alexandria. It is worth while to realize how the work of great men goes far further than they think, or their contemporaries suppose; for it lives for centuries, and influences the minds of countless generations. The reader of these pages owes more to Alexander than he will very quickly find out.

While he was still in Egypt, Alexander took a step which has greatly puzzled those who study his story. About five hundred miles to the Westward of the Nile valley is an oasis, to-day called Siwa, not an attractive spot, a shallow circle of gardens and palm groves on a lake or swamp. A modern professor who visited it took eighteen days to reach it on camel-back; later on, he went again by car in two days. In this oasis in ancient times stood a temple of the Egyptian god, whom the Greeks called Ammon. It was of much less account among Egyptians than his temple at Thebes; but somehow it had interested the Greeks who made pilgrimages to it. And now a longing seized Alexander to go to the place, because Perseus and Herakles had visited it, the great legendary heroes of the Greeks; to both of them he was akin by blood, he believed, and he felt some rivalry with them; and he had some dim notion that he was somehow descended from Ammon. So says the sober historian Arrian. So Alexander marched across the desert; and among other strange miracles, we are told, he was favoured with rain. He reached the temple; he consulted the god; he "heard what was to his mind, he said."

> High things were spoken there, unhanded down;
> Only they saw thee from the secret shrine
> Returning with hot cheek and kindled eyes.*

> * Tennyson.

He returned to Egypt, and for some time no more was heard of it. Then it got about that Alexander was really the son of Ammon; the Macedonians had always thought him the son of Philip, their own king, whom they very reasonably preferred to any foreign god. All sorts of questions rise which we cannot answer. Who told what the god said to the king? Did he wish to think he was the son of a god? Did he wish others to think so—Greeks, then, or Orientals? We can only guess what was in his mind; but the story hints at a wish to think himself in some special way the child of heaven. He was indeed romantic, they say.

The third great victory of Alexander was at Gaugamela (331 B.C.), which was really the end of the Persian King Darius, and of the Persian kingdom for six centuries. It rose again in the third century A.D. Alexander had now done what he set out to do—he had overthrown the Persian kingdom; Persian kings should no more keep Greeks in perpetual strife by sending subsidies now to one city and now to another to enable them to attack one another. Alexander swept onward into Persia, and captured Persepolis, the ancient capital of the Persian kings (331 B.C.). It was burnt; and it has been assumed that Alexander gave the order for this; but it has never been decided why he should have done so, if he did. Some have said it was no more than a freak of drunkenness; some that it was a great symbolic act of vengeance on the Persians, because a hundred and fifty years before Xerxes had burnt Athens. The latter explanation chimes in better with the romantic temper that men find in him. But it may possibly have been an accident, for some tell us he tried to have the flames extinguished. It seems certain that he never did such a thing again; and, if it be said that there was no other great city whose burning would be a symbol of Greek vengeance, it remains true that after this he tried to harmonize all the races he conquered into one great state that should be as big as the world. It looks as if he really understood what Sophocles had said, and tried to get the whole world to "join in loving".

B. THE FAR EAST

He was not satisfied to have conquered Persia, and "avenged Greece", as people put it. He marched on Eastward, and Eastward again, through Afghanistan and into the Panjab. There occurred one of the great moments in his career. After a stiff battle he captured an Indian king, whose name the Greeks wrote as Poros. "And how do you expect me to treat you?" asked Alexander, through an interpreter. "Like a king", said Poros. And Alexander did it. But now his soldiers would go no further. He had led his troops hundreds of miles further from Greece than an army had ever gone before; they were tired of fighting, and they wanted to get back to Europe after eight years absence, and, no doubt, to spend at home the heaps of money they had won; it would be a pity, they thought, not to reach Macedon again, when they had done so well.

Alexander was grieved, but he had to yield to his soldiers, and to return. But before he set out Westward, indeed before he had quite reached his furthermost point in India, he did an interesting thing. He was on the river Indus, we are told, (326 B.C.) and he noticed the crocodiles. The only river which he knew to have crocodiles was the Nile; and we are told that he wondered

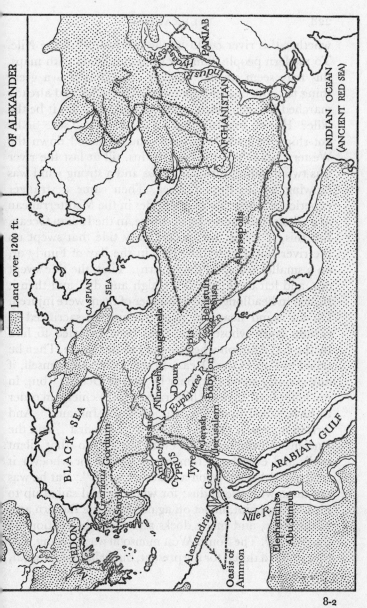

OF ALEXANDER

Land over 1200 ft.

BLACK SEA

CASPIAN SEA

CEDON

Granicus

Gordium

Sardis

Miletus

Issus

Antioch

CYPRUS

Tyre

Sidon

Jerusalem

Gaza

Nineveh

Gaugamela

Dura

Opis

Tigris R.

Euphrates R.

Babylon

Susa

Behistun

Persepolis

AFGHANISTAN

PANJAB

Indus

Hydaspes R.

Hyphasis R.

INDIAN OCEAN
(ANCIENT RED SEA)

ARABIAN GULF

Nile R.

Alexandria

Oasis of Ammon

Elephantine

Abu-Simbul

whether this river could be the headwaters of the Nile. To modern people, familiar from childhood with maps, this may seem strange enough; but (and it is a great thing to think of and remember) Alexander had already marched his men clean out of all maps. Could it be the Nile? He was told not; but he would go and see. So he got ships, or had them built, and he sailed down the Western branch of the river Indus, till at last the river was two hundred furlongs across and a strong wind was blowing up it—from the sea. Then came a stranger experience: there are no real tides in the Mediterranean as a whole, but there are, of course, in the Indian Ocean. But this, it seems, was no ordinary tide that swept up the river but a bore (like that in the Bay of Fundy or, on a smaller scale, on the Severn). First, the tide swept out, and left the king's ships high and dry, and then it rushed in headlong, and a number of them were injured. On an island near the river's mouth he sacrificed to certain gods, whose names had been revealed to him by the god Ammon when he went to the oracle. Then he sailed out on to the Ocean, to see, as he said himself, if any country stood out, near by, in the Ocean; "but, in my judgment (says the historian Arrian) chiefly in order to have sailed upon the sea *beyond* the Indians." And Arrian may well be right. "We were the first", said the Ancient Mariner, "that ever burst Into that silent sea"; and everybody remembers Cortés (or whoever it really was) "silent upon a peak in Darien". But he was not done with the Indus; for when he had sailed up to his starting point, he set off again down the Eastern arm of the river, and made docks and took observations of the country. The South-West monsoon was blowing, and that stopped things for the present, but at last his admiral,

the Greek Nearchus, was able to start on the voyage of
exploration that Alexander desired. He should sail Westward along the shore, till he reached the Persian Gulf,
which was a known region.

Alexander marched back by land, through deserts,
with dreadful sufferings. It was long before he heard
a word of Nearchus, and he began to be very anxious
about him. Day succeeded day, and he sent out search
parties to the Gulf. At last, after much disappointment,
seven or eight people were met, with long hair, un-
washed, covered with brine, wizened and pale with
sleeplessness; they were not recognized till one of them
said: "I am Nearchus." They were set on waggons and
brought to Alexander, who hardly knew them again.
Where were all the others? No, said Nearchus, fleet and
men were safe; and the great exploration was accom-
plished, after wonderful adventures (which are still to
be read) among islands and savages and whales—much
larger whales, too, than are seen in the Mediterranean.

The ancients tell us what a great soldier, what a
conqueror, Alexander was. These stories of his own
voyages and that of Nearchus tell us something else. It
was not all love of fighting that stirred him; like all the
greater Greeks, he "wanted to know", and this for two
reasons, a real scientific desire to learn about the world,
and the wish to link up the nations whom he was conquering. Sea-routes, as we have seen, are sometimes
safer and shorter than land-travel. For now we have to
consider from another point of view what Alexander had
in mind, if we can learn it from what he said and did.
First of all, as we saw, it was plain enough to him (as to
many others) that there would never be peace in Greece,
till the Persian king left off hatching wars and revolutions

among the Greek cities. So he conquered the Persian, and he found himself king of Persia as well as of Macedon; and a new view of the world seems to have dawned upon his mind—why not one kingdom of all the world? Not for mere ambition's sake; a smaller man might have fancied it something to be caught at, to look at himself as King of Mankind. Alexander perhaps felt this also, for he clearly loved to see himself in the royal robes of the Persian king. But he was more than a spectacle to himself; for he lived a life more crowded with business and government than any Persian king since the first Darius. Few people can imagine what a range and width of government he had to undertake. He had to keep an eye on Macedon, and on all the Greek states, and the doings of the politicians in the Aegaean, hundreds of miles away; he had to arrange for the maintenance of law and order in all the provinces that had been Persia's, to appoint governors, and to make as sure as he could that they would govern wisely and justly; and he had to plan for the future—to think of new cities to be founded (they say he founded some seventy), of roads to link them together, of harbours and seaports (Alexandria was only one of them; he had to create nearly everything anew on the Indian Ocean);— and for what?

Let us try to see him alone, in hours of dreaming. One story is that he drank too much; and so now and then he did; but he was never a drunkard or anything like it. We saw how greatly he was interested in Troy, and we are told that the one book he read all through his great journeys and campaigns in Persia, Afghanistan and India, was Homer. We are even told that among the loot of Darius was found a box of exquisite workmanship and just the right size; and the king took it as part of his share, to keep his Homer in it. He looked to the great past of Greece, to Achilles and Herakles his ancestors; but he saw much else in Greece; Greece was the only really civilized land, and he began to plan to Hellenize his whole empire, to give it Greek institutions, Greek amusements, athletic, literary, musical, intellectual. The barbarian was a dull sort of creature, the Greek said; he should be waked up to a higher life. This idea Alexander never gave up; but, as he came to know barbarians better, he liked them better, and began to feel that the Greeks had not all the virtues and advantages; some of these Persians were real men, and the Indian, King Poros, who would be treated "like a king", was indeed a king among men. Could he bring East and West to understand one another better, to share their gifts,—the Greek to introduce the Oriental to intellectual life, and to learn from him something of the dignity and the princeliness and the royal outlook that Greeks so terribly lacked? Someone has called it "the marriage of East and West"; and he certainly made some thousands of his Macedonian soldiers marry Eastern wives, and he took an Eastern princess himself. Greek cities in Eastern lands, with Greek *agora*, Greek theatre, Greek athletics; freedom of travel and trade Eastward and Westward, safe roads and a safe sea; after all his wars and conquests, he seems to have looked to a reign of peace, to harmony among nations, to a fuller interchange of arts and ideas, to a new growth of the human mind.

And then he died of a fever at Babylon, scarcely thirty-five years old; and what became of all his great ideas?

C. THE OUTCOME

It is possible to look at the matter in either of two ways. It seems likely that many of his Macedonians got rid of their foreign wives, and packed back to Macedon or to Greek cities in the neighbourhood of the Mediterranean. Alexander left no heir, apart from an unborn son and a half-witted brother of some kind; and his generals made themselves guardians of his empire for Roxana's son when he should be born. He was born, and he reached boyhood; but by then the empire was torn asunder; the generals quarrelled among themselves, and became independent princes, and at last those who were left took the name of "King"; and one of them killed the little prince and his mother, and the royal house of Philip was extinct. In place of one empire there were several; and ere long India was lost, and then much else; and, if you look at things in a matter-of-fact way, Alexander's ideas were wrecked, his life-work undone, and the world had fallen back into war and chaos. We shall see the same thing again in ancient history, perhaps in modern; but we have to look deeper.

One thing that Alexander had done could never be undone; he had given a shock to all the old ideas of mankind. The Greek, as we saw, could think no form of national life quite natural unless it were the city-state. Alexander had made an end of the city-state; plenty of them continued to exist, to show party-factions at home, and to quarrel with the neighbouring city ten miles away. But over every one of the city-states now loomed something bigger, a kingdom ruled by a prince; and further afield were other princes and kingdoms; and the great issues in world-politics (if we may borrow a modern phrase) were decided by the princes and kings. They made the wars and the alliances; and the famous old city-states, where they were at all free to act as they liked, were mere make-weights. Life in the city-state was not what it had been; the free and independent politicians and citizens took orders from outside; and if a man wanted a big career, he might do better to leave Greece altogether, and go to one of the new big cities which the Macedonian kings were building in Syria, in Egypt, and on the Euphrates. Little local wars of the old type might occur, and did occur; the wars of the period after Alexander were on a greater scale. But we have to remember that if great kingdoms swallow up little ones, it is not all loss. Since Great Britain became one kingdom, there has been far less fighting in her fields, and we never expect to see it. So in the world after Alexander there were more wars than enough, but probably there was more peace than before over larger areas, better government (not as good as it might have been, but better than it had been, unless indeed it is better for people to govern themselves badly than to be governed well), and more prosperity. If the rabble of Alexandria, as a Greek historian says, were a horrible and brutal lot, who enjoyed riot and murder, when they got the chance, they did not get the chance every day, and they were not the only people at Alexandria.

All sorts of intellectual life throve in Alexandria. A great library grew up there, the influence of which was felt in all the literature and science of the World. New styles were struck out in writing, whether prose or poetry; there was a new conscience about careful production of books. If there were fewer men of genius—none to compare with Euripides or Plato—there were men of science and learning, and they drew their knowledge from wider fields. It was not left to modern days and Copernicus to tell us that the earth goes round the sun. That was taught long ago by Aristarchus, of Samos, at Alexandria; and Plutarch and the orthodox of his day counted him as heretical as later men counted Copernicus and Galileo. Nearchus had not made his voyage in vain. Hundreds of mariners followed him on the Indian Ocean; one hundred and twenty ships in a year, we are told, might sail for India, about the time of the birth of Christ. All the world knew the rest of the world far better than it had ever done before. For in this period men travel more widely than Herodotus, and if they have not his genius and his originality, they learn what he has to teach—how interesting the world is, and how clever and pleasant and useful foreigners may be, how it sharpens your mind's faculties to find your set notions and best ideas contradicted and no harm resulting. Men begin to exchange ideas over a far wider area and to think new thoughts.

They had to find new thoughts. Man only lives by picturing the world as a tidyish sort of place, where he can fit in somehow, and where he can do his proper work with a reasonable hope of some result. In the old days there had been the little Greek town, and how all-important were its politics! All that is over and done with in the great kingdoms. What has a citizen left to think about, when all home-government and all foreign politics are taken out of his hands? He will indeed need new thoughts, to re-shape the strange new world in which he has nothing to do but obey the police or the captain

of the troops in the castle. The words of Pindar, pleading
for an exile, come back:

> The bitterest fate of all, men say,
> Is his, who clearly hath descried
> The right thing, and no part may play
> But stands, perforce, aside.

The citizen may see the right thing, the true course;
but he is passenger now, not pilot. Men have to find new
interests, to think out a different sort of framework for
the world they live in. Some became Epicureans; "give
to me the life I love; let the lave go by me"; pleasure
was the thing—not necessarily the English public's idea
of pleasure, but something more refined, yet still only
pleasure, some way of fleeting the time, of "playing
patience till the hearse comes". Some became Stoics,
and thought of a larger world than the little old republic;
they pictured all the universe as one great polity. Who
taught them that? It was Alexander. So they thought
of all mankind as one republic of human beings, all
citizens, Greeks or barbarians, women or slaves, all one
great state of Humanity, where every citizen has a man's
duty to do, to serve all mankind; where the gods are
citizens too, and the air and the sea, and the atoms—
all One, all related, all kin, all friends. Then a man's
part is to be a friend to all, to be a good citizen of the
City of Zeus. With these wider conceptions we may
surely link the widening of the range of art and literature
—fresh proof that their function is the interpretation of
life. Alexander had indeed done something very real,
if he induced men to think like this.

But that is not yet all. Mankind had had many gods,
local gods, city gods, river gods, gods of hill and dale and
fountain, and heroes too who were half gods. But the

local god had not very wide power after all. Alexander enlists a man and marches him all across Asia into India; will his old home-god be able to help him there, if the Indian's local god grows angry with him? The old tribe-goddess, a nice old figure in the temple in the home town hundreds of miles away? So men began to think, and at last to ask themselves a question of this sort. One world, one king (Alexander, of course—and might he not somehow have a successor who would make it one world again?)—one race, all men of one kind, whatever the colours of their skins, the differences of their languages and stations in life or on the earth—everything one—unity the one idea that explains everything—then ought not God to be One somehow? This does not quite (so to speak) un-god the local gods; they may be like the king's governors, the captains of his troops in the citadels; but would it not be a tidier sort of universe, more thinkable, safer and happier, if there were no rivalries, no civil wars, among local gods, but all were united under the supreme rule of One Divine Being? This, too, was a line of thought which men very largely owed to Alexander.

Before we leave him, let us remember that life is not all politics, philosophy and theology. Think of all the tales and legends and marvels and questions that Alexander let loose in the world! Begin with his horse Bucephalus and the tale of his taming it, of its carrying him to India and dying there, and the king founding a city to commemorate it. Remember the Gordian Knot —a proverb for cutting problems you cannot untie, and being done with them. Remember the Brahmin sages. Remember how the stories grew and were translated all over the world. Remember—remember a thousand anecdotes; and the outcome was that Alexander was the most wonderful man who ever lived.

D. THE PRECIOUS METALS

One result of the conquests of Alexander remains to be noticed. The hoards of the Persian kings fell into the conqueror's hands, and in large part went westward. We are told variously that the treasure obtained in Susa and in Persia was forty or fifty thousand talents, or from all sources as much as one hundred and eighteen thousand talents. Reckoning roughly four talents to £1000, and remembering that the purchasing power of gold was perhaps five or six times what it was in 1900, even if we allow for exaggerations, we can divine the effect of such an addition to the stock of precious metals current in the Western world, and the changes it produced by shifting (as it were) the political centre of gravity. A short survey of what we are told about gold and silver at various stages of ancient history will bring this out, and may suggest reflexions.

Homer, of course, is full of gold. Mycene was "rich in gold", heroes were always giving lavish gifts of gold; one prince wore golden armour, which however he did not keep;

> For then was Glaucus, both in mind and deed,
> Robbed of his wits by Kronos' son divine,
> To change arms with illustrious Diomede.
> Thus gold for brass it pleased him to resign,
> Arms worth a hundred oxen for the worth of nine.

But it was not till the days of Schliemann (see p. 41) that people really believed in all this Homeric gold.

"As a matter of fact", we read in Athenaeus (see p. 354), "gold was really scarce among the Greeks in old times, very scarce indeed; and the silver to be found in the mines was scanty. For that reason Philip, the father of Alexander the Great, always (so Duris of Samos says) kept a little gold saucer he had under his pillow". Herodotus, with his eyes as ever open, notes mines and mining methods as he goes about the world; and we hear of Pisistratus' interest in gold mines at Pangaion, of mines of gold and silver worked for a while on the island of Siphnos, of gold in Scythia, and of the earlier Alexander of Macedon drawing a talent of silver a day from the mines he controlled. But when the Spartans wanted gold to make an image, they had to go to Croesus of Lydia for it, who gave it them for nothing; the river Pactolus, in Lydia, "flows through the middle of the Sardis market, carrying down gold dust from Mt Tmolus". We have seen how Croesus used it to control the movements of Greek states (see p. 78). Xerxes encountered a Lydian whose wealth in gold and silver ran to some four millions sterling. But by the time of Christ Pactolus had no gold left to roll.

What gold men had was not in circulation; it was hoarded in temples; and on these accumulations the states drew when they went to war, as Athens did in the Peloponnesian War. But the King of Persia was the greatest hoarder of all; and Herodotus gives us a detailed account of the treasure in gold that came to him year by year from the provinces—Indian gold dust among it, captured from among ants the size of foxes—and how the King cast it into ingots, and could draw on it at will. King Darius, he says, issued gold coins of peculiar fineness—a fact borne out by modern analysis

—coins of about the weight of a guinea and stamped with the famous "archer" (see p. 155). What saved Athens, as we saw (p. 103), in the Persian wartime was the great discovery of silver in her Laureion mines, which Themistocles induced his people to spend on building a navy. From then onward Athens issued silver drachmas, of a very pure silver, current (we read) all over the world, and everywhere recognizable by the queer archaic owl they bore on one side, and the scarcely less archaic goddess on the other. They were popularly known as "owls", and they played a part in the recovery of Athens after her disasters, for she was wise enough not to debase them. Coinage (properly so called, as opposed to lumps of metal stamped with their weight) was, according to the Greeks, a Lydian invention (see p. 78), but Greece very quickly took it up. When the Athenian empire fell, her late subjects at once began to mint their own currencies[1]—a fact that may help to explain the contemporary rise of banking in Athens; the multiplication of currencies can have helped few beyond moneyers and bankers. The Phoenicians and Carthaginians were late in starting to coin, and Egypt never had a currency of its own till the Ptolemies ruled it; but Persian money would be current there. The early history of Montreal and of Winnipeg reveals that a great trade may be carried on with no local currency, partly in commodities, partly in foreign coinages.

We have seen already how potent Persian "archers" were in Greek affairs (see p. 173). In Philip's time another source was used, and quickly exhausted; "when

[1] We may remember the epigram of the Cynic philosopher, whose advice was "mint your own coins"—i.e. be independent, and do your own thinking.

the shrine of Delphi", says Athenaeus, "was looted by
the Phocian tyrants, then it was that gold blazed up
among the Greeks, and silver came romping in. And
later when Alexander the Greatest brought away the
treasures from Asia, then indeed rose the sun of wealth
with far-flung might, as Pindar would say." The immense sums liberated from the Persian hoards altered
the balance of the Greek world; regions poor before became rich, such as Aetolia and Elis, while Greek states
once wealthy were now by comparison poor, if not also
actually poorer than of old. Prices of course were
altered; the cost of living rose and the middle classes
suffered. We may compare the extraordinary changes in
Europe in the sixteenth century that followed from the
looting by the Spaniards of the gold accumulations of
Mexico and Peru, changes in prices, industries and
standards of living which few then understood. Sheep,
says Latimer, had become terrible creatures—i.e. it
became suddenly profitable to raise wool in England for
sale abroad at the new prices; arable land became
pasture and labourers were turned adrift. But the
greatest part of the Persian wealth remained with the
Successor Kings; and nothing could stand against it.
They could make war on a gigantic scale with mercenaries and elephants; and even their squandering
(see p. 249) could hardly exhaust their wealth. One
of Cleopatra's charms for Antony, they say, was her
treasury.

Gold-washing (placer-mining), as in the Pactolus,
and elsewhere, is described by the ancients to have been
done much as it was in California in 1849. Strabo is
particularly interesting on the mines of Spain (book III,
C 146, 147). Gold was found in veins in quartz; and the

historian, Diodorus, has preserved an account of the process by which it was obtained. Here again the methods necessary are familiar to moderns; but the absence of machinery and the substitution of convict and slave labour meant an immense amount of human suffering. All the ancient methods involved a certain loss of metal, which in some cases has been recovered in modern times by various scientific processes. At one time we read of forty thousand men being employed in gold and silver mines in Spain. Strabo quotes from Polybius the story of a fall of 30 per cent. in the value of gold in Italy in two months as a result of the opening of a new mine.

To anticipate a little the story that follows, and to end our digression, the conquest of the Mediterranean lands by Rome brought about, as Cicero said, the concentration of all the wealth of all the world in few hands. The loot of war, the spoils of peace, and the abominable misgovernment, denuded the provinces, and gave the Romans "money to burn"; the slang phrase never came nearer the truth. For cosmetics, silks, spices, Rome, says Pliny, sent a million sterling a year to the Orient; "so much", he adds, "our luxuries and our ladies cost us". This does not include the cost of procuring wild animals from Africa and Asia for the absurd and cruel "games" in the amphitheatres all over Western Roman lands. Rome manufactured nothing that the Orient wished to buy—neither guns, nor cars, nor gramophones; and everything had to be paid for in the precious metals, and not only in them—Roman coins of low value have been found at Ootacamund "by the coolie load". The result was by 400 A.D. a shortage of precious metals in Europe, and various debasements of the coinage in the desperate attempt to keep going. A great discovery of gold near the Rhine about 900 A.D. relieved things; and since then, as we all know, gold has been found in large quantities in California, Australia, Kootenay, the Yukon, and South Africa; but currency problems are still with us. It is curious to note that a momentous presidential election was fought in the United States in 1896 on the question whether a single government could fix by law the relative values of gold and silver, at 16 to 1; and then to find that Philip of Macedon had tried to do it at $12\frac{1}{2}$ to 1. Thus does History repeat itself. Nor only so; for just as the problem was solved in antiquity by Philip's son flooding the world with Persian gold, we are told that the American question was solved by greater gold production resulting from the cyanide process. But here we should perhaps stop, and return to the ancient world, perhaps with a heightened feeling of kinship.

Alexander the Great

Chapter XI

THE HELLENISTIC WORLD

A. THE SUCCESSORS OF ALEXANDER

ON 13 June 323 Alexander the Great died of a fever at Babylon. He had been king for a dozen years or so, and, as a modern historian suggests, it would be hard to name any period in history, in which in so short a time so large a part of the civilized world underwent so sudden, so momentous and so permanent a change. Till then the great empire of Persia confronted the city-states of the Greeks, which it kept in a chaos of war and uncertainty; now that empire was with the past, and Persia had not again a king of Persian stock for six centuries. The Greek city-states continued, some with Macedonian garrisons in their castles, some leagued in new federal unions, some under tyrants, some maintaining an uneasy semi-independence till it suited some monarch (or at last Rome) to give orders that none dared neglect. New Greek cities, in fifty places of the Orient, invited Greeks to leave their old parishes and parochial feuds, and to live in a new atmosphere and new ideas. These new cities were the creation of kings, but two at least of them, as we saw, counted now far more than the age-old cities of Greece.

But what of the empire of Alexander himself? It had died with him. As he lay dying, and was asked about the succession, he was heard, or was thought, to murmur: "To the strongest." At another moment, with Homer as always in his mind and the funeral games that Achilles held for Patroclus, he predicted "great contests at his burial". He left no effective heir; and his generals were well enough aware that, whoever could control the army, would be master of all; but for the immediate present a plan was devised of holding the provinces for the successsor. A dozen years saw the end of the plan and of the heirs. Into the maze of intrigues, alliances, quarrels, wars and deaths that followed, it is not needful here to give a clue. Gradually three kingdoms emerged, and three royal houses. Ptolemy, son of Lagus, had from the first made sure of Egypt; and there his family ruled for nearly three centuries till Antony's Cleopatra had herself killed by the asp after the battle of Actium (31 B.C.). The house of Seleucus ruled Asia—a vague phrase; for the frontiers were never very certain or secure; India was early lost, and the Parthians cut off other Eastern portions in the middle of the third century. Still Syria was left, with Antioch as its capital, and as much else as the Seleucid of the day could get or keep; and the family held on till Pompey came to the East in 65 B.C. In Macedon, after a good deal of disorder, the house of Antigonus made sure of the throne and kept it till the Romans overthrew Perseus in 168 B.C.

In 306 the several rulers took, one after another, the title "King". A modern would expect the name of a country to follow in each case; but it does not. Partly, because perhaps it was not the ancient way in any case to mention it; partly, because the bare name "King" seemed to leave it open to any man who bore the title to re-unite the heritage of Alexander, and be king of all—and we know that this ambition was cherished. Possibly another reason may be given; not one of these kingdoms had any strong or wide racial unity underlying it. If the king of the Macedonians had limited himself to the Macedonians, that might have been a kingdom on a really national base; and indeed it came nearest to it. Egypt had two races, Greeks and Egyptians; the dynasty was Greek, but the mass of the people were Egyptians. They had had two hundred years of Persian rule, and they preferred the Greeks who mixed with them better and accepted more of their religion; and as time went on, Greek influence in Egypt was slighter, and the native Egyptian was stronger. But, if the Ptolemy of the day held Palestine, or Cyrene, or Cyprus—and he had reasons for wishing to hold all three—there could be still less national unity about such a realm than in an Egypt with a foreign dynasty. Cleopatra was Greek, not Egyptian in any sense, even if Shakespeare calls her a "gypsy". A kingdom in this period came to look like a large series of big estates, where the one common feature was that the same man owned and ruled them, and took as much money out of them as was safe.

In 124 the last king of Pergamum died without an heir. He bequeathed his kingdom to Rome; and a glance at the bequest and the testator will explain much. We have seen (page 175) the strange origin of his dynasty. Little might have been expected of such a kingdom and such a house, but it did valiant service for art, literature, learning and civilization. Pergamum had one of the famous libraries of antiquity—it is said 200,000 volumes, which at the last Antony gave to Cleopatra. When the rival book-collector, the Ptolemy of the day, refused papyrus to his enemy, parchment (Pergamene; the name is still in the commodity, misspelled a little) was devised at Pergamum. The kings of this house did much to save Asia and Hellenism from the Gaul invaders. Thus this curious kingdom, created by an off-chance (it was a world of off-chances, few so well used), gives us two lines of study —a succession of kings whom we shall for the present neglect, and a great contribution to the forward movement of mankind. In both ways it resembles the other kingdoms. Their kings and their quarrels, the extension and contraction of their boundaries, their wars are of little interest to mankind—not quite battles of kites and crows, for the kings had ideas. They never forgot Alexander, nor his united world, nor his interest in Greek culture and Greek city life; and whatever their wars of aggression or defence, their wastefulness (some were among the colossal squanderers of History) and their private folly and worthlessness (and some were neither fools nor worthless), still the common note is loyalty to Hellenism, and that was in truth service to mankind.

If the wars of the Successors, and of those who succeeded them, stood in the way of the Hellenization of Asia, war, as we have seen (page 175), was less savage than it had been among the city-states; a whole population was less likely to be exterminated or sold into slavery. The soldiers themselves took a different view of things—they were mercenaries, and war had become a science—a complicated and intricate game; and a defeat and surrender might mean merely a change of paymaster. Mercenaries have never had a good name, and little injustice has been done them in this matter. But the combination of hereditary monarch, world-ambition and mercenary soldier, wearisome and wasteful as it was, and productive of too many wars, was not so ruinous to the parts of the world affected as the furious hates and massacres of the independent Greek cities.

At least so much is arguable, without committing our-selves to the view that peace is the only thing that matters.

For those who love the dramatic in History, the moving accident, the picturesque, and the catastrophe, yes! and the succession of extraordinary royalties, kings, captains and princesses, of striking personality, often of marked ability and seldom with any scruples at all, the stories of these royal houses and their amazing ups and downs are full of incident and interest. Thus in 316 Seleucus had lost all he had of Alexander's empire; with fifty horsemen he fled from the conquering Antigonus to Egypt, perhaps thinking as he rode that his conqueror had once been in the same plight. Ptolemy received him in Egypt. In 312 a decisive battle at Gaza lost Antigonus the control of Syria. Ptolemy gave Seleucus 1000 men (200 being cavalry), to recover his lost dominions; and from that year for centuries men reckoned their dates; it was "the year of the Greeks", when Seleucus became master of the Empire which he and his family kept. But we need not multiply instances. "How does Fortune banter us!" The cry of the Irish dean on the death of Queen Anne, rises from half the thinkers of these king-doms and these centuries. Stoics and astrologers might talk of Fate; but surely there was a lot of fluke in the control of the world. To this we shall return.

So far then, we have captains turning kings, thrones lost and recovered, three outstanding dynasties (or four, if the humbler but useful monarchs of Pergamum should be counted), wars, mercenaries and surprises—a picture of confusion, which, so far in English education, has been little studied. There are no great writers such as wrote of Xerxes and Pericles; and the threads are hard to find. Two threads we have noticed—the dream of universal dominion and the ideal of the Hellenization of Asia, both fitfully pursued, and neither wholly achieved. And yet we are told, and told truly, that few periods of history have contributed more to the development of all that is best in mankind. These kings, as the first great English student of the period emphasized, if they destroyed the liberties of the city-states, yet laid the foundations of the universal intellectual dominion of Greece, an incalculable blessing. They threw open the whole world to Greek ideas and made the Greek language universal, and thus they did more than any other single cause to open the way for the preaching of Christianity. Asia Minor, Greek and Christian, with its capital at Constantinople, was the real safeguard of Western Europe against the Turk. Results so significant for mankind we may be sure no Ptolemy nor Seleucid ever dreamed of, but these results came from ideals to which they devoted themselves, well aware that they were the highest known. If their courses were devious, they knew why they sought their goal.

B. GREEK LIFE IN THE NEW ERA

Whoever discusses the work of Alexander must pause upon the foundation of Alexandria. We have seen, in brief outline, something of what that city has contributed to the civilization of the world and to the advance of thought; and till that is realized the meaning of Alexander will only be imperfectly grasped. But, apart from its scholars and thinkers, sometimes too far apart, Alexandria was a centre of Greek life and the world's trade. The Greeks had a feeling that a city like

Chicago, hurriedly grown with a great population of miscellaneous origin and lacking the ties of common blood and common belief, must be disorderly and unpleasant; and they pointed to Syracuse and to Alexandria —to Syracuse with its repeated alternations between reckless democracy and the rule of tyrants, to Alexandria with its Jews and Egyptians and mercenaries, "wavering between apathy and ferocity", as an English scholar puts it. Polybius was shocked by the brutality they showed in their fights, in their political rioting—the spectacle of which would "fill not only the level spaces but the roofs and steps, women and children mingling with the men, in hubbub, clamour and confusion. For in Carthage, and also in Alexandria, the children play no less a part in such tumults than the men". So he ends a horrible story of the mob's massacre of a king's minister and his family, stripped and done to death in full view of the populace; one of the murders was done by young girls. Under the Ptolemies, and even under the Romans, Jew-hunts were a standard amusement in this city. Perhaps cricket has a humanizing influence, or at least saves us from seeing what we are. The later Ptolemies were not much better in their pleasures than their subjects. A pageant given by Philadelphus, the second Ptolemy, a man with a real taste for art and for literature, is described for us at great length; forty satyrs with golden wreaths, escorting a great statue of Bacchus, pouring wine from a golden goblet, on a car, amid a lot more golden furniture; a statue representing the place Nysa, on another car; more cars still, carrying a huge winepress, a huge bottle made of panther skins, containing 27,000 gallons of wine; women representing cities set free from Persian rule; a god on an elephant; five hundred girls in purple *chitons* with gold belts; elephants, ostriches, camels, negroes; spices, ivory tusks, parrots, a rhinoceros; the royal army; much else, but probably this is enough; and the cost of it all can only be conjectured.

The city itself greatly interested the Greeks. It was a new creation on a new site; a good site, they said, on two seas, the Mediterranean and Lake Maeotis. The overflow of the Nile in summer made it healthy by filling and clearing out the canals, and the Etesian winds from the North or from the sea tempered the heat. The harbour was secure at once from the silt of the Nile and sheltered from the West wind, so that ships had little difficulty in getting in. The city was divided into five quarters called after the first five letters of the alphabet (the Jews lived in *Delta*). It was full of impressive buildings, notably the Gymnasium, with porticoes more than a furlong in length. The streets were on the rectangular plan, and two of them very broad, 90 ft. in width (Main Street, Winnipeg, is 132 ft. wide); one, the Canopic Street, they say, was four miles long, and lit at night—so well lit, that an ancient writer in his enthusiasm calls it "the sun in small change"; oil-lamps only, we remember with something of a start. Broadway, in New York, is many miles long; but the ancient world was impressed with a street four miles long; the cities they knew were much smaller and far more cramped. The palace with the famous Museum and Library ("the bird-cage of the Muses", a satirical epigrammatist labelled it) fronted the sea, and may have covered a quarter of the area of the city. The lighthouse was counted one of the wonders of the world and gave its name *Pharos* to all lighthouses; it was not at all so far from shore as Menelaus in the *Odyssey* tells Telemachus.

In the last thirty or forty years immense discoveries of written papyri have "put new blood into the veins of learning", as a German scholar has phrased it. Certain authors have, as it were, risen from the dead, two of whom might have stayed there without much loss of reputation; but the poems of Bacchylides and the *Logia* (Sayings) of Jesus are real gains. Perhaps little less important is the revelation that our printed texts of Classical authors are substantially what the ancients read in the reign of Augustus; the often maligned "copyists of the Middle Ages" had done their work faithfully, if we concede a certain margin for spelling mistakes and fatigue that all of us may claim. But the German scholar meant something else, and very different. He lays the stress on non-literary finds. Here in a bunch were found the accounts of an Egyptian estate; there a broken collection of family letters; in fact, the papyri include anything that men might wish to write—memoranda, agreements, protests, all sorts of things—covering a stretch of about a thousand years. Much of it is as dull as the average contents of a thousand modern waste paper baskets, if taken in detail; but the whole reveals how people lived, ate, drank, amused themselves, quarrelled, lied, and loved, and hated, in one of the most interesting communities of the world.

Ordinary people without culture, quite commonplace and vulgar—here we find what interested them. A schoolboy writes to his father that he is quite angry that he was not allowed to go with him; another sends a longer letter with a postscript, "Remember our little pigeons". The working man writes to Alis, his wife, to tell her he is still in Alexandria; she mustn't be anxious; he will send some of his pay when he gets it; if the baby turns out to be a boy, keep it; if a girl, throw it out; "how can I forget you? don't be anxious"; and he dates the letter 29th year of Caesar, 23rd day of Pauni (= 1 B.C.). An agent writes wanting money for wages, nails for the gutters, a jar of gum for mending; the hippos have done no damage; and he will see to the boat. A cook's bill gives the day by day expenditure on meat—so many trotters, tongues, kidneys, snouts and breasts. Some one writes to a castanet dancer to engage her, and two more, to perform at his house for six days from the 24th of Pauni (old style), at 36 drachmas a day (a drachma had roughly a dollar's purchasing power; this would be about £7); with rations, so much barley and so many loaves; and the use of two donkeys both ways (one perhaps could walk). A man makes a contract to have his slave taught shorthand for two years; but the last of the money will not be paid till the end, and then only if the boy can write and read from prose of all kinds without blunders. Artemidorus has escorted the princess to the frontier, and is returning; will Zenon buy barley, get the house roofed and take care of the pigs? Sarapion is well; he is going to marry the daughter of Hesperus in the month of Mesore; please send half a *chous* of oil; "P.S. Come for the wedding-day. Apollonius". Another writes to his father: "you tell nothing but lies and your gods the same, for they have plunged us into a deep swamp where we may die; and when you have a vision that we may escape, we go over head and ears (literally: we are baptized)....I can never hold up my head at Tricomia for shame that we have given ourselves away and come a cropper, all through being deceived by the gods, and trusting dreams. Farewell".

It seems that in early days the Greeks and Macedonians

in Egypt fetched wives from the home-lands, at all events married Greeks; but for their children this would obviously be less possible, as every emigrant discovers; and they would marry in the country native Egyptian women. This meant that the upbringing of the children became more and more Egyptian and less Greek. In the three big cities of Egypt it was perhaps illegal for members of the citizen-body to marry natives; but in the country generally it is probable that large numbers who called themselves Greeks were mainly Egyptian in blood. Eurasians in India may be very Indian in blood, but yet cling to their Portuguese names. When Greeks made these mixed marriages, the variety of names in the family betrays it; and, perhaps we might add, the names of which an Egyptian god's name is part, e.g. Isidorus (gift of Isis). It may not be forgotten that the mating of Portuguese with natives was one of the things which weakened the power of Portugal in India.

Alexandria was above all things a centre for Eastern trade. Some part of the goods of the Orient came overland to Antioch in Syria; the sea-borne part came up the Red Sea (as we call it), and was distributed over the Mediterranean from Alexandria. It was, says Strabo about the time of Christ, "the greatest *emporion* of the inhabited world", the greatest gathering-place for merchants and centre of distribution; and he adds that Cleopatra's father, who administered his kingdom in the worst and most careless way, derived 12,500 Talents a year from it. (A Talent = roughly £250, but in purchasing power perhaps five times as much.)

Traders, soldiers, adventurers—Egypt called them all, as Southern Italy had once called them, as America called to Europeans of spirit in the eighteen-fifties. A man is luckless in love; what should he do? And his friend advises, "Ptolemy is the free man's best paymaster. Indulgent too, the Muses' darling, a true lover, the top of good company, knows his friend, and still better his enemy. Many a gift to many a man he gives; refuses nothing he is asked which it befits a King to give; but we must not be always asking. If you have the heart to plant yourself on both feet and stand steady against the bold targeteer that bears down on you, to Egypt with you full speed!" "Egypt", says another, "Egypt is the very home of the goddess. Everything that exists the world over, or ever was, is in Egypt—wealth, wrestling grounds, power, peace, glory, philosophers, cash, young men, the temple of the Brother and Sister gods, the king's a good one, the Museum, wine, everything good you can wish."

C. INDIA AND THE ENDS OF THE EARTH

A curious story is told of the battle of Raphia fought in 217 B.C. between the forces of Ptolemy IV of Egypt and Antiochus of Syria. Only a few of Ptolemy's "beasts" (elephants are meant) ventured to close with those of the enemy. Quite apart from the men in the "towers" on their backs, the elephants engage in battle, forehead to forehead, with tusks interlocked, using all their weight, till one gives way. But most of Ptolemy's elephants were afraid of the battle, as African elephants commonly are; for they cannot stand the smell and the trumpeting of the Indian elephants, and are terrified of their great size and strength, and turn tail and fly. Modern naturalists have told us the Indian are the larger, and that the African cannot be tamed; the latter statement is disproved by now, and the specialists must decide whether North Africa once knew a smaller variety, as some people say.

The Greeks themselves remarked that, though Homer was very familiar with ivory, he seemed never to have heard of the elephant. It was in India that Alexander met them. Porus set two hundred in battle array against him. We read also how pleased Alexander was with the elephant-catchers, and how he took part with them in a capture and added the animals to his army. From this time onward the elephant figures in Europe; Pyrrhus and Hannibal took them into Italy; the Ptolemies caught them in the Sudan; even the Britons at the world's end had a fancy for ivory necklaces, which they imported from Roman Gaul. It is interesting that the driver of the elephant is called an Indian (the *mahout*, as he is named to-day).

The great Empires opened up the world. Through the Persians the Greeks had gained their first knowledge of India, in the curious stories passed from man to man. Such talk centres on strange and unfamiliar things and will get them out of all proportion. Our modern knowledge is very different, and we owe it to men of another stamp, explorers, missionaries, civil servants, men long resident in the country and familiar with its many languages and its famous books; and some of them have high praise for the sobriety and truth of what Herodotus records of India. His tale of ants as large as foxes, from among whose burrows the gold is gathered by adventurers on camel-back, was not his invention; it comes from an old Indian story. Similarly, the anecdote of the young man who first danced on a table and then stood on his head, and so "danced away his bride", appears in

Indian fable, though the dancer there is a peacock. But when Herodotus says that in India it is hottest at dawn, and cooler in the afternoon, he proves to people who have been in India that he had not; it is a deduction from a flat earth and the sun rising over the Eastern edge of it.

Alexander's expedition really linked India to Europe in many ways. The Panjab was part of his empire, and after him fell to Seleucus, in whose reign an ambassador was sent further into the country. Megasthenes went to the court of Sandracottos, in whom to-day Chandragupta is recognized, whose capital is being excavated at Pataliputra (Patna on the Ganges). Megasthenes wrote a book about India, which was widely read and gave the geographers and tellers of marvels most of their matter. If some of it was still fabulous, it represents Indian legend; but his account of the administration of the kingdom is confirmed by an old Sanskrit book. Indeed, a most competent authority says we are more fully informed as to the political and municipal institutions in the reign of Chandragupta than in that of any Indian ruler down to the time when Queen Elizabeth's envoy visited the Great Mogul Akbar. Four hundred years after Megasthenes' day, Arrian drew largely from his book, when he added a still extant supplement on India to his history of Alexander. In time India was lost to the House of Seleucus; but for long a royal dynasty in Bactria to the Northward coined gold coins on the model of those of Alexander and his successors. Greek art made its way Eastward, and the sculptures of Buddha found in the Swat valley, and as far North as Turkestan, make him look more like a Greek god than could have been expected, a most welcome contrast to Indian art.

It is said (but this is disputed; much, however, is disputed in Ancient History that still may be true) that Indian architecture largely derives from Greek, and that stone was not used in building before Alexander's coming. In later days Italians had a hand in art supposed to be Indian, as in the Taj Mahal at Agra. The story of Buddha in turn reached the Greeks; Clement of Alexandria calls him *Boutta*, which, with its doubled T, is nearer the true sound than some English and Americans get to-day; and Buddha's story was later on worked into the strange Christian romance called *Barlaam and Josaphat*. It was not the only book that the author or authors of this work inserted, whole and intact, into their narrative.

But perhaps the most famous voyage to India was that of Thomas the Apostle. It may be doubted whether he ever really went; but his *Acts* tell of his being sold, as a carpenter, to a merchant sailing to India, and of his surprising adventures among princes in that country. Near Madras, in an old church on a hill, they still show a cross carved by St Thomas, with an inscription in a strange tongue round it; but the inscription belongs to a later century than the saint, and so may the cross. The *Acts* belong to the third century, and they contain amazing legends that seemed altogether without rhyme or reason, till it was suggested that the clue lay in the wholesale adaptation of the stories of the Divine Twins of the ancient Indian hymns to Thomas and his twin brother, who, we are told explicitly in these *Acts*, was Jesus Christ himself. The whole story is so fantastic, so alien to all our ideas (and indeed so very unlike those of the New Testament), that many people have refused to believe a word of it.

But whether St Thomas ever went to India or not, there is no doubt that it was perfectly possible for him to go. This does not prove that he did go, any more than the finding of graves at Mycene proves that Agamemnon went to Troy, or the certainty that there once was a King Charlemagne proves that he went on a crusade to Jerusalem. Strabo, in the time of our Lord, tells us that ships would sail from Egypt to India up to the number of one hundred and twenty in a year. In the first chapter we saw how in the Mediterranean, a sea of fitful and irregular winds, Greeks ever kept the shore in sight, and in their longest voyages would seldom go far out of sight of land if they could help it. But about the time of Christ, a Greek sea captain, called Hippalus, realized that at certain seasons of the year a regular steady wind could be counted on that would safely take a ship across the open Indian Ocean, out of sight of land for days together, to the West Coast of India. This wind, which we call the Monsoon, was in compliment to him named Hippalus by the other seafaring men, who used it more and more, and found that, by setting their helms aright, they might make points further and further down the Malabar Coast of India. South of India they found Ceylon, or at least heard it was there, called it Taprobane, and drew it on their maps far larger than it is. Whether by land or sea, they met merchants from China, and silk was more and more used in the Roman Empire, and called *serica* after the *Seres* (Chinese); but people in the West were not very clear where or how the Chinese got it. In the reign of Justinian silk-worm eggs were brought to Constantinople; and the silk industry grew to great importance in later Greece. Roman coins are constantly found in Southern India, sometimes in great quantity. Thus, in October 1915, when foundations were being dug at a cotton factory at Madura, a little parcel of Roman gold coins bearing the heads of Nero and Domitian were found. Their good condition (so very few signs of use being on them) suggests that they may have been buried while the Christian *Revelation*, the last book of the New Testament, was being written in the reign of Domitian. The tiger was familiar to the Romans, an Indian beast, and the giraffe, an animal of Central Africa; and one of the Roman Emperors kept a herd of elephants in Latium, at the place from which Virgil said Turnus came.

Long before this, Herodotus had told of sailors sailing South from Egypt and circumnavigating Africa in about three years. One lie they told which particularly stirred him—that at certain stages they had the sun to the North of them; but the modern sees in a moment that it must have been, if they really went round the Cape of Good Hope, and from Herodotus' comment concludes that this story about the sun was not likely to have been invented.

Finally, to round off our story, old Greek coins are found all through Russia along the routes to the Baltic. Coins of various Greek minting reached Britain, too, and were imitated there; and very curious coins they minted on this island, as the original device of horses and chariot wore down and became unrecognizable to the man who was copying it. None the less the coins tell a story. One more famous voyage remains to be mentioned, but that will come better when we discuss Britain. (See page 320.)

These travels and voyages are not all of one decade or one century; knowledge grew from more to more. In Alexandria there were men who studied all that was brought to them of these new discoveries of sea and land, and they linked them up with astronomy. They had not the implements of the modern astronomer, but they had brains and they used them to some purpose. We saw that Aristarchus of Samos reached the conviction that the sun, not the earth, is the centre; that the earth does the travelling round the sun. They got away altogether from a flat earth, and pictured a sphere, mapped it into zones, hot, cold and temperate, drew latitudes on it (not yet longitudes) and then reached a splendid deduction. Suppose, said Eratosthenes about 250 B.C., you sailed out from Spain, straight out on to the Atlantic, and stuck for ever to the same latitude, you would come to India; only, he implied, the sea is so huge, you would never get across it; for they had calculated not far amiss the circumference of the earth. This suggestion of the voyage from Spain Strabo quoted; and it is worth remembering that Strabo's book was translated into Latin and printed several times before 1492, when Christopher Columbus tried the experiment, and reached what he called the Indies till he died.

D. HELLENISTIC ART

Early in the year 1820 a Greek peasant was digging on the island of Melos and came on a statue in several pieces. It was Aphrodite. What followed makes a curious and complicated story, full of doubts and contradictions. Some French naval officers reported the discovery; and at last the French ambassador at Constantinople proposed to buy it. Someone else had bought it, or thought so, but had not paid for it. In May the Secretary of the French Legation appeared with some force to take it away, which he did, though in the scuffle on the wharf, it is said, the goddess' arms fell into the harbour. Part of the plinth, with the sculptor's name on it, was missing;

Plate V

The Dancing Satyr

but some say it was deliberately knocked off to make the work pass for that of Pheidias. Since May 1821 the statue of the Venus di Milo has been in the Louvre. Probably few statues have been so frequently reproduced in every material and every size; and few can have given so much real happiness to mankind. At one time perhaps the Belvedere Apollo (discovered in the fifteenth century) might have been said to represent Greek art to the world; but he is dethroned by the Venus. Some readers will recall the description of her in Thackeray's *Newcomes*, and how she left Clive Newcome "breathless with the sense of her beauty". The late Bishop Westcott of Durham, the great Cambridge scholar, discussing the relations of pagan and Christian art, speaks of "the pure sovereign majesty of the Aphrodite of Melos, which is worthy to be an ideal of 'woman before the Fall'". "The statue", says a more critical writer of a later date, and rather more coldly, "is not only intelligible from all points of view, but also appears to equal advantage."

In an open court at Pompeii stands the statue of a dancing satyr which is described as "a masterpiece of rhythmic movement". He is snapping his fingers, he tosses his beard in air, his tail curls behind. He is all life and elasticity, he seems unconscious that there is such a thing as physical weight, as if the straining and use of every muscle of his whole body were sheer delight, while he dances and forgets the world and himself. And, again, from whatever angle you look at him, he pleases.

Add to these the famous dying Gaul, a warrior naked, as Gallic warriors were, save for his golden necklet, shock-headed, rough-skinned, wounded with a deadly wound in the chest, dying—noble in every aspect; a monument erected to commemorate a Pergamene victory over the Gauls, but one that, after all these centuries, when the men of Pergamum are all forgotten, makes Celt and Gael proud of their race.

All these works of art belong to centuries after Alexander; each of them, besides the craftsmanship to be seen in every line of them, speaks of the spiritual side of Art; they are interpretations, one feels, of things still alive in our kind, that make human nature seem greater and better than the common run of us suggest; and they are new interpretations. The head of the Aphrodite is said to be *inspired* by work of the fifth century, but she herself belongs to this later Hellenistic age, which English people so rarely study, but to which we owe so much. In the great age they chose other subjects; no boy dragging a goose, then, nor the lad taking the thorn from his foot. But now Art is finding subjects further afield, it has left the temple for the world, and in ordinary things finds new beauty as new sensitiveness develops. The age has lost much, but it is finding compensations, in country scenes and country people, such as the poet Theocritus describes, in a closer and more affectionate study of human nature. The experience was not wholly new; Euripides, it would seem, found peace in the sound and smell of the sea, the call of the sea-birds, and later on in the woods of Macedon; nor is it wholly of the past, for something very like it is written in Wordsworth's *Prelude*—

> The earth
> And common face of Nature spoke to me
> Rememberable things.

Art and Poetry found, like the English poet,

> Once more in man an object of delight,
> Of pure imagination, and of love.

Plate VI

Venus di Milo

Character is found where it was not looked for in the great centuries, it is interpreted, and speaks. The slave becomes a man, and common things interesting. What have trees and flowers to teach me? asked Socrates. This later age began to be able to answer that question. Little of their poetry can be called great; much of it was formal, dull and learned; but they had caught some new secrets, which they told to Virgil; and Virgil's poetry gathered up the discoveries of the Hellenistic age and left them, undying, to mankind.

Bucephalus

Chapter XII

GREEK, ROMAN & CARTHAGINIAN

A. SICILY, CARTHAGE AND PYRRHUS

FROM time to time in this history we have had glimpses of the Carthaginians and their ancestors. Homer speaks of traders from Sidon in Greek waters; shy traffickers, Matthew Arnold calls them; they are not so shy in Homer. They sailed the whole Mediterranean, and at one time they were supposed to be the pioneers of civilization; to-day we are told they were not so much pioneers as middlemen, like the Lydians on land, who lay on the confines of civilized lands and passed on to simpler regions what they learnt or bought from peoples more advanced. Too much may be made of them; thus, when we are told that the habit in some South Sea islands of setting up huge stones (monoliths) must have been introduced by the Phoenicians, we need not at once believe it. Yet there are curious facts that seem to tell of their wide range in seafaring. For instance, they made a purple dye that all mankind admired. Its manufacture was really very simple; a certain shell-fish (the murex) was caught in large numbers, piled in heaps and left to die, and from the dying shell-fish ran the purple liquid. As happens so often when Nature offers an easy way to wealth, the fishing was overdone. In modern times buffalo and seal have been all but exterminated by hunters; and in those days the Phoenicians seem to have over-fished the murex beds, and had to keep moving on and on to find fresh ones. One thing always to be remembered about fish is the depth of water which they like; the depth affects the warmth of the water and the food supply; and the murex liked shallow water. So the Phoenicians have been tracked about the Mediterranean by murex beds and the remains of murex-shell heaps. Another clue, perhaps less certain, is offered by traces of their shrines and peculiar worship.

We have no records of Phoenician settlement in Sicily, but they went there, and at the Western end of the island they long held their ground. In North Africa they planted their most famous city and gave it the most commonplace of names, New Town. Greek and Roman were not expert in foreign names and turned Kirjath Hadeshath into Carchedon or Carthago, which gives us our Carthage. Readers of Virgil remember how Dido founded the town; the ancient commentators said it was founded a hundred years before Rome, and that Virgil's dates and story are all wrong together; but commentators always say this kind of thing. Carthage was Phoenician, Semitic, a nest of traders in North Africa, with a firm foothold in Sicily, something of an empire among the peoples of North Africa and eventually in Spain. They tried to keep the Greeks out of Spanish waters, and to prevent the Romans from finding the sea-route to Britain; and in both endeavours they failed. The Greeks swarmed Westward in numbers too big for them; Carthage was one city and a great one; the Greeks had many cities in Greater Greece, but they could not get the Carthaginians out of their fortress in Western Sicily. Again and again the Greeks of Sicily had to rouse themselves and drive back the Carthaginians in self-defence; the Syracusan tyrants did it best, men (we are told and can believe) of great ability; but until the fortresses were taken, the Carthaginian peril was always there.

About the year 284 B.C., the Greek town of Tarentum on the Southern shore of Italy chose to fall out with Rome; no doubt there were pretexts, but perhaps as real a reason as any was the Roman road reaching South-East into Lucania. Then came the need for help against Rome, and Tarentum sought it from Pyrrhus, king of Epirus. This was all in line with a hundred years of tradition. The Greek tyrants (who might have been called kings) of Syracuse had built up great military states; that of Agathocles extended to regions of the Adriatic; Alexander (scarcely forty years dead) had created an immense empire Eastward; Pyrrhus' own uncle had fought in Southern Italy; and Pyrrhus had moved among kings and princes and princesses, and seen and heard of strange changes. Why should he not build a Greek empire Westward, deal with the barbarian enemies of the Tarentines, cross to Sicily and at last drive out the Phoenicians, and then—other dreams, men say. So he came, and brought with his army strange beasts never seen in Italy—Lucanian cows, the Romans called them, huge creatures with a tail at both ends, which made terrible trumpetings and carried castles on their backs. At first the Roman soldier was scared, but he discovered that the elephants could be wounded with iron and put to flight, to spread disorder in the king's ranks. Pyrrhus won victories over the Romans, but they cost too much; and "Pyrrhic victories" became a proverb. So he tried negotiation.

He had with him a very clever Greek diplomat, old enough to have known something of Demosthenes and the reign of Alexander, familiar too with the courts and kings that, since Alexander's death, had ruled in Macedon, Syria and Egypt. This man he sent to Rome. Cineas was to meet the Roman Senate; he had known all about Greek senates from boyhood, and he expected perhaps a group of chattering busybodies, of no great weight, who might be bribed or bullied. But he found no such thing; he told his master the Roman Senate was "an assembly of many kings"; and the word *king* in those days, when men knew Alexander, and Ptolemy and the rest of the generals now kings, meant more of practical wisdom, political sense and real power than ever before or perhaps since. The "assembly of kings" might listen to Cineas, but a blind old man told them to make no peace with a foreigner in Italy. So Cineas had to go; and ere long Pyrrhus gave up fighting the Italian barbarians, and crossed to Sicily to battle with the Carthaginians, but here too he failed. He left Sicily saying to his friends: "What a wrestling ground we are leaving for the Carthaginians and Romans!" A battle or two more in Italy, and he went back to Greece, a defeated man. All the world knew Pyrrhus and his story, the brilliant happy adventurer, husband of princesses and once king of Macedon itself, "the lucky player who never quite knew how to use his good throws". He and his mercenary troops, the pick of Greek soldiers, had been beaten by tribal levies of a "barbarian" people! All the world knew at once that this barbarian people had, in our modern phrases, arrived, had a place in the sun, and was going to be heard of again. Ptolemy II, king of Egypt, sought relations with Rome; he knew something about Carthage, and he understood Mediterranean politics. Carthage, too, can have had no doubts as to what was coming; and the trouble began, as was foreseen, in Sicily, but far more than Sicily was at stake.

Pyrrhus, once he was gone, the Romans forgave and admired. He was the one figure among their enemies for whom they had something of what moderns might call a romantic feeling, a generous princely foeman. Ennius, the Roman poet (of about 200 B.C.), writes of him, and Cicero quotes "a famous and splendid passage" about the ransoming of prisoners. "I ask not gold for myself," says the king, in the epic, "nor shall ye give me a price. Not shop-keeping but fighting, with iron not with gold, let us settle the war, and whether a man shall live or die. Whether Fortune wills that you shall reign or I, whatever her will, let us find out by our valour. And take thou this word therewith: Whose valour soever the fortune of war has spared, their freedom I am resolved to spare. I give you them; take them away; they are yours with the blessing of the mighty gods." The Latin lines are rough, but most readers will agree with Cicero when he calls it "a royal thought and worthy of his royal race". But Carthage—the Romans never liked Carthage, never respected and never forgave the Carthaginians. Yet among them was a greater than Pyrrhus, the ablest and most brilliant foe that Rome ever met.

B. THE CARTHAGINIAN WARS

In the story of Nelson we read how important to a power with a navy are the islands of Corsica and Sardinia; and Sicily, too, is in the annals of our wars with Napoleon. It was the same Mediterranean on which the Romans looked out; the same winds blew or suddenly dropped; and British and Romans alike used sailing ships. Sardinia was held by Carthage; and Sicily lay between the rival powers. Italy was by now almost entirely Rome's, and its coasts lay at the mercy of Punic fleets with naval bases in these islands. Some years after Pyrrhus left, it was touch and go whether Carthage seized Tarentum. In ancient days a balance of power was never secure; and, whatever the occasion or pretext, Rome and Carthage fell to fighting for control of the Western Mediterranean. Control does not necessarily mean conquest.

Neither side was very clear what to do. A famous historian says there was no war which the Romans managed so wretchedly and with so much vacillation. We have to remember that the Roman scheme of government was really one devised for a canton or a city, and was now applied to a whole country. An annual term of office for Consuls was very well, when a campaign was against neighbours and lasted three days, when the neighbours, too, were much the same sort of people. War, again, was one thing, when the legions could go swinging down a Roman road; but to put an army across the sea, if it is only the Straits of Messina, is not the same thing as to get it across a river, troublesome as that may be. In war, too, it is not enough to carry out successful raids by land or sea, nor to win victories even in great battles; if the beaten enemy gets his forces away, the victory may be of little value. The essential thing is to deal such a blow that there is no recovery. A fight at sea may look like a drawn battle; yet sometimes the side that has the heavier loss and has won no obvious laurels, may have effected so much that the enemy fleet will not leave harbour again in a hurry and will do nothing more. The question is always, Where to strike? And it would seem that the Roman Senate did not know, or wavered. In spite of the story that Rome had hurriedly to model her warships on one of Carthaginian build wrecked on the Italian coast, and to practise her rowers ashore, she was not and never had been without some knowledge of ships as ships. But a ship is not a fleet. The Greek historian, Polybius, says one of Rome's mistakes was "trying violence against sea and sky"—a shrewd phrase; there are things that cannot be done with ships, however important it seems to do them. Sum all this up: uncertainty as to war policy; a new and unfamiliar field of war (the sea); consuls (commanders-in-chief) who held office for a year and might have been elected for any reason rather than military experience, and might know nothing whatever of the sea, or of ships; finally the enlistment of soldiers for one year, after which they might return home, essentially untrained men, of little initiative, more apt to obey orders steadily enough than to think for themselves what to do.

On the other side Carthage was ill-prepared. Rome was a city sovereign among tribes of one blood with herself; Carthage was sovereign over an alien race that hated her. Rome's soldiers were ill-trained and ill-led, but they were of her own people; Carthage's soldiers were mercenaries, well enough for a campaign against other mercenaries, but a dangerous kind of army for their employers. Carthage again suffered from a deep mistrust of her military commanders; the civil authorities were not sure what a general with mercenary troops might do; he might, they feared, suddenly try to make himself despot. We have seen (page 175) how, coming in a dark hour, the Spartan Xanthippos restored the fortunes and the spirit of Carthage; so much, says Polybius, can be done by one man and one man's judgment—and then he left. We shall see Caesar saying something very similar. But the main trouble was that Carthage's most effective weapon, her navy, was not in good order; it had been neglected, as the British navy was in the years before the American revolution—always a fatal thing for a naval power.

We shall not here follow the course of the war which dragged on for twenty-two years, or deal with its battles. Rome won some naval victories, and then attempted an invasion of Africa which was not successful. (Out of it she developed the story of Regulus, the Roman general taken prisoner, and sent to Rome on parole to plead for peace, and pleading against it.) Then came a period of slack and fitful warfare with the loss of fleets. The last period saw the long and unsuccessful siege of the Carthaginian fortress of Lilybaeum in Sicily, till both sides were exhausted. Carthage lost a fleet in 242 B.C., and began to expect fresh trouble in Africa. Both peoples were weary of war; so peace was made. Carthage, after all the centuries of her holding Sicily, gave it up for ever, and agreed to the surrender of the islands between Sicily and Italy, the little volcanic isles. The clause was badly drawn; and when disasters broke upon Carthage, with Africa in revolt and her mercenaries mutinous, Rome chose to say that the islands intended were Corsica and Sardinia, and insisted on having them. Carthage could not refuse them; another war with Rome in the midst of her present troubles was not to be thought of; and she surrendered them. This unjust demand was recognized as one of the main causes of the Second Punic War. Carthage fought through her troubles somehow, and the great Carthaginian house of soldiers, whose head was Hamilcar, began to build her a new empire in Spain, of which the town of Cartagena is still a reminder.

Nearly a quarter of a century passed, and the Second Punic War began. Its story is quite different from that of the First. Carthage had a general of genius this time, with a clear and thought-out plan of campaign, which he intended to carry out, though unsupported at sea, but unhampered by the home government. His plan, reduced to simplest outline, was to march overland into Italy, to get there by swift movement before the Romans could stop him, and then to deal such a series of quick and smashing blows to Roman military prestige that the Italians would revolt in response to his promise to give them freedom again, and in view of the breakdown of Rome. It was a daring design. Let us hear Polybius again; for he is fairer to Rome's enemies than Livy, and a greater historian, nearer the times and more experienced in military and political life all over the Mediterranean. Rome and her allies, he says, had seven hundred thousand men, and seventy thousand cavalry; Hannibal entered Italy with less than twenty thousand; so mighty was the power he came to attack, and so near did he come to achieving his purpose.

"No one", Polybius says, "can withhold admiration for Hannibal's generalship, his courage, and his power in the open field, who remembers how long his invasion lasted, who reflects on his greater and smaller battles, his sieges, his marches, who thinks of his great design, and how he fought the Romans for sixteen years, never broke up his forces or dismissed them from the field, but kept them to-gether under his personal command, without mutiny or quarrels, though his troops were of seven races, peoples differing in laws, customs and language. Yet the genius of the commander kept men so different together, obedient to his sole word of command, submissive to his sole will; and all this, not merely under simple conditions but very complex ones, sometimes with the gale of Fortune with him, sometimes against him. We cannot but admire Hannibal and with reason."

That is well said.

How near did he really come to overthrowing Rome? He won great battles, Trebia, Ticinus, Trasimene, Cannae, one after the other, smashing the Romans in place after place. But he did not break Rome; no, as a late Roman poet wrote, never did Rome give way to loss; no wound made her afraid; after Cannae and the Trebia, her note was greater. Claudian in those lines tells the solid truth. Hannibal was fighting against yeoman farmers, against citizens who were defending their own country, while his troops were of seven foreign races. But the main source of his failure was a miscalculation; some communities in Italy abandoned Rome, Gauls at once and Greeks by and by; but in the main the Italians preferred Rome and her law (as we saw) to freedom offered by an invader and supported by mercenaries. Rome, too, controlled the sea; and, though Hannibal might swoop on to the hills that overlooked the city to attempt to scare the citizens, there was not a chance of his taking it, nor of starving it out while it was fed from the sea. At last, he had to throw up his endeavour, and return to Africa; and the battle of Zama ended his career, his hopes, and the war, and, says Polybius, "gave the world to the Romans".

They pursued the fallen enemy over land and sea, and drove him to death. Perhaps it was better for him than St Helena. After nearly fifty years they made war again upon Carthage, and destroyed the city. Polybius stood

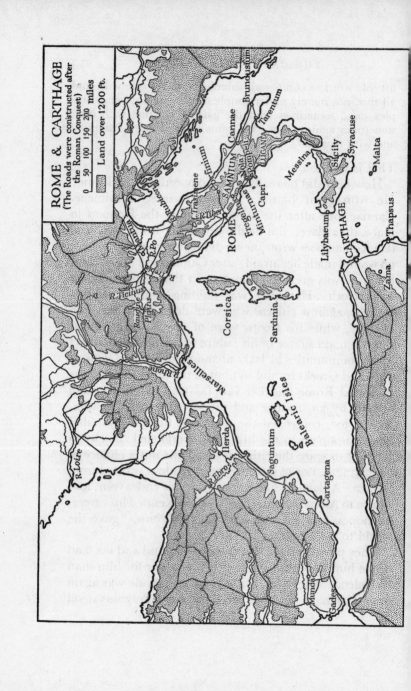

ROME & CARTHAGE

(The Roads were constructed after the Roman Conquest)

0 50 100 150 200 miles

Land over 1200 ft.

R. Loire

R. Rhone

R. Ebro

Ilerda

Saguntum

Balearic Isles

Cartagena

Munda

Gades

Marseilles

R. Ticinus

Placentia

Trebbia

R. Po

R. Rubicon

Corsica

Sardinia

Ariminum

R. Tiber

Trasimene

Clusium

ROME

Fregellae

Minturnae

SAMNITUM

Capri

Compsa

LUCANI

Tarentum

Brundusium

Cannae

Messina

Lilybaeum

Sicily

Syracuse

Malta

Thapsus

CARTHAGE

Zama

by Scipio, the conqueror, as it burned—and you need to see a city burning to understand what it is like, with wooden houses and wooden roofs ablaze, the masses of smoke and glowing ash in the air, the heat and the horror of the galloping flames, and the sense of man's helplessness. As they watched, Scipio turned, and took the Greek's hand, and quoted Homer—

The day shall come when holy Troy shall fall.

"It is glorious, Polybius," he said, "but, I know not how, I am somehow afraid, and I have a foreboding that another hereafter may give the same order about my city."

In the same year Rome destroyed Corinth (146 B.C.); Greek freedom was finished—till 1834; and half the Mediterranean, all the shore lands west of the Aegaean belonged to Rome, and the turn of the East was coming. But here we must look back again.

C. ROME AND THE GREEKS

Yet once more we turn to Polybius, so often quoted. He was born somewhere about the date of the battle of Zama (the end of Hannibal) and he lived to be eighty and to die of a fall from his horse—an active, shrewd, old man, who had lived almost all over the Mediterranean, with Greeks and with Romans. He even did a bit of exploring along the Atlantic coast of Africa. From boyhood he had been among politicians and generals. He kept his eyes open and he saw great changes; but, in the sentence we have so often borrowed from him, it was not so much *what* happened, that interested him, as *why* it happened. The soundest education and training for an active citizen,

276 GREEK, ROMAN AND CARTHAGINIAN

he said, as Oliver Cromwell also suggested, is the study
of History; and at the very beginning of the history, at
which he was busy, off and on, when travel and political
business gave him time, for some fifty years, he sets a
great question. Who is so worthless and lazy as not to
wish to know how, and under what constitution, the
Romans in less than fifty-three years brought nearly the
whole world under their sole rule? There were people
who said human affairs were governed by Fortune; it
was mere chance that set "worlds whomling up and doon,
bleezing wi' a flare", it was accident that raised up one
king or people and brought down another. No, said
Polybius, though he recognized that strange chances
made stranger changes, no, there was a reason for Rome's
predominance. She had a sound constitution, she
managed her military affairs well, she studied the world
that faced her, and her citizens were honest beyond
anything seen in the Greek world, men of affairs, who
studied situations carefully, and genuinely served their
country rather than themselves.

His fifty-two or so years must run from 198 to 146 B.C.
Hannibal was driven from Italy, and Carthage was well
beaten; and Rome looked round. One matter remained
to be settled; Philip V, king of Macedon, had given her
a lot of worry during the war with Hannibal. Perhaps
he gave Hannibal more; for he seemed always likely to
come in and back him; but he never did. So Rome now
called Philip to account, and it was time; he was an
incomparable meddler, who by war, massacre and
treachery, in his futile ambition to be universal king
(Eastward probably), had done ceaseless harm to the
Greek states that remained. The Roman general
Flamininus put an end to all this, by beating Philip in

the battle of Cynoscephalae (197 B.C.); but he left him king in his own country, to prevent Celts and other barbarians from the North invading Mediterranean lands, and to remind Greeks that there were others in the world. He made a great sensation by proclaiming at the Isthmian Games that all Greeks should be free. Wordsworth wrote a sonnet on this, in which he lays his finger on one weak spot. Flamininus made to the Greeks

> A gift of that which is not to be *given*
> By all the blended powers of Earth and Heaven.

Freedom has to be taken, not accepted, as the Greeks knew when they fought the Persians; but by now one of the Successor kings after another would begin his reign (and his manœuvres) by "liberating" the Greeks, in this not unlike the "liberators" in Spanish American republics. Once we read in Polybius of two rival "liberators"—so much liberating did the Greeks take, and so little liberty did it ever give them. It was like the candidate for Parliament promising the millennium to the unemployed; it made no difference.

A very few years passed, and another of the Successor kings engaged Rome. Antiochus "the Great" came conquering from Syria, and went back, beaten at Thermopylae, that famous scene (191 B.C.); he was followed up by the Romans and beaten again at Magnesia in Asia—their first great fight on that continent (189 B.C.). Rome treated him as she had Philip; she cut down his kingdom, gave him a frontier and strengthened the powers between her territory and that of Antiochus. Twenty years later there followed another revelation to the world of what to expect from "the clouds in the West", as a shrewd Greek had put it. Another Antiochus,

Epiphanes this time, decided to invade Egypt and annex it, if he could, for the Ptolemy king was a baby. Rome heard in time. The king was encamped somewhere on his march to Egypt, when he learnt that a Roman Senator had landed and was coming to see him. He met the Roman out of doors; there were the usual courtesies, and an inquiry as to the purpose of his coming. Popillius said bluntly that the Senate wished the king to go home. This was abrupt; but what followed was still more abrupt. The king would consider it and answer. No, said the Roman. He had a stick in his hand—the dignity of History requires us to say a staff, but the common word tells the tale better. With this walking stick he drew a circle round the king's feet; "answer me, before you get out of that". The king went home, and the world was shocked at such a rude way of doing things to kings; but it understood. So did Epiphanes; for he knew that, a few weeks earlier, the Romans had fought and conquered Perseus of Macedon, the son of Philip (168 B.C.), and that the Macedonian kingdom was finished, and he stood next. The small republics and princedoms of Asia did not count, nor the infant Ptolemy.

Again twenty years, and Rome put an end to political freedom in Greece. Corinth was destroyed, and its treasures of art were taken to Rome. Here it is pleasant to read that the Romans used Polybius to draw up plans for the future government of the various Greek city-states, and the comment that, where they took his suggestions, all turned out well.

So in fifty-three years, or nearly, Rome was in control of the world; and it was the luckiest stroke Fortune ever made for the Greeks, that they were knocked over so quickly and so easily. So said Polybius, and no one was more qualified to judge. Who could have foreseen all this? Two generations ago Rome was fighting for her very life against Hannibal in Italy; now Carthage was gone, Macedon was gone, Greek freedom was gone, and Rome was setting up kings in the East and in Egypt, and bringing them to heel with a walking stick. It was offensive, but it deserved explanation, and every reader must try to explain it. The chief of the answers lies in the points already collected from Polybius, and in the immense capacity of the Senate. That "assembly of kings", as Cineas called it a century before, was more royal than ever—royal in an Alexander's sense. The Senate was the real conqueror of Hannibal—the Senate and the steady Roman legionary, that "unknown soldier", on whom falls so much of the cost of every triumph. Everything had come into the hands of the Senate, and they were capable enough. It was recruited from ex-magistrates, generally of families which for a generation or two (or even many) had produced magistrates. There is much to be said, and it is said often enough in a democratic age and in democratic countries, for the canal-boy or rail-splitter who becomes president; there is really more to be said for the boy of ancient and honoured stock who keeps up the family tradition of service to the state; for the Roosevelts rather than the Garfields; there is more background, more tradition; *noblesse oblige*, as people used to say. Such men in Rome became candidates for magistracies, and the people in time weeded out the weaker ones. The Senate was a sort of House of Lords, for which the constituencies picked the better sons as against the merely eldest son. In no other assembly in Rome was real discussion of public business possible, and this is immensely important.

Nowhere else could things be thrashed out as they need to be, if the State is not to suffer from ignorance or haste. Every kind of business came to the Senate—public finance, all contracts for the building of roads, forts or other public works, or for the conveyance, arming or feeding of troops; all diplomatic affairs with foreign powers, terms of peace, alliances, annexations; the raising of troops; the organization of provinces and the appointment of provincial governors; and in some cases courts for special trials were nominated by the Senate.

The assemblies of the Roman people were unhandy for the taking of votes (which had to be done, all the same) and impossible for proper discussion. The mass of the citizens, too, became less and less fit to handle the business of the state; partly, because in Rome they were not the men their fathers had been; partly, because a large part of the citizen body lived outside Rome, more and more of them at greater distances, and very many abroad; and partly, because the business to be done was so much more complicated, and involved so much more particular and special knowledge. What British voter knows, or can know, the issues that concern negroes in Barbados, the gold mines of Kootenay, and the Digambara Jains in India? Yet every British voter has been taught geography at school and reads daily papers full of the latest foreign and imperial telegrams; but the Roman had neither advantage. He was too much the useful solid type that makes good corporals; and he had to rule an Empire which he did not know, and the end was that the Empire ruled him. This may sound like a mere quip, but there are few things in History so amazing as the re-action of the conquered provinces. An imperial people refused to understand its responsibilities, and it lost its liberty as a result.

The eighth chapter of *First Maccabees* gives a vivid picture of the Roman Senate, as it looked to people across the sea—"none of them did ever put on a diadem, neither did they clothe themselves in purple, to be magnified thereby", but "three hundred and twenty men sat in council, consulting alway for the people". The writer rehearses the triumphs of Rome, the conquest of the Gauls (of North Italy), of Spain with its mines of gold and silver, and of "the kings that came against them from the uttermost part of the earth", in particular Philip and Perseus and "Antiochus also the great king of Asia"; "and whomsoever they will to succour and to make kings, these do they make kings; and whomsoever they will they depose".

D. GREEK AND OTHER FOREIGN
INFLUENCES ON ROME

While we ask with Polybius what was the explanation of Rome's unprecedented predominance, all achieved in fifty-two years and some months, we have to note, as he did, some of the results that followed from it. There is nothing in our modern world that answers to it; Britain is not owner of the Dominions and takes no tribute from them. In the ancient world, with the exception of noble old towns like Athens and Sparta, left "free" out of compliment to their ancestors, and, later on, of certain princedoms, priestly and secular, in or near Asia Minor, Rome owned her provinces absolutely and drew capital from them. Some of this was legitimate tribute; but the agents, who collected it, did not always limit themselves to the legitimate tribute, nor did all of that reach Rome. Tiresome, stupid and tyrannous as a civil service may be, we have to recognize that for some kinds of state business a civil service is absolutely necessary; Rome had none, or next to none, till a century or so after Augustus began to reign. She leased the building of public roads, or the feeding and transport of an army, to contractors; then why not the collection of the taxes? She did this, also, and horrible abuses crept in—the utmost was squeezed out of the provincial taxpayers; big profits were made by the contractors, but the state (it is argued) was not much better off.

A new class of financiers rose into importance, known as the Knights (*equites*). Every now and then to-day, as in President Jackson's time in America, a community falls foul of its bankers and its company-promoters, or even of the middlemen in trade; but neither trade nor national business can be carried on without them. A government wants money suddenly (and quite legitimately); where there is a strong banking system, which cannot exist without a reliable government, the money can be supplied quickly; but where there is no faith in the government and little faith in one another among private people, there can be no strong banks. At the same time the organization of capital may alter the balance in a state. Money talks, as people say; and in second-century Rome it came to be talking far too loud. "Capital", said Theodore Roosevelt, "is a good servant, but a mighty poor master."

What the nineteenth century A.D. saw happen in the United States of America, the second century B.C. saw in Rome; certain people, certain classes, grew suddenly rich, and rich beyond all the dreams of their fathers.

War and the spoils of war, the provinces and the spoils of peace, as well as honest business and banking, gave immense wealth to people who had little or no experience of wealth at all. Men need to be used to wealth, as to other things, if they are to handle it with safety. Great wealth, unexpectedly put into the hands of people unaccustomed even to very moderate wealth, is a danger to its possessors, to the people who have to live with them, and sometimes to the state. An old aristocracy, rich in land, may have its drawbacks; but sudden wealth in cash, out of other people's pockets, is very difficult to handle; and so Rome found. What would you do (let us put it directly in the second person) if you quite suddenly became a millionaire? Rome gave various answers to this question, and most of them included eating, dressing, building, and amusing oneself on a scale never heard of in Rome before. Better cooks, larger houses, immense gardens, the multiplication of slaves, luxuries, the theatre, beast-shows, gladiatorial games, consumed a great deal of the new wealth; and it was all (or nearly all) unproductive expenditure; it did not increase productive power; the capital was wasted, and lost to mankind.

Ennius, whom we quoted in Chapter VIII, once wrote in a famous line—

Moribus antiquis stat res Romana virisque.
On men and characters antique Rome stands.

But now the antique character, the hard old citizen virtues, of the grandfathers, are seen no more, or less and less frequently. "Why shouldn't I do it?" says the young man in one of the stage plays of the period. "Why shouldn't I?" And the old man's answer that it will sap your character and injure society, seems very old-fashioned. As Aristotle said of Greece, in a democracy everybody "wants to live as he likes". How is that demand to be answered, when the young man has wealth that will buy him everything? All sorts of people drifted to Rome to help him to spend the money his father had got from the provinces; and his mother and his wife egged him on. Cornelia, the mother of the Gracchi, was quite unfashionable, when she said her sons were her jewels.

Sometimes the effect was an improvement in taste. There were men in this period who set a new fashion in collecting Greek works of art. Plenty were to be had, when a good Greek town was sacked. Polybius, at the sack of Corinth, saw Roman soldiers using one of the most famous pictures of the ancient world to throw dice on. But the Greeks did not like having their pictures, bronzes and sculptures, the work of their great artists, taken from their cities and temples to decorate private houses in Rome or near it. Polybius says that anybody can understand a conqueror taking away capital or munitions, or anything that might make further war or rebellion possible; but pictures are different, and to take them was odious. But the pictures went to Rome all the same. Several times in recent years divers in Greek waters have come on statues, which were being taken to Rome, but the ships were wrecked; and to-day in Athens and Rhodes one may see these beautiful things cleaned from the creatures of the sea, which have incrusted them for over two thousand years. Often the Roman had to be content with copies, of which also we may be glad, when the originals are lost.

Greek books went to Rome, Homer and the plays of Euripides, the writings of Plato and other philosophers; and Romans read them more and more—and this was a great gain for mankind. The conqueror of King Perseus refused any share in the loot of Macedon, with one exception; he took the library of the king for his sons. One of these sons became the intimate and life-long friend of Polybius, Scipio Africanus the younger, the conqueror of Carthage, the centre of a group of very interesting people, among whom were Terence, the Roman dramatist (quoted just now) and certain Greek philosophers. Nearly everything that was good, and that lived, was in this circle.

One instance of the influence of Greek thought is of special significance. In a former chapter we glanced at Roman law. There were various strains or sources of law in Rome. There was the old *civil law*, which embodied the immemorial usages of Rome, but there was also another type of law, or another idea of law. As Rome's rule spread, law-suits rose very naturally, which involved Roman law and with it the law of some very different city; how were they to be settled? Such cases still occur; we can imagine an English ship, carrying wool from the Argentine (the property of a citizen of the Argentine), being run into on the Atlantic by a Greek steamer with an Egyptian's goods; both have to jettison cargo (i.e. to throw part of it overboard) to keep afloat; one is salved, towed to a French port, by a Norwegian ship; the other by a Japanese steamer, and taken to a Spanish port. Now solve these questions; who was responsible for the collision, who pays for the goods jettisoned, who pays the two rescuing steamers (or their owners) for loss of time, etc. and under what law, English, French, Spanish? Roman lawyers had cases where various state codes seemed involved, perhaps at first sight contradictory; and they devised what they called *the law of nations*. They took the rules common to all the states, or to many of them, and saw how far they overlapped, or how far the underlying principles were the same; from this comparison they drew a body of rules for deciding cases such as we have imagined.

In the second century B.C. there came Stoic philosophers to Rome; and the Roman lawyers (the greater ones) found them very congenial minds. The Stoic asked the Roman why he supposed there was so much overlapping among the laws of various states; and he answered it himself. Nature makes all men of the same stuff and the same instincts, and gives them common ideas; these ideas are embodied in the laws of the various states, so that the real foundation of law and justice in any state is the *Law of Nature*. No state perhaps gets quite all of it into the local code; hence the value of the Roman's plan of comparing codes. But Nature says deeper things than any state. To take one case; a slave was sold by a very curious procedure under *civil law*, but like anything else under the *law of nations*; but what does Nature say about slaves? Nothing whatever; Nature knows no slaves. This was startling doctrine and new; but it gradually told, and the Stoic idea of a *Law of Nature* modified and bettered law in Rome through the centuries; and to this day we are debtors to the Greek Stoic and Roman lawyer who exchanged ideas in these friendly discussions. For year by year the Roman praetors, in virtue of their office, issued *edicts*, which may be described as short codes of law by which law cases in the year would be decided. It was a simple way of mending law, in a state, where legislation was so cumbrous; and it served well. The last praetor's edict was issued in A.D. 130, and it kept the name of the praetor of the year, *Edictum*

Salvianum. To describe how Roman law was codified again, till Justinian gave it final shape, lies beyond our limits; but on that great code rests much of modern law in every civilized country of the Western World. English law and Scots law still differ, and the great source of the difference is that Scots law draws far more from the Roman.

A Carthaginian coin

Chapter XIII

A CENTURY OF CHANGE

A. THE DECLINE AND FALL
OF THE REPUBLIC

IN 31 B.C. Augustus (as he was soon to be called) won the battle of Actium, which left him unchallenged master of the Roman world. Four years later he "restored the republic", as he put it, and as he wished men to believe; thenceforward he reigned till the end of his life. The date of the end of the republic it might thus be difficult to decide, if it mattered. The beginning of the end was a hundred years before the battle of Actium; and for a century Rome knew little but the alternation of experiment, reaction, and civil war, with a growing feeling that a great change must come. It is a world, as Virgil pictures it,

> Where wrong and right are blent,
> A world that teems with war, a world that reeks
> With countless crime, where evermore the plough
> Lacks its due honour, and the hind is forced
> Far from his desolate fields, and reaping-hooks
> Are straightened into swords.

Several factors were early recognized in the gradual break-down of the republic. Agriculture in Italy was being replaced by cattle-ranching, and the native free Italian farmers by foreign slave cowboys. There was growing indignation among the Italians at their exclusion from the rights of Roman citizenship; the public assemblies of the Roman people were becoming a farce. The great mass of the citizens were by now spread over Italy; thousands of them were always overseas, in trade or in the army. The inhabitants of the country towns North and South, and the citizens abroad, could obviously not come much to Rome to take part in elections or in legislation. The Assemblies of the Roman People accordingly came to be in the main mere gatherings of the least Roman of the burgess-roll, the town rabble, of the most mixed origins, slave and free. The Senate was losing its *morale*, and was less and less to be trusted; its great days were over, and its competence and even its honesty began to be doubted. Meanwhile the task of government became more and more complicated, as province after province, race after race, was added to the Empire, and every addition meant a new frontier and fresh enemies beyond it, save where the frontier was the Sahara or the Atlantic. That the republic broke down is less surprising than that it lasted so long. To bring it to an end, a combination of certain things was needed; there must be a man who controlled an army, a man who might reasonably be trusted by quiet people, a man who had the insight to see what the state wanted and the genius to do it. This combination was found in Caesar, and by a strange good fortune once again, in large measure, in his nephew Augustus. It is difficult to imagine the strain with which good citizens watched the break-up of their institutions; but the relief with which the world accepted Augustus gives some measure of it.

B. AGRICULTURE AND THE GRACCHI;
EXPERIMENTS IN GOVERNMENT

Tiberius Gracchus, a young Roman of noble origin, found with some consternation that the men he met on the country roads of Etruria spoke no Latin, and that it was much the same over large parts of Italy. The population had changed, and danger was easily to be foreseen. The Italian farmer and his family were being replaced by foreign slaves; Italy, like New England, saw her own people move out, and die out, while foreigners, of strange tongues, traditions and religions, took their place. But if this process went beyond a certain point, what would become of a country, where homes and children were no more, and slave-barracks or slave-prisons were the only habitations? Of course it will be said, it was not so bad as this; alarmists are always wrong; there is always enough evidence on both sides of a question to enable you with good conscience to do nothing. No, it was not yet so bad; but what was to stop it becoming so? "There is a lot of ruin in a nation", said Adam Smith; yet nations do come to ruin.

It was not a new question. Hannibal and his army had maintained themselves in Italy for a dozen years or so, at the cost of the Italian population. Analyse that sentence, and it means that his troops consumed the food, destroyed the property, mishandled the people, and left ruin and death behind them in many places, and in all devastation and something like despair. It is despair that kills a countryside. "Let the Astrologer", wrote John Milton, "be dismay'd at the portentous blaze of Comets, I shall believe there cannot be a more ill-boding sign to a Nation than when the Inhabitants are inforc'd by heaps to forsake their Native Country." And this befel in Italy. Roman vengeance on disloyal areas made things worse; life in Rome, in the army, in business in the oversea provinces, grew more attractive; more and more Rome got her food from abroad. Cheaper and more abundant wheat came from Sicily and, by and by, from Egypt; for, as we have seen, transport by sea is generally cheaper than by land; an extra thousand miles by sea, experts tell us, adds comparatively little to the cost; and in Sicily and Egypt there was (what in modern phrase we may call) mass-production of wheat. The passion for big estates in Italy led Roman nobles, we are told, to acts like Ahab's, in clearing Naboth out of his vineyard; the dispossessed no doubt, if they were foolish enough, might go to law, but they had better go to Rome or the provinces. Cattle-raising began to replace wheat-growing; and English farmers bid us remember that "to make a field may break a man, to break a field may make a man". The slave-market supplied the cowboys, and they made the countryside still less pleasant for the honest farmer people. Altogether, as we are told, it was fewness of numbers that overtook the Italians, a "failure of the man-crop".

Tiberius Gracchus gave his mind to it, and his purpose was "not production of wheat but production of men", to re-establish farming and farm-houses and farmers' families. He found no sympathy among the land-owners and the Senate, which we can perhaps understand; young men in a hurry have much to learn. However, if the Senate would do nothing, he would go to the Assembly. It was the rule—the established practice, but *not* the law—that nothing should be put before the Assembly without the previous approval of the Senate.

Tiberius hoped nothing now from the Senate, so he availed himself of the law, and made proposals for allotments to Roman citizens. This meant that the State should take back for this purpose lands which indeed were State property, but had been, often for many years, held by the big land-owners. The lands did not *belong* to the occupants, but it had come to be understood that they would never be disturbed in their occupation of them; and they were freely bought and sold, even with this tacit reservation of State rights. Gracchus proposed some compensation for them; but the taking of the lands at all seemed outrageous interference with honest people. A fellow-tribune was put up to veto further procedure with Gracchus' proposals;—Gracchus had chosen to be strictly legal; this veto was strictly legal; and there was an end to Gracchus and his meddling. Not quite, said Gracchus; and he proposed the "recall", as Americans name it to-day, of the hostile tribune; he should be deposed. To this point democratic government has had to come to-day; to secure the people's will, the people must be able to "recall" its own elected if the elected representatives frustrate, or misconstrue, the people's will. It is a dangerous doctrine, but it may at times be necessary. It has often been said that this act of Gracchus, the deposition of his colleague by popular vote of the Comitia Tributa, was illegal, unconstitutional and revolutionary. It may be questioned whether a thing is illegal which has never been seriously discussed nor decided; "unconstitutional" is of course a vague word; and "revolutionary" is vaguer still; but it was a hint at least of great changes that might come. However, whether the Assembly was entitled by law to depose its tribune or not, it did it; and Gracchus' laws were carried.

When Tiberius sought re-election as Tribune for the next year, the question was raised whether this was legal. Excitement grew intense in Rome; it was proposed that the Senate should pass the famous resolution that the magistrates "see to it that the State take no harm"; but only a consul could move that resolution, and the consul Scaevola was a lawyer; he hesitated. Others did not hesitate; and, led by a hot-head, they dashed from the session of the Senate, and found Tiberius; they clubbed him to death, and threw his body into the Tiber. Three hundred of his followers died with him (133 B.C.).

Nine years later his brother Gaius took up his work. Gaius was an abler man, a clearer thinker, and one of Rome's greatest orators. Looking at his laws we find (as usual in legislation) that some dealt with his great objects, others with the obstacles in his way. The chief obstacle was the Senate, and his aim was to weaken it. By one law he tied the hands of the Senate; the citizen should have the right of appeal against a death sentence to the Assembly; the Senate should appoint no more special judicial commissions such as tried and condemned his brother's adherents. He had next to make sure of allies against the Senate. He got laws passed establishing a system of wheat-purchase by the State, to secure the poor against the risks of famine or of extortion by dealers (a popular law, and a good one in itself, but liable, as time showed, to dreadful abuse as a precedent); transferring certain law courts from the wicked Senators to the Knights; arranging for a lease of the taxes of the new province of Asia to financial companies. The last two measures were defensible enough in the abstract, but they also served to give him the backing of the financial classes against the Senate. Then he renewed his brother's laws as to land-allotments, and proposed oversea colonies in addition, one to be at Carthage. But his time was running out. His views in favour of enfranchising the Italians were not popular. And once again violent death overtook a Gracchus.

"He died the death", says a modern scholar, "of the pseudo-reformers of this period." The name Gracchus became a proverb for revolution. "Who", asks a Roman satirist, "will stand a Gracchus complaining of sedition?" When all such language is duly weighed, we find that Julius Caesar adopted and developed nearly all that Gaius Gracchus did or proposed. He regulated wheat prices, assigned land-allotments, founded oversea colonies, extended Roman franchise. When the greatest political genius of Rome repeats a man's acts and re-affirms his ideas, we may be less ready with sweeping condemnation of the man as a mere demagogue and pseudo-reformer. But that is not all. A striking phrase is used by the Greek biographer of Gaius Gracchus— "a certain monarchic power had grown up about him". Monarchic—not in the old English royalist sense, but in the Greek and philosophical sense of the word. Gaius made the first real experiment in Rome of the rule of one man. He meant, it would appear, to be tribune in successive years, and, supported by Knights and commons, to carry out the reforms that Rome sorely needed. But his foundations were not strong enough; more was needed than popular goodwill. The Senators saw clearly enough that his continuance in power meant the end of their rule; and his death restored it.

They governed badly. A Berber prince in North Africa, Jugurtha by name, gave a lot of trouble; however hemmed in, he always escaped; Roman troops could never catch him; but why? men asked. Because, they answered one another, he simply bribes the noble generals we send against him. Had he not, men said, described Rome as "a city for sale, and soon to perish, if it can find a purchaser"? A commission had to be appointed to look into these charges against the Roman commanders; but people said their report was so much whitewash; what was wanted was a real general, who would not be bribed. Marius became consul, a "new man", no noble, a man of the people; and the Jugurthan war was soon over. Meanwhile barbarians, Teutons and Cimbrians, had come over the Alps in a huge migration; and again and again the aristocratic generals were defeated by them, and discreditably too. A war of revolted and runaway slaves dragged on in Sicily. Pirates swarmed about the sea and did what they liked. On the Black Sea a hereditary half-barbarian king, Mithradates, was building up a great empire. Incompetence all round marked the rule of the restored Senate, and danger every day to Italy and the Roman people.

Once again the Roman people acted. Contrary to all precedent, they kept Marius consul year after year. After an interval spent in harrying Spain, the barbarians moved Eastward; and Marius, with his Roman army, remodelled and properly trained at last, cut them up in two great battles at Aix in Southern France (102), and on the Raudine plains in Northern Italy (101); and the peril was past. It was not monarchy in the nineteenth-century sense; but the six consulships spelled the failure of the old system of successive commands and of Senatorial control; they showed that men began to feel the need of an effective brain to organize and control government. The Empire was by now too big, and too complicated, to be ruled by a degenerate Senate, without the intelligence to realize a whole world and its needs at once, and without the public spirit that had saved Rome so often in earlier days. The Senate was doomed; but when Marius tried his hand in politics, he failed disastrously. He made it clear that, if there was to be a "monarchic" ruler, that ruler must have, in addition to military glory, some real political capacity. The Senate had a fresh lease of power, but not a long one.

But a word must be given to Marius' army reforms. Briefly, he re-arranged the legion in ten cohorts; he enlisted all and sundry, "paupers" included, without reserve as to social rank; and he developed drill. Every soldier should be a swordsman, every cohort a unit and efficient. Three things are to be noted. The Roman legion became a more effective tool than ever, as his victories showed. But the new recruits had little civic feeling; it was soon clear they did not think much about constitutional government; they were soldiers rather than citizens. Lastly, the silver eagle, which Marius gave as a standard to each legion, marked the final democratization of the army; but within a century (indeed much less) it meant something else. "Rome's standards and the people's—till the battle of Pharsalus", wrote a Roman poet. There the eagle became the standard of Caesar, and so it remained. Kaiserdom, Tsardom, Napoleon, all used the eagle as an imperial symbol; and now, oddly enough, whether taken from Washington's arms or from Austrian imperial dollars, the eagle has become republican again in the United States of America. If the Austrian dollars are the source, it is the very eagle of Marius.

C. THE ITALIAN QUESTION

For something like a century the Italians had been ambitious to receive the full Roman citizenship, instead of the half measure they had. They provided more than half of Rome's armies; but they were excluded from magistracies and from the Senate; they had no part in governing provinces and in the wealth that came from such government; they had no share in shaping national policy. For Italy was a nation or on the way to becoming one, as Pyrrhus and Hannibal in turn had discovered. There were also personal immunities which made the full citizenship desirable. But there was a dullness and a jealousy prevalent that barred their claim. The more enlightened Romans admitted it; but to advocate this Italian claim was to ask for death. Scipio Africanus the younger had been the champion of the Italians, and was murdered. Gaius Gracchus had proposed enfranchisement of the Italians, and was murdered. Marius, indeed, on the defeat of the barbarians had conferred the citizenship on two Italian cohorts; and when he was told it was illegal, he had said that the noise of battle was so great, that he could not hear the laws. From time to time there had been anti-Italian laws and measures. A premature uprising by the town of Fregellae in 125 had been ruthlessly crushed. But at last, when in 90 Drusus, who once more attempted legislation on their behalf, was murdered, the Italians rose, and civil war followed (90 B.C.).

The Italians fought, says Cicero, "not to deprive us of the citizenship but that they might be received into the citizen roll". Failing that, they would have a new Rome of their own, a federal capital. There are not many records of attempts made at federalism in ancient times: the Achaean league is the most famous, and deservedly so. But this Italian scheme deserves notice for its curious anticipation of federalism in the British Empire. The Italians chose for their capital a fortress town, with no very noticeable history, Corfinium, and they re-named it Italica (or Italia); the Canadians chose "the lumber village nearest the North pole", as a satirist put it, actually By-town, an obscure place (named from a British Colonel By), and re-named it Ottawa from the river on which it was to be; the Australians took a new place altogether. Two languages prevailed among the Italians, Latin and Oscan; both were to be freely used, like French and English at Ottawa, English and Dutch in South Africa. In general the constitution was a copy of the Roman, but it had no long life or development.

For a year's hard fighting showed the Romans their mistake, and some clever legislation ended the war. One law gave full citizenship to every Latin or allied state that had not taken up arms; another gave it to any individual citizen or resident of *any* state in Italy, domiciled in Italy, who would apply for it in sixty days; a third enabled a Roman magistrate in the field to confer citizenship where he saw fit—a simple but efficient device to detach troops from the revolted armies on the eve of battle. Fighting went on in Samnium; but the war was over, and Corfinium was no longer a capital. Rome, so to put it, had become the competing "Italica". Citizenship had been gained, but not federalism (89 B.C.).

This victory for Italian citizenship is signal indeed; but perhaps equally signal is the fact that, though now the citizen body comprised a population spread from the Rubicon to the Straits of Messina, the Roman constitution was not changed. All the elections took place in Rome; to vote for tribune or consul, the Italian must go to Rome. It is as if in Britain no vote could be recorded except by personal attendance in Trafalgar Square. There was no dream of a representative system. The Roman constitution had for generations been less and less fit for its purpose. Originally the system of a clan, or (if the stories of *plebs* and tribunate be trusted) of *two* clans, it had been possible and workable, by good sense and conciliation, in a city. But every extension of territory meant greater distances to be covered by voters, and, more and more, the non-attendance of voters; that is to say, the Assemblies held in the city contained ever a smaller proportion of the citizens. The admission of practically all Italy to citizenship meant again a reduction in that proportion; it meant that no Assembly ever really represented the "people", nothing but a mere fraction of them. Magistrates were elected as before, and laws passed, by the same Assemblies—technically Assemblies of the People, in reality anything but that. The constitution was by now a mockery. But a Roman manoeuvre made it worse. Every citizen was assigned to one or other of thirty-five "Tribes", distantly like our constituencies; for each tribe voted as a unit when legislation was proposed. Now a Roman law packed all the Italians into *eight* of these tribes; there could thus rarely if ever be a decision taken in which the Italian vote could count; the old citizens held a permanent majority. It was what in America has been called a "gerrymander", an arrangement of constituency borders to secure a safe result. Suppose, if it is not too fanciful, that on the extension of the suffrage to women, Parliament to neutralize the concession had enacted that women voters should be enrolled, whatever their actual domicile, in the Cornish constituencies; it would have produced the same effect —the irritation of a concession neutralized by a dodge.

The extension of the Roman citizenship, with the "gerrymander" that followed, weakened the Republic. The coolness, to give it no worse name, between Rome and the Italians continued. The Italians had as individuals citizen-rights; but what loyalty could be expected to such a constitution, so monstrously out of key with all realities, once a genuine thing but now unreal; or to magistrates and laws deriving their power from a mere section? The addition of the Plebeians in the old days had reinforced the government; this much greater addition of citizens could only destroy its credit. When the later civil wars followed, there was no real reason for the Italians to take up arms for a constitution which deprived them of any real voice in government; why should an Italian be hot for the rights of the Roman Senate or the Roman mob? Virgil, in many ways a most representative Italian, is frankly for the Caesars; he came from Cisalpine Gaul, and from the North side of the Po; and till Caesar crossed the Rubicon, Latin rights were all that the men North of the Po had; they owed their full Roman citizenship to Caesar, who thus re-affirms Gracchan statesmanship.

D. THE GREAT REACTION AND ITS FAILURE

But peace did not last long. In 88 B.C. a proposal was made to redress the wrong done to the Italians and to distribute them more equitably over the "Tribes". At the same time a popular vote transferred the command in the war against Mithradates from Sulla to Marius.

For, when Italy rose against Rome, Asia rose too.
A massacre of (it is said) 80,000 Romans and Italians
took place, and Mithradates became master of most of
Asia Minor, including the Roman province, and, before
long, of Greece too, where also rebellion flared up.

Sulla was at Nola, encamped with the army he was to
take to the East. He announced to them his deposition;
they could draw their own conclusions. The soldiers
elected, as he intended, to follow him to Rome, to cancel
the transfer, and to secure the expedition for themselves.
It is to be remarked that most of the officers refused to
go with the troops—an indication, at least, that the
motive of Sulla was not taken by them to be the more or
less honourable one of giving a real constitution or something like order to a disordered state; he is not the
"saviour of his country", he is an adventurer striking
for his own hand. It was a new thing in Roman history
for a Roman to lead Romans against Rome.

Sulla duly drove his enemies out of Rome, and published a list of persons whom he wished to have murdered.
This also was a new precedent. Men long remembered
the story of the hunted Marius—in the swamps of
Minturnae—in the jail, when the Cimbric slave (his old
captive) was sent to kill him and feared to do it—and
among the ruins of Carthage. Sulla arranged for the
government of Rome and left Italy for the East, to fight
the armies of Mithradates in Greece, and to recapture
Athens. At once his enemies returned to Rome, and
Marius had the seventh consulship which the prophetess
had promised him, and very soon died—a great man for
all the savage half-madness of his last few months, and
reckoned by Virgil (as Sulla was not) among the glories
of Italy.

In Greece Sulla had a hard fight, but at last he took Athens. He made a sort of peace with Mithradates, assigned him frontiers and took an indemnity from him. But from the Roman province of Asia Minor he exacted ten times as much. Then he returned to Italy; but it is well to look at what he left behind him. Mithradates recovered from his defeat and the loss of Greece which had never been his. Asia Minor did not recover, till the Roman Empire gave the country peace and good government. The Asian massacres may be cited in defence of Sulla ruining the communities; but it remains that he failed to complete the reduction of the enemy. Brutal vengeance and inconclusive work are his record in Asia; and in Rome it was little else.

He fought his way into Rome, massacred his victims in cold blood, and set up a revised constitution. His object was to secure the Senate in its government of the Roman world, and protect it against all who might threaten it. There was to be no more legislation by revolutionary tribunes. To put tribunes for ever out of action, he enacted that no man who had once been tribune might stand for a higher magistracy; that would keep energetic and ambitious men out of the tribunate, and the tribunate in futile hands could do no more harm. But he realized that higher magistrates than the tribunes might menace the power of the Senate—men like Marius, or like Sulla himself. So laws were carried to prevent it; no man might heap up consulates like Marius; a slow upward ascent with intervals was decreed for magistrates. The financial class, the enemies of the Senate, were deprived of their control of the law courts. Various comments are made on all this. Sir Richard Jebb did what he could for Sulla, who "made the best on his own principles of an almost desperate situation", who "built the fortress, but he could not answer for the garrison". No, for there was an enemy outside with golden bullets; organized capital was ranged against his constitution; and how many of the Romans really were for it? It lasted till Sulla died; and then it began at once to crumble. The election of Pompey to the consulship marked the end. Pompey's career, far more than any idea of his own, was fatal to Sulla's constitution. He extorted a triumph in his youth from Sulla, though he was not a magistrate and not entitled to one; he was sent against Sertorius in Spain, though still no magistrate, for a soldier was needed and there was none whom men really trusted so well; and his first actual magistracy was this consulship in 70 B.C. Once consul, he let legislation go through that restored the tribunate to its old powers. It was as though another Sulla had Rome in his hand; but Pompey was no Sulla—a better but a weaker man.

The great German historian of Rome has another comment on Sulla's work; it contained "not a single new idea of statesmanship". We have seen Rome grow from a city to a country, a national state covering a land six hundred miles long, and ruled by an ancient constitution, good enough for a canton, possible for a city, absurd for a country. But the city ruled an Empire and controlled the politics of the Mediterranean; provinces East and West and South had to be administered; the machinery was obsolete, the finance was outrageous, the government was bad. (There is never trouble on the scale of the Asian massacre without cause.) In short, the whole aspect of the world has changed; and Sulla thinks that the Roman world can be ruled by the Senate that fought Pyrrhus. Perhaps it could have been; but that assemblage of many kings had been dead nearly two centuries. To quote once more the line of Ennius, "on men, and on character of the old stamp, the Roman commonweal stands". The old type of character was gone; there were not the men; all was changed; and Sulla had no single new idea of statesmanship. His work recognizes nothing; it is not creative. No one needed it, and it passed.

E. CICERO

It has often been remarked that the historian Thucydides, in writing the history of Athens, ignores most of the politicians. In this he reached the point of view that posterity would take. In that respect his example has been followed in these pages, where the endeavour has been made to show the Roman Republic, rocking (as it were) on its base, steadied a little, and then set swaying again; it fell, and posterity is content to forget most of the men whose actions and whose characters brought it down. The Gracchi were men of ideas; Marius was a man indeed, and had a career increasingly picturesque; Sulla concerns us no more than any other reactionary who for a while is successful. All of these, with Pompey and others, play their part in bringing about the great change from republic to empire; the movement is more interesting than any of them. It is one of the great illuminative changes in History, and deserves the deepest study.

But among the men of the time, who, for their day, caught the public eye, or who really contributed to shaping events, there are two who counted far more with later ages even than with their contemporaries—formative men, who shaped the thinking of generations for centuries, whose influence is still upon us. It will not be debated here, though it is an arguable question, whether Caesar or Cicero had more effect, more control upon the minds of men. All action is the outcome of thought and belief; what you think, and sometimes the way in which you think it, shapes your life; make a community, a nation, think certain things, or think them in a particular way, and you have shaped its story. Darwin has done more than propound a few theories, right or wrong, about human origins; he has given three generations the mould for their thoughts. To Caesar the next chapter in this History belongs; here we have to think of Cicero.

Cicero's is a curious story, in life and after death. Men despised him in life because he was a "new man", self-made (as moderns say), a middle-class person from a country town, and not of noble stock. They despised him as a man who made his career by his talents; without any great wealth; a pleader; a man of words and books; a man who, from timidity or from conscience, seemed uncertain of his political course. Moderns of coarse texture have despised him, as they have despised Jeremiah, because they have had access to intimate records of his mind. His letters were published, masses of them, by his secretary after his death; and those which he wrote to his friend, Atticus, for no eyes but those of Atticus, reveal a temperament highly sensitive, destined (some would say) to fail in days of revolution; he feels the horror of the times too acutely, he loves the old traditions of the Republic too intensely, he hesitates between two parties neither of which he trusts. He is too facile, his critics say, speaks too easily, writes too quickly, hardly thinks deeply enough, foresees the future as little as the rest of us; all of which may be true, to some extent. Some have not shrunk from calling him insincere, and a great German brutally, and rather foolishly, labelled him a journalist.

That Cicero was however a real power in Rome and in Italy is shown by Caesar, the shrewdest judge of those days, when he was not called on to suspect treachery in his friends. Caesar, says Plutarch, "continued to show him honour and kindness, and praised Cicero's eloquence and his life as resembling that of Pericles and Theramenes. Further, when Q. Ligarius, an enemy of Caesar, was being prosecuted, and Cicero appeared for him: 'Ligarius is a rascal, condemned already,' said Caesar, 'but why not, after all this time, *hear* Cicero?' But when Cicero was speaking, Caesar's face kept changing colour, and it was plain that the emotions of his soul were all stirred. At last when Cicero touched on the campaign of Pharsalus, Caesar was so deeply affected that he trembled, and dropped some of his papers. At any rate he acquitted Ligarius, as if compelled to do so". More than once Caesar made overtures to Cicero for his support. Thus, after he crossed the Rubicon, he wrote to Cicero: "Above all I beg of you, since I trust I am shortly to reach Rome, that I may see you there, and be able to avail myself of your advice, your influence, your high character, your help in everything". Discount such a document as we may, it shows that Caesar knew that Cicero counted; that honest men all over Italy were looking to see what course would be followed by a man of genius, known to be patriotic and honest.

Few of the ancients lacked faults; and Cicero had the defects of his qualities. Ambitious and nervous, he was accused of "trimming"; but, for all the doubts and fears to which he was open, he had moral courage, as his stand at the last, his campaign against Antony, reveals. He had a genius for friendship, and conceded perhaps too much to his friends. He loved young men, clever young men above all, and generally over-estimated them (a rather lovable fault in a great man), and he wrote them delightful letters. Nobody in the ancient world wrote letters with the liveliness and charm of Cicero, perhaps nobody in the modern world; and the charm of the letters is that they so clearly reveal the man writing them, in all his mind and in all his moods. You might say he never wrote a clumsy sentence. Like all the great letter-writers, he seems to see the man to whom he writes, and talks with him. The same grace is in his other writings.

He wrote a great deal beside letters and speeches— books on oratory and on philosophy. A quiet laugh at himself in a letter to Atticus has been used to dismiss these books as of little account. "They are copies [from Greek originals]," he says; "they don't cost me much trouble; all I supply is, words;—and I have plenty of them!" Plenty of them! A man's laughing criticism of himself may not be the final judgment the world passes on him. Another quotation will show something else. Four centuries or so after Cicero's death, St Augustine, as a young man, came on one of Cicero's books, the *Hortensius*, now lost; he repeats a conventional judgment on Cicero and then gives his own personal experience—"a book of Cicero, whose tongue nearly all men admire, but his heart not so much. That book changed my mind, it changed my prayers to Thee, O Lord, and made my petitions and desires quite other than they had been. Of a sudden every vain hope became cheap for me, and I yearned for the immortality of wisdom, with an incredible surge of heart, and I began to 'rise that I might return' to Thee". No man in a good dozen centuries did more for mankind than St Augustine, and he owes the beginning of his thinking life to Cicero. So did hundreds of readers for centuries.

Cicero introduced Western minds to Greek thought, "supplying the words", and beautiful words. He is one of the great factors in training the West to think, for centuries—a real contribution. He is also the first non-Greek, and the first man of affairs, whose re-action to Greek ideas we know—again, an important contribution in both ways. Ideas have to be tested by life; and here is a man, who has lived a large and full life in a great community in an age of appalling difficulty, and who gives us his judgment upon Greek thinking. It may not be a final judgment, it will not be; but it is a judgment and a serious one. He gave the West a philosophic language in which to think; for all men in the West he created ideals of writing, of handling ideas, of style and order, and so forth, so that whoever writes a good sentence in French or English owes something to Cicero. "Ciceronian prose is practically the prose of the human race."

From a bust of Cicero

Chapter XIV

CAESAR AND AUGUSTUS

A. CAESAR AND POMPEY

SOMETIMES a stray fancy may suggest some real thought more quickly and securely than a deliberate judgment might. Suppose the reader of this book, with some knowledge of European history and some acquaintance with the great words of the centuries, were transported back to Rome in 80 B.C., and put this to an intelligent Roman: "For centuries the greatest men in all Europe, in the greatest and most intelligent races, yet to be developed, will take to themselves as their supremest title the name of a Roman now living, whom we saw to-day on the streets"; would it not be almost certain that the answer would have been: "Sulla"? Ten years later, or even twenty, it would have been: "Pompey". To our ears Pompey Wilhelm or Sulla Nicholas is merely ludicrous; Kaiser and Tsar wake no laughter, they suggest an immense vista of history. At this very day King George is Caesar—Kaisar-i-Hind. Once more, as Polybius said, the interesting thing about history is not *what* happened, but *why*. *Why* did *Caesar* come to be a name so significant for a thousand years and more of modern history, from Charlemagne to George V?

To answer this question in a word—because he realized the world in which he lived, the great changes that the extension of the Empire had made, and the need for a real government; because, so realizing the world's conditions, he was able, in virtue of supreme gifts as soldier and statesman, to give the world what it actually needed, to lay down the lines on which it was to be governed, and, in fact, to be better governed than by far the largest part of it had ever been governed before or much of it has ever been governed since; because he gave the world peace and order, made it possible for the outrages committed during two centuries by kings and demagogues and soldiers to be healed, and did all this with the minimum of bloodshed; because, Roman as he was, he thought (like "a lover of Alexander", as they describe him) in terms of humanity.

Legend or anecdote grew in abundance about his youth. In the bad days of Sulla's tyranny, for instance, he refused at the dictator's bidding to divorce his wife (the daughter of a man once foremost among Sulla's enemies); he would marry or divorce as pleased himself; it was a domestic matter. This got his name on the list of the proscribed, to be murdered. Friends begged him off—he was so young; Sulla consented but shook his head, "he saw many Mariuses in that young man". If Sulla said this, it was a rare example, in his case, of insight. Then again, when Caesar voyaged East, he was captured by pirates; and when they fixed his ransom, "No," said Caesar, "I am worth more than that"; and men told the story of his living with his captors and airily telling them his plans; on his release he would charter a ship, and himself catch *them*; it would be the end of their piracies, too, for he would crucify them; and it all came true. So early he showed himself what the poet Lucan described, "Caesar, whose way it was to hazard all on a throw".

His great rival Pompey became a consecrated legend, afraid of his own reputation, anxious as to men's opinion, irresolute. The anxious, says a German scholar, are always egoists; and so was Pompey, and his nervousness led him astray. Thus, to anticipate an event or two—in the civil war, Pompey's troops defeated Caesar's at Petra; but that was all; and Caesar's comment was: "To-day the victory was in the enemy's hands, if they had had the victor". It was a defeat for Caesar, but it did not lose him the war; the enemy did not know what to do with their victory. Indeed, they lost by it; for Pompey let his people kill the prisoners; Caesar's rule had been to let them go. Of course some of the men whom Caesar released would fight against him again, and they did; "let them!" was Caesar's attitude, and his clemency achieved more than Pompey's victories. On the great final battlefield of Pharsalus, Pompey, conqueror of half the world, of Spain and of Asia, made another mistake. He ordered his troops not to charge; Caesar's should cover all the distance; but they did not, for of themselves they halted, got their breath, and charged again when ready—no doubt a little pleased to see Pompey's device frustrated and Pompey's men fidgetting. "No," says Caesar, "Pompey was wrong; there is in all men a natural spirit, an instinct for battle, which the ancients would heighten with shouting and trumpets; Pompey damped it down."

But for years Pompey overshadowed Caesar. Spain was still in the hands of Sertorius when Sulla died; and Pompey, as we saw, though not a magistrate, was sent to subdue the country, and he did. As he returned he intercepted and destroyed Spartacus the brigand, who had long held the mountains of Italy, but was now in full flight from Crassus. His consulship of 70 B.C. followed, and a strange retirement into private life. Men wondered why he did this; one solution was that, much as he would have liked a position resembling Sulla's, he hesitated, and then plunged (in an endeavour to maintain his dignity), and regretted it. It is clear that he regretted what he had done; but the way opened for his re-emergence. A special law (66 B.C.) gave him a new command, with huge forces and immense range, to crush the pirates of the Mediterranean; and he did it quickly and effectively. The command of the war against Mithradates was then transferred to him (65 B.C.). He overthrew that king, and how many more! He carried the Roman frontier to the Euphrates and to Gaza—a second Alexander, conqueror of the Orient. And what would he do when he came back? men asked anxiously. He would not again retire.

The interval in Rome, while Pompey was in the East, was a nervous time; one manœuvre and another were tried, to make ready against his return. The conspiracy of Catiline took place and gave Cicero "the glory of that December day". Men said absurdly that Crassus, the great financier, was in this bankrupt's plot for looting Rome; that Caesar was *proved* a fellow-conspirator of Catiline's, for did he not try to save the lives of the guilty prisoners? What he actually did was to urge the Senate not to lose its head and do an unconstitutional and unwise thing in its fright. There is nothing so obviously unpatriotic, some people always think, as to keep calm and sensible in a national emergency. So Cicero gained great glory, and Caesar lost credit. At last Pompey came home. On landing in Italy he dismissed his army, and he was in the hands of his enemies in the Senate. They would not confirm his arrangements in the new provinces he had won, without minute discussion; they would not give land-allotments to his soldiers. The Senate had

Pompey at their mercy, when they foolishly quarrelled with the financial magnates. Then Caesar struck in; he, if elected consul for 59, would get a concession which the financiers wanted, he would have Pompey's acts confirmed, and he would carry a land-bill for the soldiers. He was elected, but with a hostile colleague, who tried to veto all he did. But Caesar left him to veto what he would, and carried a series of laws embodying the plans agreed upon. The wags said the two consuls of the year were Julius and Caesar.

After being consul, Caesar went as proconsul to Gaul, as everybody knows. "All Gaul is divided into three parts"—it is perhaps the best-known Latin sentence in the world; an insignificant sentence in itself, why is it so famous?

B. DE BELLO GALLICO

In the *Cambridge Review* in 1909 a "Song of the Lecture Room" by R. F. D. was printed, and one stanza of it raises in more charming form the question just asked.

> A lecture-room in the middle of Spring
> Is a god-forsaken and desolate thing,
> When winds are blowing on Madingley Hill
> And waters are flowing at Trumpington Mill.
> > For what can it matter at all,
> > And what can it matter to me,
> > That Caesar conquered Gaul
> > In 58 B.C.?

A severe critic, or a French patriot, would tell the poet that it took Caesar far more than a year to conquer Gaul, or might even insist that Caesar in his nine years did not do all we are going to attribute to him; nor did Alexander

Hellenize the Nearer East. No, for many co-operate, but Alexander and Caesar create; and it "matters" to every thinking man. Caesar (to speak in our abrupt way) turned Gaul into France, and that "matters" to all mankind; and, more than we sometimes realize, Gaul made Caesar—the Caesar who built the framework that saved the Greek and Latin civilization, of which we are heirs, every one of us, however forgetful or ungrateful. Homer, Pericles, Alexander, Caesar—there is a golden cord running through History. So it does "matter to me, that Caesar conquered Gaul".

The details of his nine years in Gaul may be read in his own book. It is not always realized what a huge task Caesar had in a country, roughly six hundred miles square, a land of forests and great rivers, with only primitive roads; a land of warlike tribes, of first-rate fighting men, a race (as other men said) "war-mad", with able chiefs who had their own tactics and could copy Caesar's. His force was 60,000 men. He had to beat the Gauls all round, and then conciliate them; and he did it, though (as a French historian points out) he nearly failed, and he does not disguise it. But the Gauls, as ever, were divided, or imperfectly united; they had not, says the same historian, the faith that makes a nation; they had no faith in the language they gave up, or in the religion which they disguised, or in the institutions they hastened to Romanize. No doubt also Caesar's policy of keeping out the Germans helped him to win Gaul. He had to make the Germans understand they were not to cross the Rhine; and this, too, he did; it was three hundred years before they became a real menace again; Mommsen, himself a German, says four hundred years. Freed from German invasion and linked to the

Roman empire, Caesar made Gaul "entirely and for ever Roman". A people, quick and intelligent, touched already with a sympathy for things Greek, "had faith in civilization"; and almost as soon as conquered, they grew Roman in heart and instinct. Celts and Italians were always nearer akin than one might gather from the superficial look of Gaelic and Latin. The Gauls, said Sainte-Beuve, early found their way to the Capitol. The French genius is essentially Latin. There is truth in the wicked quip that the French language is "merely the Latin of a Gaulish slave trying to talk like a Roman centurion"; but the Frenchman for centuries has thought like a Roman, with a clearness of mind and a lucidity of speech (and a grace) which perplex the Englishman who muddles through. It was a great thing for Gaul that Caesar, a big-natured and sympathetic conqueror, won it for Rome; it was a great thing for Caesar that he did; and it remained that Gauls and Caesar believed in one another.

The conquest of Gaul won Caesar great prestige in Italy; it lifted him clear out of the ranks of the clever politicians: it made him for all Romans a figure on whom the imagination could dwell. History is made by imagination; no man creates till his own imagination is touched, and till he touches the imagination of his fellows. Here was a whole new world added to the Empire; even Britain had been invaded; and it was obvious to all that Pompey (who during these years was managing affairs in Rome very ill) was *not* Rome's only general. The adroitest of politicians is turning out to be a great soldier; Caesar would rank with the greatest names in Roman history. So men talk and think, and form for themselves pictures of great men; they had done this ten years before for Pompey. Far more important it is to ask what was the influence of those years on Caesar himself? Can we justify what was said above, that Gaul made Caesar?

We have seen that it was a huge task; and tasks such as this break or make a man. They call out all that is in him, and develop the faculties they draw out. Night by night, day by day, Caesar in Gaul was handling great problems; the distances, the shape of the country, the spirit of the people, had all to be realized; and his tools, not altogether strange to him, had to be realized as well. The handling of great armies, all that strategy and tactics mean, was part of his task; where should he send his troops, how should he place them? But there was more to be done; he had to weld his forces, and to make them his own; and this he did. When Caesar leaves Gaul, he takes with him an experience wrought into his nature that has made it over again; he has had to think on a great scale; he has done it, and he knows he can do it again. Pompey no doubt had had some such experience in Spain, perhaps also in Asia; but experience means more to genius. By the time they were both dead, it was plain that Pompey was one of Rome's most capable generals, and Caesar one of the world's greatest soldiers. Could his genius have grown to such greatness without the nine years' discipline in Gaul?

But the soldiering was not all. Caesar in his book tells chiefly of his campaigns and battles, strategies and tactics; it is not a civilian record. But all through those years, questions of civil government must have risen; such and such tribes of the Gauls make peace, or are conquered, and, as each is added to the Empire, questions arise as to the future; what must be done at once, what must be devised against years to come? It meant a close study of the problem of government in a new field. An analogy may help; Alexandria has to be built, it will not be like Athens; or in our own country Winnipeg begins, and Dr William Cowan plans the wide streets—streets for a real capital: in the two new cities the mistakes of the past are avoided. London to-day would be better for straight and wide streets like Winnipeg; but who could make them? The scene is not open prairie. The Roman world needed a new system of government, and nobody saw how it could be made out of what existed. Caesar in Gaul is giving a great country a government, and he can do it with a free hand; it was like town-planning on the prairie. One feels, as one looks at Caesar's later work in the government of the whole Empire, when it became his, that he has learnt to handle great issues with a freedom which he could never have learnt in Roman streets. No Roman governor or general had ever been away from Rome for so long a consecutive period. "The great open spaces" change a man's thoughts; and a new world sends him back a new man to the old world. The Caesar, who crosses the Rubicon, is ready for the greatest tasks, and he is not afraid of them. In the years that followed, men grumbled that Caesar had "said the *republic* was *nothing*, a phrase, just a phrase without substance or shape". Perhaps he did not say it; but if he thought it, he was right. Reality, as we have seen, had gone from the old system; it did not answer to the facts of the world; and in Gaul Caesar had been handling facts of all sorts, building on realities and doing it with freedom, without fear of traditions; and he came back into the old world, prepared to do it again. If "monarchic" power had made such work possible in

Gaul, he was clear (as most people were becoming clear) that something like that was needed in Rome; and he was prepared to take it, and to use it.

By inheritance Caesar belonged to the party that had favoured the inclusion of the Italians among Roman citizens. He was a humane man, as Robert E. Lee, the great general of the Southern States, was humane; either of them was ready to sacrifice human life on a large scale, when it was necessary, but not otherwise. Caesar, as we saw, was ready enough to spare opponents who would be sensible. After the battle of Pharsalus they tell us he walked over the field, strown with the dead; among them he recognized men he had known in earlier days; "it was *they* who wished this", he said. In all his work, fighting or organizing, one feels a genuine humanity, above all a new sense for the provincial, a new sympathy for people, who, if subjects of Rome, are fellow-citizens, and have the same right to honest government and decent treatment. In this he is not unique altogether among Romans, but supreme power had never been before in the hands of one so large-minded. Can it be thought that his nine years among the Gauls did nothing to enlarge his outlook in this way? He had had (in Roman phrase) "to do without his country" for nine years, to live among men who (apart from some section of his troops and officers) were not Romans; and just as Alexander had discovered, and then acted on his discovery, that there are other people beside Greeks, Caesar grasped the value of men who were not Romans. When he crossed the Rubicon, he gave Roman citizenship to all in Italy up to the Alps, and to some outside (e.g. to the people of Gades), and Latin rights to Sicily. When he became master of the world, he tightened up the administration of the pro-

vinces; there was not to be free spoliation of the pro-
vincials by bankrupt governors. Every governor shall
be in effect Caesar's legate, answerable to him, and
Roman rule shall mean peace and justice. He even made
certain Gauls members of the Senate—an act that shocked
common Roman opinion, but revealed Caesar's mind.

In great communities with long traditions men take in
new ideas slowly. Alexander had revealed a new world
of the East to the world of the Mediterranean and had
linked them together for ever. Caesar did the same thing
in the West. Britain suddenly comes into literature.
Catullus addresses two friends who will go with him

> Where breaks on Ind's remotest shore
> The sea with far-resounding roar;
> To arrow-bearing Parthian horde,
> Or where, through sevenfold channels pour'd,
> Nile stains the Ocean with his hue,
> Or cross the skyey Alps to view
> Great Caesar's trophies, Gallic Rhine
> And savage Britain's far confine.

Horace speaks in the same way of "Britons savage to
strangers". "It was only a late posterity", wrote
Mommsen, "that perceived the meaning of those expeditions to England and Germany, so inconsiderable in a
military point of view, and so barren of immediate result.
An immense circle of peoples whose existence and condition hitherto were known barely through the reports
—mingling some truth with much fiction—of the mariner
and the trader, was disclosed by this means to the Greek
and Roman world. This enlargement of the historical
horizon by the expeditions of Caesar beyond the Alps
was as much an event in the world's history as the
exploring of America by European bands." The reader

will think of Alexander sailing down the Indus and out on to another Ocean.

C. BRITAIN

If this book were being written for Russians or Spaniards, Mommsen's words would furnish an excuse for a digression to Britain; British readers will expect it.

Caesar was not the discoverer of Britain. Centuries before his day, Celtic tribes had made the island their own. Goydels (Gaels), still in the North, and later on Brythons, still in the West, dispossessed or absorbed the people they found—the Picts perhaps. The name of the Picts has a Latin look, perhaps they were "painted" men, who used wode; or it may be Romanized spelling, for something Gaelic or Welsh meaning "the little people". But the first real explorer of Britain was a Greek from Marseilles, called Pytheas, who came here about 330 B.C. His own record of his travels is lost, and we have only broken quotations, cited by geographers who knew less of Britain than we do, and were so much more sure that Pytheas was a liar. He sailed (he said) from Marseilles, rounded Gibraltar and followed the Atlantic coast to Brittany. Then he crossed to Britain and sailed round the North of Scotland, where he heard of an island or islands beyond—"the sleeping-place of the sun", he was told; and whether one say Shetland, Norway or Iceland, it seems a first hint of Arctic winter. He records the huge spring tides of Pentland Firth. He describes the habits of the natives, their mining tin, their threshing in barns (there is so much rain and so little sun), but as you go North there is less and less agriculture.

About 90 B.C. another Greek traveller (who did not

visit the island) tells about it, again noticing the tin trade. From time to time, as we saw, gold coins are found in England, made on the model of Macedonian coins, but sadly degenerate. Traders from Gaul came over a good deal, and reported many things about the savage people in the land of fogs. There were, it would seem, close relations between Druids in Gaul and Druids in Britain; this may have been the cause of Caesar's expeditions— to let the islanders know that Romans could cross the sea, too, and intended to stand no interference and no oversea plots to disturb Gaul. As to the Druids, their wisdom, their poetry, and their sacrifices, are famous, and perhaps lost nothing in telling. One Roman poet says epigrammatically of them that "they alone know the gods—or do not know them". No other race had quite the same sort of religion; and when the Romans, a hundred years after Caesar's day, added Britain to the Empire, the Druids were the first religious group to find Rome hostile, as the Christians did a generation or so later, and for the same reason; both groups were too independent, and both refused to blend.

Everyone knows how intensely Romanized the land became, how full it is of villas and baths, tombs and temples, and every kind of inscription and relic. Professor Haverfield was once talking with Mommsen of the Roman Wall; "Ah!" said Mommsen, "you have such wonderful inscriptions in your North Country; no land tells us more about the Roman army". One point is worth noting, which follows from this. The Romans did not shift their troops about as Britain has done from Quebec to Bangalore. Legions and cohorts and cavalry remained in their stations for generations together, sometimes for centuries. Finally, as Mommsen says, it was not Britain that broke loose from the Empire, but the Empire which gave up Britain. And here our patriotic digression must end, and we return to the Rubicon.

D. THE CIVIL WAR AND THE MURDER OF CAESAR

In January 49 B.C. Caesar crossed the Rubicon, and began his march upon Rome. The course of events leading up to this is intricate. In a civil war, as in other wars, both sides have good grounds for fighting, and Caesar could "play politics" as well as Pompey and the Senate. The last stroke was the flight of two tribunes, whose veto and, of course, their persons were in gravest danger—or, at least, they took care to advertise their peril. To a Roman, taken prisoner, Caesar explained that he had not left his province for any evil purpose, but to defend himself, to restore the expelled tribunes to their legal position, to reassert his own freedom and to give freedom to the Roman people, which had been ground down by an oligarchic faction. So he might speak to the man with whom he sat, but his thoughts were deeper. If these are to be divined, he realized that he was indeed fighting on the issue of his own life and death; he saw that a government was needed for the world, and that Pompey and the Senate had made a mere chaos of it; he saw, as nearly everyone else was seeing, that the government must be monarchical, and he was ready to undertake it. Deeper still, as we have seen, though he did not say so to Romans, his acts show that he thought of the provinces in a new way, not as his opponents did; that the Roman world was more to him than the city on the Tiber. How should he think else after nine years in

Gaul? France is wider than the Campus Martius as the prairies are larger than Trafalgar Square. To those who follow his acts, it is clear that he relied upon moral and political support from the provinces rather than from Italy.

Pompey had boasted that he need only stamp with his foot, and armed men would spring from the soil of Italy; but, in spite of his boasting, he was not ready for war. He soon realized that Rome was from a military point of view untenable, and he evacuated it, moved South to Brindisi, and there prepared to cross to the Balkan peninsula, where, as he rightly judged, he could carry on the war better. It was a soldier's act, and a political blunder, as Cicero said in a letter to Atticus. Caesar, of course, saw it, too; and he swept down through Italy and was master of Rome at once, and there he had about him enough Senators to be able to hold in due form a meeting of the Senate to give constitutional colour to his acts. Pompey conspicuously refused every overture, every concession, which Caesar offered, as Caesar probably foresaw that he would. In these manœuvres for peace he did much to throw the odium of war on Pompey. It is to be remembered that Pompey had the larger part of the Senate along with him, to which he must defer or seem to defer; and they may have hampered him in negotiation as they certainly did in the conduct of the war. Caesar had a free hand; his Senate was composed of his partisans.

Pompey got clear away, Senate and army and all, and left Caesar no means of crossing the Adriatic. But he had plenty to do. Spain was held by the Pompeians, and Caesar hurried there—"to meet", he said, "an army without a leader, and I shall return to meet a leader without an army". He had to besiege Marseilles, which he took, and he beat his enemies at Ilerda (the modern Lerida) in Spain. In 48 he crossed the Adriatic, landed, united his forces, and tried to force Pompey to fight. Pompey would not fight; his position was stronger than Caesar's and would be stronger yet. But we have seen already Caesar's comment after Petra; it is the *man* that counts. At Pharsalus Pompey, whether of his own judgment or stung into it by the taunts of the aristocrats with whom he had to live, fought and was utterly defeated. He fled to Egypt, and was murdered in a row-boat while landing. Caesar followed, and became involved in all sorts of adventures. He also met Cleopatra for the first time. The queen reached his camp rolled up in a carpet.

Next year he had to defeat an army of Parthian invaders at Zela in Asia Minor; in 46 Pompeians at Thapsus in Africa; in 45 Pompeians again at Munda in Spain. So he swept about the world—fighting battles, writing books, collecting gems and antiques, legislating, governing an Empire, preparing for future work.

Typical of the man, and of the mind with which he worked, is his reform of the calendar. Ancient calendars, outside Egypt, were very amateur affairs; so many days to the month, and if the months did not work out quite right for a year, extra days were added; "intercalation" was the term. Agriculture obviously depended on some kind of calendar, and with it worship of the gods, festivals and ceremonies, were interwoven. All depended on astronomy, and priests who were not real astronomers regulated the calendar. In Rome the calendar had been freely played with for political purposes, and it was by now ninety days wrong by the sun. No wonder Virgil in his *Georgics* tells the farmer to watch sun and seasons;

it was practical as well as poetical; the calendar would
not help him. Caesar put this right for ever. He obtained
from Alexandria the best astronomy the world had, and
"adjusted the year to the sun"; it should always have
365 days, with an extra day every fourth year; and no
more intercalations. His calendar remained in use in
Greece and Russia till the war of 1914; and after nineteen
and a half centuries it was only some thirteen days wrong.
Contrast the Mohammedan year. Mohammed found
the same sort of muddles as Caesar found; but he fixed
his year by the moon and forbade intercalation; his year
was not a true year. His fasting month, Ramadan, moves
about all through the seasons; it is appalling in summer;
and in some thirty years is back again where it started.
There is no calculating a Mohammedan date without
reference to a hand-book: no one can guess whether a
given date means winter or summer.

Caesar in all he does fixes his eyes on the facts. What is
the situation, what are the forces at work, and how can
they be used and harmonized? The world's need of
honest and intelligent government was the chief thing; so
he saw, and he intended that the world should have it.
He carried a bankruptcy law in Rome to settle money
difficulties there. He reduced the number of persons who
in Rome received free grants of corn to less than half.
He planted his soldiers on farms—80,000 of them—to get
them off the national pay-roll, to set them at real
productive work, and to lessen the chance that organized
legions always offered for more civil war. He broke up
the political clubs that had kept Roman elections corrupt
and disorderly. He refounded Corinth and Carthage,
which the Romans had destroyed in 146; and both
became great centres of commerce—Carthage also of

letters and, by and by, of Christian Theology. Augustus is often regarded as the founder of the Roman imperial system, and he certainly gave the world peace and good government; but would he ever have done what he did, had he not been Caesar's nephew and adopted son? He saw shrewdly enough where Caesar went wrong, and avoided his mistakes; but the genius was Caesar's.

On the Ides of March 44 B.C. Caesar was murdered. What is to be made of that murder? A stroke for freedom or the most foolish thing done in antiquity? It cost the world proscriptions, civil war for years, the rule of Antony, despair, till at last Augustus restored the system of Caesar.

Shakespeare's play, *Julius Caesar*, deserves the study of those who wish to understand the ancient world. At every appearance on the stage some weakness is seen in Caesar; he is deaf, he vacillates, he has cramps, fevers, epileptic seizures, he reads character at a glance and reads it wrong; he is not, it would seem, a heroic figure. Yet at the beginning:

> Why, man, he doth bestride the narrow world
> Like a Colossus, and we petty men
> Walk under his huge legs and peep about.

And at the end it is the same thing:

> O Julius Caesar, thou art mighty yet!
> Thy spirit walks abroad.

Look more closely at the play. Every man's life there depends on Caesar, living or dead, on his attitude to Caesar, friend or foe; Caesar is in all their thoughts; Caesar is the test of all their mind and manhood; Caesar, as they judge of him and act for him or against him, shapes

Plate VII

Rome: the *Via Sacra* and the Palatine Hill

their destinies. That is History as well as drama—the history of the world.

We need not here follow in detail the struggles of the wretched "liberators". Cicero had to stand in with them, to try by any and every means to save the state—though he saw (and wrote it in a private letter) that, when they killed Caesar, they had shown the political sagacity of babies. "Be your own Senate!" he wrote to one of the republican generals, who by and by made peace with Augustus; and it was for being his own Senate that they had murdered Caesar. Ere long Cicero is murdered, and Brutus hears of it, and sees the end; he "blamed his friends; it was their own fault they were slaves, not Caesar's or Antony's". And at the last Brutus, the hero of declaimers, the man who could not see fact or know the world he was living in, has to kill himself, and dies quoting from some Greek poet:

> O miserable Virtue, nothing real!
> A phrase at best! and I have followed thee
> In earnest; and thou art but Fortune's slave!

With Antony we need not linger long. He might well be forgotten, had not Plutarch written of him and Cleopatra, and had not Shakespeare read Plutarch in English and written a play; and what a play it is! And all the way Shakespeare follows Plutarch, only (as Heine wrote) adding genius. To that play, too, the reader will turn, and will understand why Augustus and not Antony ruled the world. Antony in truth belongs to literature far more than to history.

E. THE PEACE OF AUGUSTUS

No war, or battle's sound,
Was heard the world around;
  The idle spear and shield were high uphung;
The hooked chariot stood
Unstain'd with hostile blood;
  The trumpet spake not to the armed throng:
And kings sat still with awful eye
As if they surely knew their sovran Lord was by.

So Milton in his *Ode on the Morning of Christ's Nativity*;
and he follows Virgil and Horace. Augustus gave the
world peace, some forty years of peace, "the immense
majesty of Roman peace", as Pliny the Naturalist calls
it. He put down pirates on the sea, suppressed brigandage
on land, ended the folly and the menace of Antony, gave
the world order and government, and closed the temple
of Janus—the great symbolic act that pictures the end
of war. A new age begins, and he takes the name, which
for convenience we have given him in these last pages.
He had been Octavius; by adoption as Caesar's heir he
became Gaius Julius Caesar Octavianus; now he is
Augustus as well as Caesar, and the name is to hint at
good auguries, at everything august, at restoration and
development.

Old tradition requires that the historian shall chronicle
wars and battles, and it has been faithfully done by
Roman historians. Less attention has been given, to
what Rome replaced, to the wars, battles, seditions and
revolutions, to which her rule put an end. We have
to think of what happened in the streets of Greek cities,
such as Corcyra for instance, of Syloson's restoration to
Samos, of the bloodthirsty wars between neighbouring

Greek cities, of the ambitious wars of the kings who followed Alexander—for all which there is ample evidence, while we may be sure there were endless horrors and disorders of the same kind unrecorded. We have to recall the vague notices we have of inroads of Scythians, Treres, Gauls, Cimbri and Germans from the North and of Parthians from the East; to realize how much there was of brigandage, piracy, and slave-raiding; to think of the habit of war, the "war-madness" of the tribes of Gaul; and then to reflect that, broadly speaking, all this ceased and Peace ruled, healing the wounds of centuries, restoring spirit and giving new hope to mankind. To take two small points, as it might seem, we find in ancient writers repeated comment upon the freedom of travel which the rule of Rome gave; the journeys and voyages of St Paul are proof enough of this; and the learned remarked upon the additions to knowledge, particularly to knowledge of Nature and Geography, which the Roman Empire, like those of Alexander and the Parthians, had made possible.

In the year 27 B.C. Augustus "restored the Republic". Later generations are unable to see that this made any real difference in the government of the world. He made great parade of governing in partnership with the Senate, of maintaining old forms and traditions. Julius Caesar had introduced great innovations and had not troubled to conceal the fact. Augustus appears to have had a shrewder understanding of the little liking men have for change, and he posed as a Restorer, the guardian of tradition and usage and constitution. He had a genius for compromise; he was expert in the art of allowing other people to think they were acting and to feel all the importance their position gave. As for himself, he made a show of accepting only a temporary lease of exceptional power for a short period; but the lease was repeatedly renewed. He was neither king nor dictator; both were bad names; he was *Princeps*—not "prince" yet (that meaning was to come out of his use of the word), but "chief citizen". There was uncertainty in the system; the question was always "to-morrow"; how long will it last? will there be a successor? No one could have foreseen the forty years of his reign, nor the succession of Tiberius. But the uncertainty helped to secure Augustus, if it made others uneasy. Uneasiness haunts the reign— peace and good government all contingent on one life; and the system heightens the doubt. This most able man, says a French critic, "for fear of daggers, would do no more than organize the temporary and consecrate the fiction". We catch the note of the period in Horace; man's wisdom is ever to take the day as it comes, to enjoy the good luck of the hour, and leave the future to the future.

The world accepted the Imperial system; it had indeed no choice; but, outside Rome, or certain groups in Rome, there was no wish for anything else; here was peace, and with it justice, order and the hope of recovery. Among the old noble families the change was not welcome; they recalled a past of privilege, of which they were dispossessed, and they avenged themselves with their tongues, "at dinner tables and in private", as Tiberius said. It was what men before the French Revolution described as "despotism tempered by epigrams". In certain reigns the tattle was retailed to the Emperor by spies and freedmen; and the talkers were directed to commit suicide—perhaps an excessive penalty; but it showed how the uncertainty, which he felt (rather needlessly) in his position, might worry a nervous ruler. But once we are clear of the clubs and circles of Rome (which Tacitus represents with more genius than they ever achieved, or deserved), we find acceptance of the new order almost universal. The Jews, of course, were irreconcilable, as we have seen; and the writer of *Revelation* in the New Testament hated the scarlet woman who sat on the seven hills, drunk with blood of martyrs. But the truest picture after all is given by Virgil.

Virgil had lived through nearly forty years of the period of disorder; he was an Italian of the North, and a poet, peculiarly sensitive to human sorrow, the "tears in things", an interpreter of the human heart above all who ever wrote in Latin, even if St Augustine be named. He was for Caesar and for Augustus. If there is something artificial in the gods and goddesses of his *Aeneid*, if a prophecy in Jove's lips at the dawn of history seems superficially unreal, none the less, to those who will understand, there is meaning in it. The poet has an interpretation of History; it is coherent; and one great type of manhood makes it one—the type that serves mankind from Aeneas to Augustus.

> There comes a day
> While Rome's great ages hold their way;
> From Troy's fair stock shall Caesar rise,
> The limits of whose victories
> Are ocean, of his fame the skies:...
> Then wars o'er all the world shall cease,
> Harsh times shall mellow into peace:
> Then Vesta, Faith, Quirinus joined
> With brother Remus, rule mankind:
> Grim iron bolt and massy bar
> Shall close the dreadful gates of War.

And again, in the prophecy given by Anchises to Aeneas:

> Others, belike, with happier grace
> From bronze or stone shall call the face,
> Plead doubtful causes, map the skies,
> And tell when planets set or rise:
> But, Roman, thou, do thou control
>   The nations far and wide;
> Be this thy genius—to impose
> The rule of peace on vanquished foes,
> Show pity to the humbled soul,
>   And crush the sons of pride.

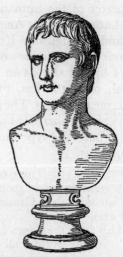

The young Augustus

Chapter XV

THE CHRISTIAN CHURCH IN THE ROMAN EMPIRE

A. MARS' HILL

THE visitor to Athens, when he climbs the Acropolis, is apt to be halted at the *Propylaea*, the ancient entrance buildings; and while a voluble guide rolls off legends of prehistoric kings, Erechtheus and Cecrops with the serpent's tail, he may well let his eyes wander over the scene. Rather to the North below him is a shoulder of rock, a round top standing up boldly. On this, somewhere about the year 50, stood a man addressing a group of dubious listeners. He spoke in Greek, but perhaps with an Eastern Mediterranean accent; Greeks noticed such things, and the word *solecism* recalls the fact that at Soloi in Cilicia (this man's country) Greek was not at its best. He was a Jew; but he began well, dealing with the no-man's land between Jewish monotheism and Greek philosophy:—God—the rather Stoic doctrine of the common human nature of all men —and then a slight quotation from an early Greek poet. But he was advocating a new religion, fresh from the East; and high above him towered the Acropolis, and high upon it stood the Parthenon.

No background for an address upon a new religion could have been found more fatal. The Parthenon was nearly five centuries old; and still (as we are told by a visitor fifty or sixty years later) the marble was as fresh as if it had left the sculptor yesterday. It was the symbol of eternal and universal religion. All mankind, if you except Jews and Druids, were of one mind, with small local variations. Ancient Stoic and modern Catholic have emphasized the weight to be given to the "consensus of mankind", to what is believed "always, everywhere and by all"; and this was typified by the Parthenon, no ruin then, but in its full beauty. Beauty, the universal mind, five hundred years of unchallenged witness—and down below on Mars' Hill the Jew was pleading for a wholly new view of life, and telling an incredible story. His listeners had only to lift up their eyes, to realize how absurd it all was. The Parthenon was itself a refutation of it all—if it needed refutation; for, when he reached the point of talking about a dead man rising from the grave, perhaps in Palestine, there was general laughter, and the gathering broke up with some unconcealed contempt. So Paul preached on Mars' Hill, with the Parthenon high above him; he left Athens; and Athens forgot him.

But Athens was to hear of him and his religion again. In A.D. 435, or perhaps a year or two later, the Parthenon was dedicated as a Christian church to the Divine Wisdom; and a Christian church it remained for a thousand years. In 1456 the Turks took Athens; in 1687 a Venetian shell (a German aimed it) crashed through the roof, and the powder stored there blew up, and left the famous building very much what we see to-day. The Turk was expelled in 1833, not to return; his minarets and his cypresses are gone; everything that man can touch that might remind us of him is blotted out as it deserved to be; and the ruin stands high above Mars' Hill, over a city of Christian churches. But how strange a history! One wonders what Stoic and Epicurean would

Plate VIII

Athens a hundred years ago.
To the right of the Acropolis and beneath it is Mars' Hill

have said, if, in the midst of their derision, it could have been told them that Christ would hold the Parthenon longer than Athena had held it or was to hold it. History, however, is hard enough to interpret as we look back upon it; and it is useless unless we try to interpret it.

From time to time surprise has been expressed that there are not more references to Christ in Greek and Roman literature of the early Empire. But much of it is lost; much that was kept dealt with matter taken from the great Classical past, which still absorbed the minds of men; and, in dealing with things nearer their own day, it was the polite fashion of men of letters to affect an antique tone. The Jews were disliked, and, as far as their rebellions and their presence would allow, they were ignored. The Christian church was long supposed to be a mere Jewish sect, an affair of the fuller and the baker, the slave on the verandah; its beliefs were not examined, but were dismissed magnificently as "Jewish superstitions"; here, as the caustic Tertullian wrote, curiosity ceased to be inquisitive. The most famous reference is made by Tacitus. A great fire laid much of Rome waste in A.D. 64; and men guessed as to its origin. "Neither human aid, nor imperial bounty, nor offerings to the gods, could remove the sinister suspicion that the fire had been started by Nero's orders. So, to get rid of this rumour, Nero shifted the blame on to others; and with the most elaborate tortures he punished those people, whom the mob, hating their abominations, used to call Christians. The source of the name was one Christus, who, in the reign of Tiberius, was punished with death by the procurator Pontius Pilatus. For the moment the detestable superstition was checked; but it began to break out again, not only in Judaea, where the mischief began, but also in Rome, where everything hideous and shameful from every quarter gathers and is welcome." Tacitus, it should be remembered, repeats elsewhere the fable of the ass's head being a part of the Jewish religion, along with rites borrowed from the Egyptians. It will also be noted that, in describing the Christian super-stition, he uses the imperfect tense, as if it were a matter of the past which educated readers might have forgotten. He adds, however, that Nero's cruelties went too far and roused a certain pity for his victims, richly as they deserved their fate. The vulgar are often more senti-mental than historians.

But if contemporary historians miss matters of their own day which are destined to be of the utmost interest to posterity, if they fail to recognize the forces and factors, and above all the personalities, which are re-shaping the minds of men, and, by changing men's central thoughts, are altering the whole of life, there is no excuse for men of later days, who look back and, from literary etiquette or whatever reason, say nothing of what has meant most. Probably few historians of fifty years ago, who wrote of the previous half century, gave much mention, or even thought, to Charles Darwin or Karl Marx, but no men of the period they studied have so much influenced the life of to-day, political and economic. Jesus of Nazareth was not of interest to Tacitus, his literary friends and contemporary historians. But when the Jews of Thessa-lonica, about the year 50, denounced Paul and his friends as "the men who have turned the world upside down", whatever the magistrates, to whom the com-plaint was made, thought of the charge, it was to prove true. The greatest rulers of the Empire had to reckon with the believers in Jesus Christ; and at last, as we shall

see, the issue had to be faced of peace or war with the
Christian church, and, after fruitless war that did the
Empire no good, a wiser Emperor made peace, and took
for his emblem what was called the *labarum*[1], the initials
of Christ.

B. THE GOSPELS

Within a few years of the fire of Rome, two or three small
books appeared, which give us a large part of what we
know about Jesus Christ. The exact years in which
Matthew, Mark and Luke wrote, are perhaps not yet
fixed, but the books are the work of Nero's generation.
They are not written in the traditional literary dialect;
but to say that they are in colloquial Greek approaches
nonsense; no one ever wrote as he spoke. It is recognized
that both Matthew and Luke used Mark; and close study
reveals with what extreme care Luke remodelled what
he borrowed. He at least was not writing colloquially.
He cuts out Mark's foreign words, like *talitha cumi, Eloi
Eloi lama sabachthani*; he writes a good Greek word for
Mark's popular Latinism for "bed"; he substitutes words
of better tradition, cuts down rambling sentences, omits
pronouns when he can, re-arranges episodes. Mark
keeps saying "immediately"; it comes nearly fifty times
in his pages; Luke has it once. Luke now and then im-
parts some hint of Septuagint language to his story.
Summing this up, we find a man writing a book which
he means to be read by educated people; he is loyal to
Jewish scriptures and to Greek taste, and above all to
Christ. Not undeservedly has his Gospel been described

[1] See the title page.

as "the most beautiful book in the world". He was a medical man, according to early tradition, and Matthew a sort of civil servant. Matthew groups his material in compartments tidily, here preachings, there healings, in another section parables, in yet another condemnations of the Pharisees.

The Gospels begin by showing us a man with ideas of his own, which he wishes men to realize and to adopt. If the word did not in English suggest so much of dullness and failure, we might call him, as men of his day did, a teacher. No one ever understood the work, the art, of the teacher better. He, as the Greeks said of the poets they admired, did the right thing and knew why he did it. His first task was to win attention, and we read that never man spoke like this man; men were astonished at the charm with which he spoke. He was simple, and people could follow him. Indeed the French thinker, Pascal, has put it that Jesus speaks so simply about the deepest things that you might almost imagine he had never thought about them. Abstract nouns of the most dismal kind fill the books of the later Greeks, even of such great men as Polybius and Longinus; but Jesus did without abstract nouns. He never speaks, like the Greeks, of "the divine" (in the neuter) or of "the divine goodness" or "father-hood"; he says plainly "God" or "your heavenly father". He never talks, like modern men, of "humanity" or "social righteousness"; he says "thy brother" or "thy neighbour". His speech, as reported, is singularly free from adjectives, as indeed the Gospels are; he checked a young man who called him "good master". He spoke —and perhaps he thought—in pictures; and his pictures are realistic. Eagles in his parables do not plant trees in market-places; lost sheep do not argue, they are sheep and not philosophers in sheep's clothing. He drives to the actual, and makes men look at it—and then take a second look, for it somehow is linked up with something deeper, something eternal; but it is still the real thing, the thing that you can see, though you never thought about it before.

Socrates was famous for making men define their thought and be clear in their minds as to what they are saying. Similarly, it is noted how apt Jesus is to use a question to make men think. Someone has counted some hundred and fifty questions in St Luke. As in Socrates and Cervantes and other great teachers and thinkers, so in Jesus, the attentive listener can catch something of humour among his most serious utterances; not wit of course, but the subtler, more universal, happier thing, that speaks of peace of mind whatever the contrasts and contradictions it sees—humour, the gift that puts men in good temper with God and the world, and tempts them to look further into things as they begin to enjoy them. There is a vivid dramatic quality about his stories. One has only to compare the commonplace sentences of the Hebrew writer (*Ecclesiasticus* xi. 18, 19)—"There is that waxeth rich by his wariness and pinching, and this is the portion of his reward: When he saith, I have found rest, and now will I eat of my goods: yet he knoweth not what time shall pass, and he shall leave them to others and die"—with the parable of the Rich Farmer. *There* we see the man, hear him talking to himself, like Robinson Crusoe, about his problems; we are challenged by his questions of what to do; and suddenly we realize that there is Another on the stage with a more awful question. Thus all the teaching has a centre, and drives to the one centre.

He realizes that, to achieve what he wants, the teacher must stamp something indelible on the memory—his words or his personality, or both; and it should be noted that, though he wrote nothing down, and though the Gospels were put in writing perhaps forty years after the crucifixion, no man's words are so well remembered. Nor so fertile; for he, like Socrates, used the analogy of sowing, and aimed at planting something in the mind that would root itself there and grow, and he trusted to its development. For he stands alone among the great figures of the past in his belief in men. In this he is nearer to Pericles than to Constantine. No one, said the philosophers, could expect the many to take in the idea of One God. Ah! but they will, is written in the whole attitude of Jesus, and in every word of his. He stands nearer to common men and is in deeper sympathy with them, and rates their power to absorb and understand and handle the profoundest ideas higher than any administrator, reformer or archbishop has ever dared to put it. But this he did, without the reformer's vague dreams; he knew what was in man, and expected men to crucify him. Like Buddha and Mohammed, and unlike some of his followers, he believed in preaching, far more than in argument or symbol. This followed from his belief in men and his belief in what he had to say; he had no doubt about the outcome. That he was justified, appears from the story of his apostles; but no practical person could have trusted such a group to do what they did. It showed how right he was in his belief in soil and seed and their fitness for one another.

Yet few canons for New Testament interpretation are so valuable as Matthew Arnold's sentence that "Jesus was above his reporters". As one studies the men and their age and their antecedents, it is clear that Jesus did not square with expectation. If men since his day have identified him with the expected Messiah of the Jews, it is because they have adapted their picture of the expected Messiah to the historical lineaments of Jesus. The Greeks identified him with the divine *Logos*, the "Word" of God. But, not to digress into explaining explanations, Jesus has always been more intelligible than the explanations men have given of him. It is not always recognized how independent he is of all tradition in religion. He comes of Judaism, and abundant efforts have been made to heighten his debt to it—both by friends and enemies. To the Jewish suggestion that "nearly everything Jesus said is in the Talmud" (the commentaries, written and recorded, of Jewish rabbis), there is one sufficient retort, made by a German scholar: "Yes! And how much else is in the Talmud!" He was criticized in his own day for his independence of Moses; and it was speedily a charge against his followers that they were overturning the law of Moses, and with it the customs, traditions and religion of Israel. The charge was more just than his followers realized. He does not try, as some Jews did, to make a blend of Jewish theology and Greek philosophy. Fate and Fortune are the two interpretations of the universe most prevalent in that day outside Judaea; neither word occurs in the New Testament. All round he is singularly independent of established and traditional ideas. He does his own thinking himself, speaks out and takes the risk of being misunderstood.

His purpose, then, it is important to understand. Men have attributed to him their own interest in organization. It is curious how much more apt to surrender to contemporary thought his followers have been than ever he was. They have tried in one period to make his teaching chime in with Neo-Platonism, in another to reconcile it with theories of scientists then popular. No wonder that, living in the Roman Empire, and thinking of it as eternal, the framework of human life for ever (for they held it must last as long as the world), men took it for certain that the church must be a counterpart of the Empire. Some indeed compared it to the schools of the philosophers, which was more apt. But Jesus laid his emphasis above all on the relation of the individual with God; and, where that is paramount, there is always less interest in organization. In the centre of every religion of that day, at the centre of Judaism as practised in the temple, though not in the synagogue, ritual was all-important; to the Roman the priest was essential, because the priest alone knew the proper words in which the gods must be addressed, and a single word astray might wreck the purpose of worship; the gods would not be bound by a blundered formula. Whether the priest believed what he said, was of no consequence, provided he said it aright. To the mind of Jesus all that is utterly foreign; not the tongue but the thought was what mattered. All life rests on belief; and no one ever realized this more clearly than he. Action is the outcome of what a man believes or disbelieves; his conduct shows his wavering in thought. The unstudied word, the unconscious act, are the overflow of what is within. Jesus addresses himself to changing men's central belief, and makes it clear, that once they have conceived of God as he does, a new relation with God follows, which will affect every thought and at last every act.

So far all is plain sailing; it is here that difficulties begin, the best clue to which, in modern times, is suggested once more by Matthew Arnold—"Jesus based himself always upon experience, never upon theory". To understand any man—the simplest politician, the man of letters, or the poet—three things are needed. You must have as full a knowledge as possible of his words, and be able to get them in some perspective. Jesus, it has been said, took the risk of being misunderstood; every man who thinks has to face that risk. Next, to understand a man, you must obviously be able to grasp what is in his mind when he speaks; that alone will interpret his words; the dictionary is useless, for it only tells you what common men mean by words, who do not mean much. With the greatest men the concordance is of far more value than the dictionary, for they use words in their own way. (Compare the words "impel" and "impulse" in Wordsworth.) When, at last you have found what his words mean, and what he really is thinking, the third and most difficult stage is reached; for now you have to ask, Why does he think so? and the answer is that the thought comes out of the experience. That is why Matthew Arnold's canon is so important. When one asks, What, then, was the experience of Jesus? what lies behind his thought? what contacts with God, or what experience of God, leads him to think as he does? the man claims a great deal who will try to answer. No such attempt will be made here. The inner life of any man is generally beyond our grasp. An amazing book has recently been written to suggest how Coleridge's mind treasured strange pictures which he saw as he read, combined them, and transformed them from odd details to amazing poetry; but the writer of it frankly owns that the process between accumulation and creation is beyond us. How much harder, then, in a case like this to say how Jesus reached his central thought! His acts we can more or less follow; his disciples and the evangelists were quite clear that the crucifixion was not an accident; he chose pain, he foresaw betrayal and crucifixion. One hint is given us here; some part of what he learnt, he got, as we all do, by suffering; the *slow* realization of what is coming from what is about him rather than any such revelation as was claimed at Greek shrines. This deepens the significance of his choice.

C. THE CHURCH AND THE INTER-PRETATION OF THE GOSPELS

The New Testament contains more than the first three Gospels. It grew slowly; and it was a century or so after the bulk of it was written before the Christian community quite decided which books were of first importance, made its list (the "canon") and called them canonical. It hesitated long over *Revelation* and one or two more; but no one can regret that it rejected the *Shepherd* of Hermas, a book like some others that might be mentioned, well enough to read once; some might even say it was the worst good book that ever survived in manuscript for thirteen centuries. To compare the books rejected with the books included will give any man a higher sense of the value of Christian instinct, for the selection was the work not so much of officials as of readers.

In the other books of the New Testament the story of the Gospels is supplemented. First and foremost, in Gospel, epistle, and revelation, the Resurrection is emphasized. The men on Mars' Hill laughed at it, as a great many other people have, forgetful that a thing is not untrue because you cannot picture it and cannot explain it. The reader must judge for himself; but History would only be falsified, if it were not made clear that on the Resurrection, on the continued life and activity, "the grace", of "the Lord Jesus", on his peculiar and individual relation with God the Father (witnessed by the outcome of that experience which we saw we could not understand), the whole Christian faith rested. The church was built on the realization that Jesus is unique. That is the origin of the church; and the historian will remark that its power to grip and to change men—and with them to change and develop the outlooks of society, the beliefs on which society rests and acts—has varied with the intensity with which it has made Jesus central, all-helping and all-significant. To men outside the church other views may be attractive and more probable; for the Christian church they have again and again been shown to be fatal. So far as the church is concerned, or its experience (as yet interpreted) is valid, the danger of over-estimating Jesus is not a real one; the danger is the other way. It is not the historian's task to prophesy, but to record, and, if he can, to understand. Here no attempt shall be made to prophesy, and it may not be fitting to attempt explanation; but the facts, so far registered in the experience of nineteen centuries, have to be recorded and have to be weighed.

With this emphasis on Jesus and this historical explanation of him, came that re-valuing of life which he sought to lead men to make. Old estimates, old ideas, passed away. The Stoics, for instance, had deprecated slavery, gravely, and sometimes rhetorically: through their teaching Roman law, as it bore on slaves, was slowly modified. The common Christian teaching put the slave on a new footing altogether; just as it abolished distinctions of Jew and Gentile, of Greek and barbarian, it refused to recognize any between slave and free; all are one in Christ Jesus. So they speak. It is not always recognized how much of Christian metaphor comes from a society in which slavery was universal; such words as ransom, Redeemer, "bought with a price", freedom, must have made the hearts of those who heard tingle. One Christian writer of the second century says that what the soul is in the body, that Christians are in the world; and the historian has to recognize that he was right—the Christian church was the most living thing in that world, and the most life-giving. Not all its members, nor all its writers, were inspired; but the new note in many of them cannot be missed; and the new experience set St Paul and St Augustine among the writers whom every age will wish to read.

D. THE CHURCH AND THE INTERPRETATION OF HISTORY

The Parthenon, as we saw, became a Christian church; and the world of Greeks and Romans and Syrians accepted Christ. The very names of the old gods are forgotten; some survive in the dictionary, some in verse, and the use of their names is a hint not to take the eighteenth-century poets too seriously. What is the meaning of the change? Let us go back to some ancient thinkers before we answer.

Polybius, then, has been quoted more than once in this book; and here we turn again to the words now familiar. It is not the fact, he says, that matters, but the reason; not *what*, but *why*. "Who is so worthless or spiritless" [these are interesting adjectives] "as not to wish to know by what means and under what kind of polity, the Romans in less than fifty-three years have succeeded in subjecting the whole inhabited world to their sole government—a thing unexampled in history?" The progress of the Romans, he says at another point, was not due to Chance as Greeks suppose; that is vulgar talk, not proper language, he says; Rome forged ahead, and it was wholly reasonable that she should. We need not here recall his explanation (see page 276), but he means that History is reasonable enough, if you will look at facts and weigh them.

Not everybody took so much trouble. Fortune, wrote the Greek, whose words were in the mind of Polybius, makes no treaty with human life, baffles our reckonings with some abrupt stroke, displays her power by her surprises; who could have believed, he asks, that Persian power would ever come to nought, or that, of all peoples, Macedonians should enjoy the world, till Chance changes her mind? St Cyprian says something much the same. A Latin bishop in Africa, a lawyer and an official, and as unreflective as any of his class in maintaining the tradition which he accepts, he writes, in his tract to prove that "Idols are not gods", that the kingdoms of this world do not depend on merit; they are thrown from one to another by Chance; Syrians and Persians; Greeks and Egyptians; and now the Romans.

Polybius is more credible here, unless the history of the world is as meaningless as a record of the fall of dice. Then how was it that the Christian religion prevailed? Was the cause in the correspondence of the faith with the facts of human life? Or was it something in the character of the men and women; but then how came it to be in their character—was that chance? A Roman poet of the fifth century finds something further to suggest; and with two quotations from him, it will be left to the reader to frame his own account of the matter.

Prudentius was indeed a poet, not a Homer, nor a Virgil, but still a poet of character, charm and power, the first, and for centuries the best, of Christian poets. This, then, is what he says: "O Christ, sole deity, O splendour, O might of the Father, O maker of earth and sky, builder of these walls, who hast set the sceptre of mankind on the hill of Rome, and dost ordain that the whole world should serve the Roman *toga* and yield to Roman arms, that thou mightest bring under one law the customs and the ways of differing nations, their tongues, their genius, and their faiths". "This" (in another poem), "this was achieved by the mighty successes, the triumphs of the Roman Empire; Christ even then was coming, and the way was made ready for him."

Byzantine coin of the later Empire
with Christian device

Chapter XVI

THE ROMAN EMPIRE

A. THE LIFE OF THE PEOPLE

THE most charming critic of antiquity records a discussion with a philosopher friend on the decay of literary genius; there is plenty of talent, but no genius, no natures with the touch of the sublime. Are we, said the philosopher, to accept the old story that Democracy is the good nursing-mother of great men, to believe that Liberty alone can breed noble spirits and give them imagination and hope? To-day, he continues, we seem swaddled from the cradle in the usages of a virtuous slavery, bred as (I am told) pygmies are in cages that prevent their growth and shrivel them up. No, says Longinus, not quite that; it is man's peculiar gift to grumble at his age; but it can't be the peace of the world that ruins great natures—far more likely the truceless war that our own passions wage within us, and our love of money; perhaps it is better for people like us to be ruled than to be free, safer for our neighbours, too. The cause of the decline lies in ourselves, in the lack of spirit that is second nature to us. Tacitus says much the same—the great geniuses have ceased to be produced.

It is with the Roman Empire as we found it with the Successors of Alexander; History halts—there are plenty of historians, but, as a caustic Greek said, of the sort whose books nobody reads through to the end. There are sad stories of the deaths of kings, and the kings fight battles among themselves, but neither king nor battle seems to make an epoch. Polybius alone stands out in one age, as a historian, a very great historian indeed, if you will read him in any language but his own. In the later age there is Tacitus, a supreme stylist, who has given an indelible colour to the first century A.D.—not its own, but his—and has left his mark on all historical writing since his day. All historians who *write* (as opposed to innocent chroniclers, compilers, economists and the like) have him, consciously or unconsciously, at their elbow. But in both cases the real history of two centuries is uneventful, without a Salamis or an Actium; disasters there are, of course, and calamities, as always in human affairs; but the historian's task here is the more difficult one of tracing changes in social ways, in outlook and thought, in attitude to life. There is a gradual transformation, the unimaginable touch of time; the changes come so quietly that a generation or two may pass before they are noticed, at any rate before their importance is realized. England is a different people to-day from 1820, and it is neither Queen Victoria's accession nor her death, neither the Reform Bill of 1832 nor Darwin's famous book, that is the one great cause of the change.

So our task now is to look at the lives of ordinary people and commonplace communities; and for our story we go to the travels of St Paul, the excavations of Pompeii, the letters of Pliny from Bithynia, the amphitheatre of Arles and the Pont du Gard.

In the *Acts of the Apostles* we find a Greek-speaking Jew of Tarsus, by birth a Roman citizen, travelling as he will by land and sea over the Empire; with peril on both elements, he tells us in a letter, but it is only incidental peril; there is perfect freedom of movement. He sails on wheat-ships. He goes to the great centres where men gather; most of his towns are still on the maps of modern politicians; Salonica and Konia are still central. He meets Greeks and Romans, and Jews with Greek and Roman names, proselytes, adventurers, philosophers. His biographer, too, has a knack of naming the right magistrates in the right places, a proconsul in Corinth (Gallio gives us our one definite date in the story, A.D. 51), politarchs at Thessalonica, Asiarchs at Ephesus, and a *Protos* (first man) on Malta. Wherever he goes, Paul is involved in controversy, but it is private controversy with the Jews; he has no quarrel with Roman magistrates, except once when the law was overstepped by them. Few books illustrate the age so well. (See the map on page 76).

Pompeii was overwhelmed by Vesuvius in A.D. 79. Excavation began there about 1748 to discover works of art; in the mid nineteenth century excavation was directed to discover Pompeii itself—the layout of its streets, its housing, its general aspect—and that in the main has been marvellously achieved. The streets run at right angles; the houses are generally small, and walled blank against the street, with courts and shrubs within, many (even humbler homes) decorated with marbles, mosaics or bronzes; and very generally the inside walls are painted, mostly with scenes from mythology. Inns and taverns are recognized, and two theatres are found. But perhaps the inscriptions are most interesting, for they comprise nearly everything that can be written on a wall—very rude things, advertisements, election notices, references to guilds. The strangest, perhaps, tells us of a schoolboy, who began to write up a line of Virgil, but somebody chased him away or he changed his mind, and all that he wrote is CONTICUEREOMN; and it came true, for "all were silent" in Pompeii.

Pliny as governor, with a tremendous long title, in Bithynia, in Northern Asia Minor, wrote ceaseless letters to consult the Emperor Trajan, and we have also Trajan's letters in reply. They are disorderly communities, these Greeks and half-Greeks, whom he rules, and unlucky. The city of Nicomedeia has twice tried to build an aqueduct, and failed both times; the new theatre at Nicaea has collapsed—not the only failure there; Prusa wants new public baths. Pliny pleads to have a Roman architect. You have plenty of Greek architects, says Trajan, who apparently does not want to see why Pliny wishes a Roman. Pliny clearly does not trust the Greek architects he meets; we have to guess why, and it is not very difficult. Nicomedeia shall not have a fire-brigade; the Emperor is quite decided; it would only be used as a political club to promote riot and faction; people can have buckets. Amisus has a right by treaty to have benefit clubs; so be it then, but not elsewhere. Apamea's public accounts are in confusion. Temple questions, questions of the postal system, and many another, are broached; notably one about Christians. They, of course, ought to be punished for their contumacy; otherwise they seem harmless if silly; a good many are giving up the religion; and Pliny seems to hint some accommodation. Trajan's orders are explicit; there must be no anonymous accusations; if proper information is laid and proved, Christians must be punished; otherwise let them alone, and don't hunt them down. Illogical! says Tertullian two generations later; if they are to be punished, it is because they are criminals; if criminals, they ought to be hunted down; if they do not deserve to be hunted down, they do not deserve to be punished. Yes, illogical! But it illustrates Roman government and Roman wisdom—the one in not suffering combinations or clubs of doubtful allegiance; the other in letting sleeping dogs lie.

The letters reveal the main factors in the life of the Empire—the growing Imperial control (the next reign saw this re-inforced by a system of civil service, which tended to kill all local and individual enterprise); the waste of labour and money on huge buildings put up by ambitious cities (think of the neighbouring amphi-theatres of Nîmes and Arles, the latter of which held a town in the Middle Ages, with a church and streets); and the religious movement.

In spite of Longinus and his friend, literature was not all dead. The centuries between the death of Nero, A.D. 69 and the fall of the Western Empire in A.D. 476 are not barren, though it is not always the fashion to read the authors of those years. "What, Sir, a good book?" said Boswell. "Yes, Sir," said Johnson, "to read once". Perhaps that might be sufficient comment on many of them, or Quintilian's dry sentence, "worth reading—if you have time". Greece and Rome, however, have better books than those to show, and much greater names. The reader, with some leisure, will find a certain curious satisfaction in the *Tour of Greece*, which Pausanias (*c.* A.D. 180) plans for him, rich in old associations and things of enduring beauty, a book for the traveller in Greece to-day. He will find real interest and pleasure in some of the *Orations* of Dio Chrysostom (*c.* A.D. 100); two in particular are peculiarly fresh and engaging, the one describing country life in Euboea (a sort of *Paul and Virginia* of the Greek world), and the other which tells of the frontier town in South Russia, where they read only the oldest Greek literature and have to be on constant guard against the Scythians. In the *Gastronomers* of Athenaeus (*c.* A.D. 180) he may well be staggered at some of the menus; but the indescribable mass of odd information about the Classical period is always good to dip into. Lucian is familiar enough, and generally over-praised. In Latin we have already drawn upon Tacitus and Juvenal; but many more readers than he gets would find Apuleius and his *Golden Ass* a living book; he is the first known teller of *Cupid and Psyche* and probably the cleverest. In the fourth century Ammianus Marcellinus is a great historian not often read through, but admired immensely by those who do read his contemporary history of the fourth century, including the reign of Julian. Or if the reader will turn to Christian writers, three are outstanding—Justin the converted philosopher; Clement of Alexandria, a writer of the greatest charm, who finds it natural to interweave his happy recollections of the Gospels with memories as happy of Greek literature from Homer to Plato; and Tertullian, lawyer, Stoic, convert, epigrammatist and Christian apologist, the shrewdest and keenest mind of the century. These are not authors "to read once", though many Classical scholars pass them by, regrettably.

Three other names are more familiar. Plutarch (*c.* A.D. 50–115) has somehow ceased to be a part of a proper education, but his *Lives* are always good to read, and his *Moral Tracts* (more amusing than the English title suggests) give a full picture of the life of scholar and thinker in his period, and endless lights upon older days. We have already seen how he contributed to English literature in Shakespeare's plays; and the French critic Brunetière, thinking perhaps chiefly of the *Life of*

Lycurgus, says "it was Plutarch who made the French Revolution". (Of course it depends whether you think revolutions are made by economic conditions or in studies.) The Emperor Marcus Aurelius kept a journal, which it is good for every man to read, but as he kept it— a little bit every day is bracing, the whole is saddening. The greatest figure of all is St Augustine, the most creative mind in the religious sphere between St Paul and Luther; his influence on mystic and churchman, Calvinist and Catholic, is incalculable; his *Confessions* and Virgil's *Aeneid* are the two most formative and most moving books in Latin.

Philosophers will remember Sextus Empiricus, most thorough-going of Sceptics. Porphyry and Plotinus, the Neo-Platonists, are more significant, writers who for a thousand years deeply affected the thinking world outside the Christian church and within it. Spenser's *Faerie Queene* is full of their teaching. In Law, the third century supplies three great names, Gaius, Papinian and Ulpian, by whose labours Roman law was progressively humanized and became at last the law of the whole civilized world.

A brief enough survey—but it should be clear that the debt of our modern civilization and of modern literatures is no slight one to the early Empire.

B. DECLINE AND DIOCLETIAN

Years ago a Cambridge historian remarked on the difference of tone in Roman life before and after the death of Nero. The successors of Augustus belonged to his wife's family. Tiberius is the villain of Tacitus' *Annals*, a gloomy man, trained to be suspicious, and full of a

perhaps natural antipathy to people whom he suspected
of a desire to murder him. Gaius, it is pleasanter to think,
was mad. Claudius was an honest drudge, an awkward
prince who made Augustus wonder whether he were not
mentally defective; "not all there" was the slang Greek
phrase the Emperor used. The prince wrote Ancient
History, and reached the throne by a strange chance.
For, while the soldiers were busy killing Gaius, Claudius
hid behind a curtain; but his feet were seen, and a soldier
hauled him out; he was recognized and suddenly made
Emperor. Nero has few apologists; the Romans would
more easily have forgiven him but for his artistic temperament. With him the house of Julii and Claudii ends;
and with Vespasian sense ascends the throne, and (but
for Domitian) sense reigns for over a century. A series
of Emperors, who adopted their successors, men of
intelligence and character—they go far to justify the
description of the Roman Emperors as the finest roll of
names in History. Nerva, Trajan, Hadrian, Antoninus
Pius, and Marcus Aurelius cover ninety-six years. With
Commodus, the worthless athlete son of Marcus, disorder
begins.

Disorder is the mark of the third century. There were
six thousand miles of frontier from the Euphrates to
Carlisle, and back again, to be guarded. Eastward,
beyond the Euphrates, the Parthian dynasty came to an
end about A.D. 250, in a native Persian revival, which
lasted for four centuries; Northward there was fresh
movement, incessantly renewed, among the teeming
tribes of Germany. This indeed began earlier; the first
book of Marcus Aurelius is dated "Among the Quadi";
he was fighting German invaders by day, and night by
night made these notes. In the third century the Alle-

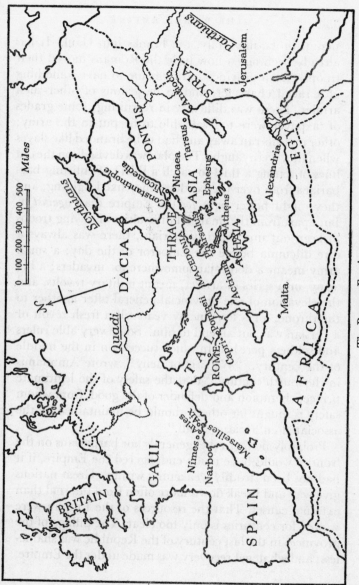

The Roman Empire.

manni broke into Italy, the Franks into Gaul. It has
already been noted how little the Romans moved their
troops. Each provincial army came to have something
of a racial character, and to be jealous of other such
armies. There was difficulty in recruiting; some grades
of taxpayer were too valuable to be put in the army;
other recruits ran away and had to be branded like slaves
when they were caught. The plan was devised (on the old
lines of setting a thief to catch a thief) of enlisting barbarians from over the borders; they liked fighting, and
they might better fight *for* the Empire than *against* it.
But apart from the financial difficulties of paying troops
to keep out unwanted barbarians, there was always a
dire dilemma before the Emperor of the day; a small
army meant a door ajar somewhere for invaders; a big
army, or a series of armies, meant military revolts, and
the elevation of one provincial general after another to
the throne, for a few uneasy years till a fresh revolt or
a Persian war put an end to him. Some very able rulers
and soldiers perished in quick succession in the middle
of the century. "We cannot deny", wrote Ammianus
in the fourth century, "that the safety of the legitimate
prince, champion and defender of the good, from whom
safety is sought for others, should be maintained by the
associated enthusiasm of all."

Probably neither rebel generals nor barbarians on the
frontier would have much endangered the Empire, if it
had not been steadily weakening within. Great nations
give way and break down more often from internal than
external causes. That the resources of the Empire were
wasted for centuries is only too clear. The pillage of the
provinces in the last century of the Republic was shame-
less; and whatever recovery was made under the Empire,

certain wounds cannot be healed. One Roman conqueror, a man of high character and repute, sold one hundred and fifty thousand inhabitants of Epirus as slaves. Sulla's furious vengeance on Asia will be recalled. The money that rolled up in masses to Rome was in large part wasted, as the wealth of Alexander's Successors was. A mania for building huge villas, baths, arches, temples; a still more wasteful mania for beast-shows, in each of which the end was the public slaughter of the animals (fetched with extreme cost from the ends of the earth); a universal desire to wear silk and to have spiced food— all these things and others wasted labour and money.

Lately the point has been well made that there was a new shortage of labour. For some two centuries, down to Actium, Eastern and Northern wars had meant a ceaseless supply of slaves in Italy. Agriculture and manufacture were carried on by slaves—a bad thing in itself, for slave labour is reluctant and careless labour, wasteful of material; there was no improvement in tools or methods (and improvement was needed); slaves generally left no offspring, and they crowded out free labour with its families. This contributed to decline in population, while land went out of cultivation. Italy began to repeat the experience of Greece. There, what with wars, and emigration, and other things, cities and islands, once abounding in people, were very largely depopulated. (Why should the gods keep oracles going, asked Plutarch, when the countryside is empty?) With the beginning of the Augustan reign of peace, wars ceased, and the source of the slave supply was cut off; and the question with each generation became more insistent, Who was to get the food out of the ground? To tend the fields, Germans were planted in Italy; and law at last tied the farmer to the soil, eventually to make him something like a serf. Law did a good deal of such tying of men and women to hereditary trades; the actress might not leave the stage. All this was not going to produce any real revival of agriculture or industry.

Gold and silver going East, labour scarce, slavery and law tying reluctant persons to trades they were sick of —it does not spell energy. Add to these factors of decline, the great plague of the later second century, famine, the roads going out of repair and so far impeding what trade there was, and, in addition, ceaseless heavy taxation; and one thinks again of what Longinus said—the curse of the Empire is want of spirit. And any symptom of energy, of freedom of mind, or enterprise (apart from military revolts) was repressed by the civil servants, more and more dominant, as the taxpayers lost heart and spirit. It is possible for people to be too well governed. Solon made Athens by setting enterprise free; the Roman civil servants wreck the Empire by killing initiative.

Thus we find barbarians at the gates, barbarian troops holding those gates, vanishing figures on the throne, triumphant civil servants, and a population declining in numbers and in spirit. And people ask why the Roman Empire fell! Why did it last?

In 284 Diocletian became Emperor, famous for three things, his re-organization of the Imperial system, his persecution of the church, and his final retirement into private life. First of all, mutiny and disorder were to stop; in order to effect this, he devised a system of two colleague emperors, each with a "Caesar", an heir, designated to succeed him—all four to be surrounded by Oriental pomp and mystery. From now onward the Emperor, aloof and above men, is a very different figure from Augustus and Vespasian, very much more of a sultan than "chief citizen". The great provinces, long familiar, were "cut into little bits" (says a critic); Gaul for instance became seventeen provinces; the legions were divided; civil and military administrations were separated; and a regular ladder of promotions and titles arranged; there should be no more concentration of power in the hands of any one who might rebel. For the time it meant order, but the system broke down on top; the plan of four Emperors, actual or future, led after Diocletian's retirement to civil war, till Constantine became sole master (A.D. 323). But the Empire had a respite of a century; and by then in the West there was no heart left to resist barbarians; there were too many of them, and they could not be more oppressive than the government they replaced. The interesting thing is the admiration the invaders felt for Rome.

It is perhaps worth noting that two of the technical terms in the new arrangement have been taken over by the church in dioceses and provinces, as other secular terms have been. From the temples it took no titles, though responsive enough to pagan ideas of religion. In time it annexed their buildings; but, when free to build for itself, it developed its own architecture on secular lines.

The last great battle for liberty was now to be fought. From the time of Nero, the state had scented danger in the Christian church; quite apart from scandals alleged (perhaps without much belief in them) against Christian morals, the early adherents did not recognize sufficiently the authority of the state; they did their own thinking; when required by magistrates to worship images, even the Emperor's image, they refused. Trajan's letter to

Pliny left their position uncertain; in one place there might easily be trouble, in another their neighbours, and the authorities, preferred to leave them alone. Thus one story is current of a Christian before a magistrate, starting to speak, when the magistrate ordered an attendant to hit him on the mouth; his speech was stopped, and, before he could start again, he was bundled out of the court—alive. Another magistrate ironically asked the Christians before him why, if they really wanted to die, they did not take ropes and hang themselves. But such rough kindness was not universal. Anywhere on the cry of a mob, there might be martyrdom. Tertullian's pamphlet *On Flight in Persecution* and his *Apology*, the one addressed to Christians, the other to pagans, repay reading, even in a translation; the Latin is brilliant. After his day (*c.* 200) there was a half century of comparative peace; the government had enough to do elsewhere; but its claim to obedience was not abandoned even if it was not enforced.

Persecution had not in the Roman world, as in Queen Mary I's reign in England, either religious conviction or an ecclesiastical organization behind it, until we come to Julian "the Apostate". The whole episode of Julian's re-action is such a contrast to all before it, that, anticipating the order of history, a few words must be spared to it. Julian was a deeply religious sentimentalist, a reasonably good soldier, but without dignity. An Emperor, who addresses a pamphlet to a hostile city populace and boasts in it that he has lice in his beard, can only command a qualified respect. Like converts, or perverts, he was a bigot, but he is not a representative figure—far from it. His attempt to deprive Christians of higher education was condemned by pagans. Paganism was unorganized; it was no system, no coherent whole;

it had many temples, many priests, but no united priest-hood, no dogmas (to speak of), no creed. Julian tried to change all this, to create by decree a virtuous, philan-thropic and propagandist priesthood; but it was not to be done. His reign was short (361–363 A.D.), and the re-action was spent. Thenceforward the only enemies of the Gospel within the Empire were inside the church, till the Moslems invaded the Mediterranean world. Roman religion was, as a French scholar has put it, a layman's religion, cool before the gods; and the most important priests were elected by popular vote. Julius Caesar was *pontifex maximus*; the title was borne for centuries by the Emperors; and, for many more centuries, it has been borne, and is still borne, by the popes.

The local persecutions of the church did not generally come from any conflict of faith; their origin was apt to be lowlier. Tradesmen were the enemies of the church; they complained of the injury it meant to their business, like the shrine-maker at Ephesus in St Paul's day, and perhaps the people in Bithynia in Pliny's time who sold fodder for cattle destined to the altar. Men grew annoyed at family dissensions, which might follow, when the Christian slave on the verandah whispered his "Only believe!" to the women of the house. The Jews, again, are indicated as the source of anti-Christian movements.

The attitude of the government varied with its pre-occupations, and perhaps with the character and temper of the Emperor. If at times it was willing (like Trajan) to let things alone, to look the other way, the fixed maxim of Roman rule was that no other authority but that of the imperial government could be tolerated. A nation must be united; Christians were welcome, as in India to-day, to worship Christ by all means, but they must also worship the gods of the state and the city. The

Emperor Alexander Severus (A.D. 222–235) kept in his *lararium* (the chapel of his household gods, *lares*) statues of certain predecessors on the throne and of "some holier souls, among whom were Apollonius [of Tyana], Christ, Abraham and Orpheus, with some others of that sort, and the images of his ancestors". He wished "to build a temple to Christ and to give him a place among the gods"; but the omens were against it, making it too clear that, "if he did, then all men would become Christians and the other temples would be deserted". So writes his biographer.

But the Christians would not compromise; neither would the State yield. It came then to war between them in the short reign of Decius. When he became Emperor (A.D. 249), the storm broke. It was the first *general* persecution. The Emperor's edict (the first *edict* issued against Christians) required all persons to "sacrifice" (i.e. to the pagan gods) by a certain day. Certificates, issued to those who did, are still extant. Here is one from Egypt, unabridged:

To those chosen to superintend the sacrifices at the village of Alexander-Island, from Aurelius Diogenes, son of Satabus, of the village of Alexander-Island, being about seventy years old, a scar on the right eyebrow. It has always been my custom to sacrifice to the gods, and now in your presence, in accordance with the decrees, I have sacrificed and poured libations and tasted the offerings, and I request you to countersign my statement. May good fortune attend you. I, Aurelius Diogenes, have made this request.

[In another handwriting] I, Aurelius Syrus, as a participant have certified Diogenes as sacrificing along with us.

[Dated by Diogenes] The first year of the Emperor Caesar Gaius Messius Quintus Trajanus Decius Pius Felix Augustus. Epeiph 2.

The church was taken by surprise, and there was a rush of time-servers to the altars. But the reign of Decius was very short. When the persecution was over, the renegades, the *lapsi*, in thousands, sought safety again for their souls; and a new question arose for the church as to the terms of re-admission for those who denied Christ. Not unnaturally there was great division among Christians upon this issue. There followed another interval of peace, for some forty years. Public opinion was less hostile, perhaps shocked by the martyrdoms, and we hear less of the mob.

For the first eighteen or nineteen years of Diocletian's reign (284 B.C.), he took no open step against the Christians. Christians were among his court officials; his wife and daughter, rumour said, were Christian. He was himself a man of high character, who took his own religion seriously, and his superstitions, too; but he was a statesman, busy with heavy burdens at home and with war abroad. But Galerius, one of his colleagues, was the enemy of the Christians; and at last in February 303 the edict of persecution was issued; church buildings were to be destroyed, the Scriptures burnt, Christian officials degraded; nothing so far against private Christians or clergy, unless they refused to give up their Bibles. But there was resistance; two fires in the palace were set down to Christians; and other edicts followed—all persons now were to sacrifice—and the edicts were executed, not indeed vigorously in Gaul or Britain, the sphere of Constantine's father, but more strenuously in Italy, and savagely in the East, there only to cease in 313, though by 308 it was clear that persecution must fail. The massacres had not extinguished the church; they had embittered its leaders, many of whom perished; and they had done the Empire no good. The secular government had still a rival; it had conspicuously failed to crush the church. The most telling comment upon this was made a thousand or more years later by a French scholar. "Sire," said Theodore Beza to the French king, "it belongs to the church of Christ, for which I speak, to receive blows rather than to deal them; but your Majesty will remember that it is an anvil which has worn out many hammers."

The only alternative was to make peace with the church.

C. CONSTANTINE

Round few names has centred controversy more bitter than about Constantine—a sure sign that he was a significant man; and his reign is indeed epoch-making, in more ways than one. He became Emperor on the death of his father at York (July 306), the choice of the army of Britain. He re-united the Roman Empire (323 B.C.), held it united for the rest of his reign, and dying in 337 he left it to remain united for some half century longer. Because he did this, he was able to do something far more signal, in reconciling church and state, and giving each the support of the other. In the next place he sought to give unity to a divided church, and called together the Council of Nicaea. Thirdly, he was the founder of Constantinople. In all three ways he made history, as none had done since Julius Caesar. It seems improbable that he was without insight, that he did not know what he was doing, or had no consciousness of what History meant.

The attempt of the state to crush the church had failed. Conscience had been involved, and had proved too strong for the civil administrators; it looked to something deeper and more eternal than an unruffled and un-idea-'d

Empire. In 313 Constantine issued the Edict of Milan, in which he granted full freedom to Christians, and to others, to follow whatever religion they pleased to think best. The edict marks the end of one age and the beginning of a new one. Long ago, Tertullian had declared that "it is no part of religion to compel religion". Here at last the omnipotent state, organized, controlled and hierarchical, recognized something beyond its reach— the domain of conscience; and conscience is above all else an individual thing, the affair of the man who thinks for himself about the deepest and the supreme things. But the alliance of church and state did not stop there. That it was an advantage to the state, few will deny; but it has been repeatedly a painful question whether the church gains by leaning on the arm of civil power, whether the first principle of the Edict of Milan is not the best, that conscience, unsupported and unimpeded, does not do more for mankind. It has always been difficult for authority, in church or state, to grasp this idea; control is always the language of the official—control, quiet, safety; let sleeping dogs lie, by all means, but no dog bark except as directed by edict or act of parliament. Yet, looking at the Roman Empire, it must be owned that the healing of the breach made for the strengthening of the state, soon to face fresh barbarians East and West.

But alas! the church was not united, as Constantine found to his dismay. Arianism was dividing it. In old days a very new and raw Roman magistrate in a Greek city found, they say, that the philosophers could never agree; as to the subject of dispute perhaps he did not very closely inquire; he magnificently bade them come on a certain day to his tribunal, and he would settle finally the points at issue, and all that disputing should cease.

Constantine was far shrewder. It was not for him, as yet unbaptized, to decide what was and what was not the true Christian faith; that he conceived to be the task of the bishops. Episcopal decision upon truth may not seem consistent with freedom of conscience; but Empire and peace are practical matters, and as a practical ruler Constantine accepted the current view as to bishops. So in A.D. 325 on his summons there gathered at Nicaea, in Northern Asia Minor, three hundred and eighteen bishops from East and West—far more from East than from West; there was no bishop from Britain. From one point of view the Council of Nicaea may be regarded as the first representative assembly, the first of Parliaments; for in those days bishops were not nominated by king or pope, but were elected by the community (and sometimes very oddly, directly and spontaneously, as when Ambrose, a military officer on duty, was elected bishop of Milan). Probably for those times, and for the purpose in hand, no better plan could have been devised. Constantine gave the assembly freedom of debate and of decision. When it came to real grips, the verbal compromise proposed by a learned bishop was decisively rejected, and a form of creed proposed by Athanasius (*not*, however, the "Athanasian creed" set out in the Anglican prayer-book) was accepted. Then, and not till then, Constantine put his foot down; this being the Christian faith, all bishops must accept it.

There has been much trivial mirth over this "dispute about a diphthong"—mirth as well based and well directed as if it had played upon the insertion or omission of the word *not* in a sentence. Was Christ *homoousios* or *homoiousios* with the Father, "of *one* nature" with God, or "of *like* nature"? How can you know? some people will say. Letting that point wait, we see at once that "of *like* nature" means "*not* of *one* nature"—the one phrase is the opposite of the other; and, in spite of all practical people, then or now, no compromise can be made between an idea and its opposite; the same door cannot be shut and not-shut at the same moment. To compromise on a practical issue is another thing; when one man wants to walk a mile and the other to sit still, a half-mile walk may be reasonable; truth at all events is not involved. It is curious how little this is realized by persons avowedly religious. A further point remains as to the Nicene creed; the late Professor J. B. Bury said —perhaps not very sympathetically—that the acceptance of the position of Arius (that Christ was of *like* nature with the Father) would have meant the "*premature* disappearance of Christianity". Historians are not always prophets, and the *final* disappearance of Christianity has been prophesied so often as to be no longer interesting. In any case Bury was so far right, that Arianism was at bottom a negation of the Christian religion; it made Christ essentially indistinguishable from the pagan gods as they were now conceived by the Neo-Platonists. That many Christians did not realize this, is natural enough. Arius himself was admittedly a man of high character; but that was irrelevant then as now; it was truth that was at stake. Nicaea marks an epoch in the history of Christian thinking; the issue is still vital for Christians.

Constantinople stands where in ancient days Byzantium stood. Very early a caustic Greek called Chalcedon, the town on the Asiatic shore of the Bosporus, "the city of the blind";—could they not have seen where the city *ought* to be, where Nature meant it to be? After the first century A.D. Rome had ceased to be a practicable capital for the Empire; it was too far from the frontier and not central enough. Tiberius had lived for long on the island of Capri, astonishing Romans by his readiness to "do without his country"; but the government of the world could be carried on as well from Capri as from Rome. Hadrian did not live in Rome; he travelled the whole Empire incessantly. So sure was the instinct of Julius Caesar that the old order was to go, and that Roman and provincial were to be fellow-citizens one of another. The same idea runs through the story of the Christian church from St Paul's day. Diocletian made Nicomedeia on the Asiatic side of the straits his capital. It was a stroke of genius when Constantine shifted the seat of government for ever to Europe and the Golden Horn. There his city stands, as it stood; for a thousand years and more it was (far more than Venice) "the safeguard of the West", and protected Europe, still imperfectly civilized, from barbarism and Islam, from Hun and Turk and Slav. It kept Greek literature and Greek thought safe for us all, till our Western world was fit to receive it. The Turk took the city in 1453, and the greatest of all historic churches, the Hagia Sophia of Justinian, became a mosque. A mosque it remains; but some, who have worshipped Christ in it, know that it still is, and will yet be, the Church of the Divine Wisdom.

D. ENVOY

Thirty or forty years ago it was said, with at least enough emphasis, that History was a science, better divorced from the literature and moral philosophy that had so long trailed about with her. The part played by men of mark, a Themistocles, an Alexander, a Caesar, a Constantine, in shaping the world's story, was, we were loudly told, exaggerated; movements were shaped by "factors", and other abstract nouns. The course of the European war from 1914 to 1918, and of the years of "peace" since then, must have shown the least intelligent historian how much a man may count. Achilles and Agamemnon quarrelled at the beginning of our story; who will deny that "ten thousand sorrows" have been laid on us all "since what time Woodrow Wilson and Henry Cabot Lodge stood apart, in quarrel", as Homer might have put it? But whether men or "factors" make History, can we see any threads running through it?

We began by looking at Geography; and throughout we find that the shape of the land, the map, controls in some measure the life of men; and men still need food, and the search for it, in field, and mine, and factory, shapes much of our history. So much is plain without a long study of the past. But man does not live by bread alone; can we not go further? The historian E. A. Freeman, of Oxford, expressed with some humour his doubt whether he should set the date for the beginning of "Modern History" at the Reform Bill of A.D. 1832 or the call of Abraham (date uncertain, but early B.C.). Another date has been suggested in these pages, but it is not important. What seems clear is that Freeman was right when he urged, more seriously, that all History is one History.

Then, we ask again, does the story, here set out in briefest outline, tell *us* anything, us of to-day anything relevant *now*, in *our* lives? No single key unlocks all the doors in Science, or in History, or in the human heart, which counts so much in History. But certain things may be traced in ancient, medieval and modern history.

Ideas are again and again the real forces, and they have strange adventures among men. Here is one—law emerges more and more as of prime importance, law based on intelligible principles, law corresponding closely with human experience, human needs and human nature, law growing more and more like Justice, the "Law of Nature" of which the Stoics taught. And again, it slowly grows clear in human affairs that inner sanctions, inner inhibitions, are substituted for authority without; or in plainer language, what Jeremiah said comes true: "I will put my law in their inward parts, and write it in their hearts". Homer and Euripides, Plato and the Stoic, Virgil and the Apostle, are all prophets of the same great doctrine; and its acceptance is the one hope of any democracy such as Pericles dreamed of for Athens or St Paul for the Christian church. Lastly, Solon set free the individual Athenian and made Athens; Constantine gave freedom of conscience to the individual in his Edict of Milan; and St Paul wrote perhaps the ultimate word upon the individual when he spoke of "him [a singular pronoun] for whom Christ died". Everything comes back somehow to the individual, his convictions and his choices.

But whether the reader of this book draw these conclusions or not from the story as here told, the story is a greater and a more moving one than any one man can tell; and there is nothing better than that a man read it for himself, wherever he find it, and see what it means for himself.

TABLE OF DATES

This Table rests largely on the Chronological
Tables of the *Cambridge Ancient History*

B.C.

597	Babylonian captivity of the Jews begins
c. 600	Voyage of Kolaios
	Marseilles founded
c. 590 or 560	Journey of Antimenidas
c. 590	Solon's reforms at Athens
586	Fall of Jerusalem
585	Eclipse of sun, 28 May; foretold by Thales; peace between Lydians and Medes
c. 570	Naukratis in Egypt founded
561	Pisistratus tyrant
c. 550	The Spartans take the Thyreatis land from the Argives
c. 550	Theognis of Megara *floruit*
546	Sardis taken by Cyrus the Persian
539–538	Babylon taken by Cyrus
c. 538–523	Polycrates tyrant of Samos
c. 530	Pythagoras *floruit*
c. 530	Xenophanes *floruit*
529–522	Cambyses King of the Persians
527	Death of Pisistratus
521–486	Darius King of the Persians
c. 510	Heraclitus *floruit*
511	Pisistratid family expelled
511	Alleged expulsion of Tarquin from Rome
5 –4	Simonides *floruit*
499–494	Ionic revolt against the Persians ending with the battle of Lade and the sack of Miletus
492	Persian fleet wrecked off Mt Athos
490	Battle of Marathon
485–465	Xerxes King of the Persians
480	Xerxes invades Greece. Battle of Salamis

B.C.

B.C.

333	The battle of Issus
332	Alexander takes Tyre
331	Foundation of Alexandria
331	The battle of Gaugamela
331	The burning of Persepolis
c. 330	The voyage of Pytheas round Britain
327	Alexander invades India
326	Alexander explores the Indus and sails out on to the Indian Ocean
323	Alexander dies at Babylon
312	Seleucus King at Babylon. "The Year of the Greeks" in later chronologies
306	The Generals of Alexander take the title of "King"
280–275	Pyrrhus at war in Italy and Sicily
262–242	First Punic War
242	Sicily taken by the Romans
218–204	Hannibalic War
218	Hannibal wins the battles of the Ticinus and the Trebia
217	Battle of Raphia
217	Battle of Lake Trasimene
216	Battle of Cannae
204	The battle of Zama
197	Flamininus defeats Philip V at Cynoscephalae
190 or 189	Defeat of King Antiochus by the Romans at Magnesia
175–164	Antiochus Epiphanes; and the Maccabaeans
168	Defeat of Perseus at Pydna, by Aemilius Paullus; and the end of the Macedonian Kingdom

B.C.

146	The destruction of Carthage and of Corinth
134–133	Tiberius Gracchus
124	Death of the last king of Pergamum
123–121	Gaius Gracchus
113–101	Teutons and Cimbri moving in the West
112–106	Jugurthan War
90–89	War of Romans and Italians
88	Massacre of Romans in Asia
88	Sulla takes Rome
87	Marius, the seventh time Consul
87–83	Sulla in Greece
83–78	Sulla in Rome; his constitution
77–	Pompey in Spain
70	Pompey and Crassus consuls
67	*Lex Gabinia* gives Pompey command against the pirates
66	*Lex Manilia*; Pompey's campaigns in Asia begin
63–62	Catiline's conspiracy
63	Pompey at Jerusalem
62	Pompey lands in Italy
59	Caesar Consul
58–49	Caesar in Gaul
55 and 54	Caesar's expeditions to Britain
49	Caesar crosses the Rubicon
48	The battle of Pharsalus
44	Murder of Caesar
42	The battle of Philippi
31	The battle of Actium
27	Augustus "restored the republic"

A.D.

14–37	Tiberius Emperor
37–41	Gaius Emperor
41–54	Claudius Emperor
c. 50	St Paul preached in Athens
54–69	Nero Emperor
64	The Fire of Rome
69	The year of five Emperors
69–79	Vespasian Emperor
70	Destruction of the Temple at Jerusalem
81–96	Domitian Emperor
180–192	Marcus Aurelius Emperor
c. 200	Tertullian *floruit*
222–235	Alexander Severus Emperor
249	The Persecution of the Christian Church by Decius
c. 250	The end of the Parthian Dynasty; revival of the Persian power
284	Diocletian Emperor
306–337	Constantine Emperor
313	The Edict of Milan
325	The Council of Nicaea
c. 434	The Parthenon becomes a Christian church
476	Fall of the Western Empire
527–565	Justinian Emperor
1453	The fall of Constantinople to the Turks
1834	Greek independence achieved
1934	The Theseum in Athens re-dedicated as a Christian church